T0208639

POLITICALLY CORRECT MORAL AUTONOMY:

CHRISTIANITY BESIEGED! STIRRING THE MELTING POT TO A BOIL

FERD WAGNER

authorHOUSE®

AuthorHouse™
1663 Liberty Drive
Bloomington, IN 47403
www.authorhouse.com
Phone: 833-262-8899

Published by AuthorHouse 06/14/2022

ISBN: 978-1-6655-5908-9 (sc)
ISBN: 978-1-6655-5907-2 (hc)
ISBN: 978-1-6655-5909-6 (e)

Library of Congress Control Number: 2022908556

Scripture quotations are from the ESV Bible® (The Holy Bible, English Standard Version®), copyright © 2001 by Crossway Bibles, a publishing ministry of Good News Publishers. Used by permission. All rights reserved.

Print information available on the last page.

This book is printed on acid-free paper.

CONTENTS

CHAPTER 1

Moral Autonomy: Vain Attempts to Escape Scriptural Restraints

"The means justify the ends" seems to be the weapon of choice for many political figures and rights activists. In order to reach an ideological goal or activate a new right, it appears specific individuals and groups are designated as fair game. Using all the tools available and doing whatever it takes becomes their mantra. Collateral damage is expected but necessary to achieve the ends of the politically correct who promote moral autonomy. Their logic is basically perverse human justification.

It is a form of situational ethics whereby specific political goals use corrupted ideology to justify harm or perverted justice when it gets them to their desired ends. If you accept that excuse to get away with evil in the process of arriving at what you consider a higher good or compensation for past sins, logical, ethical people and institutions would be aghast to postulate or condone using scripturally prohibited behavior as the means to correct something that transpired in the past. Recompence or compensation for previous wrongs must not include new wrongs or undeserved penalties. If you then proceed to commit evil in the name of political goodness or righteousness, what kind of resolution or solution will be offered to those whom you injured or attacked in the process of reaching your ends? Is your evil behavior any better than those you are condemning?

Proverbs 3: 5-6 instructs us not to use human logic or wisdom to solve human sins as neither our logic or wisdom is equal to God's always equitable justice and wisdom: "Trust in the Lord with all your heart, and do not lean on your own understanding. In all your ways acknowledge him, and he will make straight your paths." Human justice and logic are limited by the quality of the assigned authorities honor and integrity passing judgment on others. When the authorities are biased, their judgment is biased.

Objectivity in many disputed social issues is subject to personal biases and animosity of authorities who subjectively follow their legal and political ways and means to settle the matter as they see fit. Equity is not the goal. By picking and choosing selective data and designated ideological leanings, they convey a partially true, one-sided viewpoint, while shielding or hiding data or facts that negate their position. Pay back or an eye for an eye will not bring about the changes necessary for both sides to reach a just outcome. A better way is to find an equitable way to make a present enemy a future friend. The highest equitable way is applying God's instructive truth to all human conflicts. Only God is always objective and only God is always correct. Hardened human hearts are hard to soften.

"Life is like a box of chocolates, you never know what your gonna get" is a catchy phrase from the movie, Forrest Gump. But it is not completely accurate. It is true the vicissitudes of life and unpredictable weather events frequently interrupt our normal routines and plans. That is a given we all experience. However, we have commonly posited and accepted phrases such as "truth or consequences" or "you reap what you sow" which counter the unpredictable and point out much of life is predictable.

"Cause and effect" are laws of nature God instituted and enshrined that are not subject to human manipulation. They are His eternal reminders that what you say gives yourself away and what you do reflects back to you. Nothing escapes His notice, and there is nothing humanity can do to ultimately thwart His purposes. He rules, we serve and revere is at the core of Reformed theology and practice. That is being reversed by many liberal politicians who progressively believe their authority to govern and guide our moral traditions and values supersede God's authority. Self-righteous, pretentious politicians and moralists want you to trust and follow their lead, often determined by which way the public mood directs, not God. Those who apply objective observations corroborated by historically validated facts rather than biased ideology will better solve any current or future problems.

We believe in many instances, based on data and facts from former and present reputable authorities, we can pre-determine what will typically follow certain human actions or behaviors. Based on personal cause and effect experiences, typical human responses and above all, scriptural guidance, we know in advance that certain acts or behaviors result in certain negative consequences. If your physical body dominates or determines its needs must come first, your response will be emotionally self-oriented, seeking immediate self-gratification. If your spiritual body, attuned to scriptural constructs inspired by the Spirit is in control, it will help guide and control your physical behavior, finding appropriate ways and means to respond to moral challenges and the importance of self-control and respectful civility in confronting social divisions.

The eternal human problem is we deny or reject certain natural truths because it denies us the pleasure or gain we so desperately want. Consequently we suffer because of our disbelief, callousness or indifference. There is no correct way to sin and expect something good to come from it or that God will bless it. Majority rule or political party validation cannot assign merit to someone who has not earned it or something that does not already have it. Passionate, emotional belief or faith that contradicts core scriptural doctrine or practice is often a designated political ploy or gambit orchestrated to deflect or redirect the emphasis articulated in scripture to excuse or downplay bad policy or behavior that resulted from the political process that promoted it as valid.

You can only see, hear or understand what you have prepared yourself to see, hear or understand! The untrained, undisciplined or unprepared will struggle and falter to the degree they are unprepared or led astray by emotional, self-righteous indignation. Those who primarily follow acceptable human standards and parameters will always be adapting to current philosophies or ideologies that haven't been proven. As a result, trial and error predictably will generate false beliefs which some will passionately follow, hoping but not knowing if what they believe or are told to believe, will solve or reduce current social, political and moral conflicts. Trial and error, blame and shame are frequently politically correct moral autonomy's *modus operandi* for getting things done.

While we are all human, not everyone is humane. What does that mean or imply? It means we typically drag out the phrase, "we're only human, everybody makes mistakes" as an excuse or cover for our mistakes, errors in judgement, and our lack of appropriate due diligence resulting in harm to others or ourselves. The question becomes, do we learn from our mistakes or are we indifferent and make little or no effort to prevent them from happening again? When tolerance is the issue, as it is on the news every day, too much or too little is always a matter of degree. How can you and I arrive at an objective, equitable solution when everyone is using a different measuring stick with different standards and parameters of fairness? We can't!

When politically correct individuals using ever adjusting identity ideologies take it upon themselves to arbitrate the degree and kind of acceptable tolerance; our human biases and self-righteous indignation, reveal the degree of our baser nature. In many instances, uncontrolled emotions drown out the civility required for each side to convey their concerns and grievances. What individuals or groups will often attempt to get away with or self-justify, will largely depend on their legal/ideological interpretation of laws and what the governing liberal authorities will condone or allow under their "correct" supervision. Those authorities are all under God's authority and are held accountable by faithful Christian theology and practice. Their responses often reveal to God and faithful Christians their contempt for the word and will of God and their bondage to the word and will of a political ideology. A hardened heart, disrespectful to others and God, will seek its own way, unable to control its arrogance or vitriol as it erodes the possibility of reaching an equitable outcome for all involved.

Every generation takes it upon itself to redo or re-examine existing moral protocol. We continue to make the same mistakes and make bad judgements because we create laws and philosophies that allow us to do so, and in many cases, encourage us to do so. For thousands of years we have unsuccessfully turned inward to individuals, groups and institutions to find answers. It is a sure thing that we will continue to deny and attack God's truth. That has been and is a given. No doubt our assaults on core truth will result in repeating the same mistakes using "corrected" adjustments here and there, expecting different results. The word "insanity" is often used to describe the futility of doing the same thing repeatedly, expecting different results.

The state of the nation reveals we are more divided than united. Even worse, the acrimony and hostility of competing political parties is widespread and escalating. It seems each party votes lockstep yea or nay regardless of the quality of their candidate or the legitimacy of their convoluted and obviously biased position. Honor and integrity are being held hostage to emotional blackmail, entitlement favoritism and a host of identity and rights' groups coercive threats. The "rule of law" is spasmodic, dependent on who rules and the degree they will bend or subvert existing ethical standards and parameters to the will of their identity groups. If one attempted to label or define the national social and political mood or mantra of the United States at this time in history, a good candidate would be "truth by degrees and rights by decrees."

Politically correct emotions are fueling increasing personal attacks against judges, politicians, and private individuals who do not agree with their agenda. It seems individual vendettas and even violence are legitimate if they advance moral autonomy that embellishes correct ideology. Equal civility, equal consideration, and equal respect for historically accepted truths and personal accountability are now the exception, not the rule. The sanctity of and respect for all life has been a core Christian value at the ethical center of Western civilization. Today, the sanctity of individual rights and one's body, as well as the use of politically orchestrated blame and shame mantras are at the center of Western civilization. Intimidation and self-righteous indignation are used to steamroll Christian tradition, theology and practice.

Many conservatives believe we are not facing up to the truth. Individuals, institutions and the federal government in many moral issues are looking in the wrong places and scapegoating. Our point being that when the same people tasked to fix the problems are the same minds that created the problems, we can expect more trial and error that often exacerbates the problems! When politicians or civil rights leaders cannot rise above their personal biases and moral deficiencies and admit mistakes because they fear their political base will abandon them, their misplaced loyalty reveals they are willing to abandon God's truth for popularity. Judas betrayed Christ for money and we vilify him. Many of our politicians and indiscriminate tolerance, moral autonomists betray Christ for popular approval and we applaud them. Go figure!

Humanity on its own volition cannot cure its selfish-predilections nor its us-against-them polemics. Where there is no central ethical core that sets equal boundaries and standards of accountability and responsibility that apply uniformly to all parties and participants involved or affected, common sense tells you "politically correct" moral normal is dependent on individual perception and therefore a right everybody has to justify their position.

> Suppose every liberal or special interest group approached each scriptural prohibition in an open-ended manner, basing it on their standards. Eventually, every negative connotation and scriptural denunciation of a habit or practice would gradually become acceptable should they interpret them using their biased leanings. By redefining value or morality using fluid liberal parameters and standards, what is good and right is primarily based on their all encompassing theme of indiscriminate tolerance, each person is essentially given a pass to do what seems right to them. Further, they end up affirming everyone else's right to do the same, potentially affirming a lie or contrived deception.

The liberal community believes that man is basically good, he deserves more credit and praise for his social concerns and will typically do the right thing. That being their moral reality, they are less dependent on God. Their thought being man's laws and political leanings should be pre—eminent, in essence, <u>we worship our own ascendency</u>. They want you to think God is becoming more like modern man, quick to reconcile the sin and sinner, overlooking transgressions.

What seems to be ingrained in their ideology is their goodness and social wisdom attributes have somehow miraculously been ingrained into the mind of God and altered His nature to be more like theirs. By reversing roles, man, not God, is prone to make exceptions, exemptions and excuses previously considered non-negotiable. If there is a God, he is now seen as being on their side, doing their bidding or at least allowing us to do our own bidding.

We as a nation are in a power struggle for the bodies and souls of the individual and nation. When any government political ideology stacks the deck with rights, entitlements, and vast amounts of money flowing to special interests and identity groups; pandering for votes replaces finding a just solution. Today it looks like dependency and grievance are more effective crowd pleasers and have become more important than individual integrity and honor. Liberal ideology based on human implementation of human imperatives through human resources in order to eventually reach human utopia can be lumped with communism, socialism and humanism as "the spiritually deceived leading the spiritually blind." Where God is merely an afterthought in any process professed to be enlightened or correct, pride and deceit become the evil partners of those "good people."

The "rule of rights" has replaced the "rule of God's law." Self-validation is in, Christian ethics are out. Let your conscience be your guide has replaced let scripture guide your conscience. To paraphrase William Barclay, "the difference between those who look to human law for truth and guidance on relationships and law and those who look to the Spirit is this; those who proceed according to human law, treat people as the law allows and define truth as the law directs whereas those of the Spirit treat others as scripture commands and define truth as the Spirit reveals and demands." Accepting a compromised Christian truth is no better than blessing deceit.

Any Christian deference to another faith or ideology in matters of scriptural truth and trust, mocks our reverence for Christ. Ethical deference should only be offered when a superior, proven truth has been demonstrated, not where a passionate emotional affirmation is exhibited. Confusion reigns where inclusion rules. If you can keep in the back of your mind that all valid truth has been endowed with a legitimacy and strength of its own by God, one will be reminded that your representation can't add or subtract from its merit, but it could add or subtract from its reception. 1 Timothy 4: 1-2 addresses deceit when it says, "Now the Spirit expressly says that in later times some will depart from the faith by devoting themselves to deceitful spirits and teachings of demons, through the insincerity of liars whose consciences are seared."

Because we are hardwired to want more power and control, many individually and corporately are forgetting the importance of respectful, civil discourse; intimidation, heated verbal exchanges and violent protests are becoming progressively more common. If we continue to see widespread economic hardships, political arrogance and hypocrisy, rising violence, racial animosity, sexual license and anti-Christian sentiments, we will increase the likelihood of anarchy becoming a real possibility.

Are progressive political authorities attempting to govern and coerce others by instituting "truth by degrees and rights by decrees," grounded in liberal identify politics, greater moral autonomy, and political correctness? If you embrace moral autonomy, a progressive globalism that seeks to subdue and control the masses, you have made the government or your political ideology, your God. Beware of what or who you serve!

Ecclesiastes is an Old Testament book in which many biblical scholars believe was written by King Solomon. It conveys a core message for all generations, recognizing the critical importance of human responsibility and accountability in relationship to God's sovereignty.

> Ecclesiastes 3:2 declares there is "A time to be born, and a time to die." God determines both. You can't add or subtract from either.

> Ecclesiastes 3:14-15 conveys divine wisdom, "I perceived that whatever God does endures forever, nothing can be added to it nor anything taken from it. God has done it, so that people fear before him. That which is, already has been, that which is to be, has already been, and God seeks what has been driven away." All human efforts and governments are temporary and subject to God's authority. That which God posits, last forever. There is nothing new under the sun regarding man's contentious nature or creative bent to excuse bad behavior.

> Ecclesiastes 4: 1-3 "Again I saw all the oppressions that are done under the sun. And behold, the tears of the oppressed, and they had no one to comfort them! On the side of their oppressors there was power, and there was no one to comfort them. And I thought the dead who are

already dead more fortunate than the living who are still alive. But better than both is he who has not yet been and has not seen the evil deeds that are done under the sun."

Notice how the last sentence condemns the wickedness of man in that the unborn, unlike the already dead and still living, have not been exposed to the evil that awaits them, as have the past and present generations. Could it also convey a message that the evil that awaits, is an imminent threat?

The following pages address the above via a combination of holy scripture, Christian theologians Spirit inspired wisdom, and social commentaries from various discerning political leaders, journalists and writers to illustrate the necessity of civilly working together to establish and maintain right relationships with God first, our neighbors, and those who disagree with you.

To let you know up front the summation of what follows, any so-called truth or "right" that circumvents or undercuts the required sacrifices, disciplines and self-denial demanded by God in any given social issue or ethical requirement, ceases to be true, ceases to be "correct" the moment it becomes a force unto itself, outside of or independent of the scripturally required obedience. This book takes the view that Christian truth is the basis for all answers to social and moral issues dividing our nation. Further, there are not two opposing but equal answers within Christian truth that are equally valid and equally acceptable to God. Domestic tranquility will never happen as long as "domestic fidelity" is not required.

Unfortunately, a case can be made that one of the biggest obstacles to Christian influence today is the undisciplined, misinformed and unfaithful lifestyles of many professing Christians. Liberal church positions have become so indoctrinated in their aversion to any form of sexual and identity group discrimination that it has placed a higher priority on keeping the peace by compromising the Gospel than by keeping the truth by honoring the scripturally required letter and spirit intended.

When anyone presents to others, a God who mirrors their civil and legal priorities, they want you to believe their priorities and see their priorities as God approved. Remember, the source of your accepted truth will drive your truth. God's truth is unbiased, but man's representation often is not. For many Christians it seems as if we are "damned" by liberal thinkers if we hold fast to our values and we are "damned" by our theology if we know the act or practice is wrong but ignore it. The conundrum is this; if you believe and attempt to serve God as instructed in scripture, appropriate discrimination as directed by scripture requires you to faithfully reject anything politically correct that corrupts, denies or defies God's word. If you believe "politically correct" trumps the Word of God and the things of God, you have to "correct" God's Word with more tolerance and more moral autonomy.

"Be still and know that I am God"—these are among the most powerful and insightful eight words written in the Old Testament. Those words came from God, who has revealed himself and is speaking to David, the king of Israel, through the inspiration of the Holy Spirit. Even though David is a king and among the most powerful men at that time in history, God, plainly, spells out who is really in charge. He instructs David to be quiet and to listen for and discern the spiritual keys to all who seek wisdom and a closer, more faithful, spiritual relationship with him.

Those silent, inspired words that God gave to David speak loudly to all men and women today who have been blessed by God to receive words of eternal importance. Such words set the tone for an earthly and heavenly life, centered on the proper perspective, priority, and relationship dynamics of divine authority and human submission to God's sovereignty in every generation.

That inspired instruction is filled with multiple ramifications, including the necessity to trust that God knows what the best course of action in every situation where uncertainty or fear is present. Prayer and patience are required to faithfully trust and obey. Those eight words convey divine wisdom, eternal security, a command, and a warning, as God speaks to David in Psalm 46:10. He reminds David that he is the creator and in control over heaven and earth. He is the king of the universe, forcefully reminding David where his strength and security lay and where David should put his trust when personal and national conflicts test his resolve and faith.

Self-reliance, self-righteousness, and self-sufficiency are leading causes of disastrous decisions that come back to haunt or hurt us, both on an individual and national basis. By declaring your independence or moral autonomy from scripture and divine authority, you are throwing yourself under God's bus. Seeking and listening to the Spirit's "still, small voice" may seem weak or less politically correct, but in the end, any action taken that is not scripturally discerned or Spirit-influenced, more likely than not, will do more harm than good.

When you arrogantly determine that you are morally independent or autonomous regarding God's sovereign authority, you inevitably set yourself up for a fall.

Here is what frequently) transpires when we take it upon ourselves to follow human nature or human wisdom instead of divine providence:

> Well did Isaiah prophesy of you hypocrites, as it is written, "this people honors me with their lips, but their heart is far from me; in vain do they worship me, teaching as doctrines the commandments of me. You leave the commandment of God and hold to the tradition of men." (Mark 7:6–8)

> Deuteronomy 4: 2 sternly warns against reading into scripture what is not there or intended: "You shall not add to the word I command you, nor take from it, that you may keep the commandments of the Lord your God that I command you."

Chance, luck, coincidence, or fate are the words that many choose to describe or explain the unforeseen good or evil that comes their way. But does that also apply on a national scale? Are there forces beyond our control, individually and nationally, that put us at greater risk, causing us to be at the wrong place at the wrong time or the right place at the right time that have no plausible explanation? Is there an ultimate authoritative order over all things to which we can appeal? Are the various forces and authorities in the world at odds with each other to the extent that we are by varying degrees, all subject to the vicissitudes of authorities and institutions, with little or no appeal or recourse? It may seem contradictory but from a Christian perspective, the answer is yes to both.

A primary theme of this writing is that Christians are certain that God's providence precludes coincidence or so-called chance events as being uncontrolled or beyond his ability to contain. Everything happens for a reason—a purpose that God's providence controls and directs, according to his sovereign will. The good, the bad, the ugly, and all the big and small events in your life and in each nation are a part of God's plan and purpose, which come together to give God the glory and Christians, eternal joy. We may find it hard to believe or accept that the chaos we see today, on an individual and national basis, fall within His master plan. Though it is often not clear why we are experiencing such turmoil and chaos in our country and world, God determines, allows, and directs the obvious and unseen events according to his purposes.

Accidents, bad luck, or bad timing are misplaced human understandings that fail to identify the root causes and effects of many of life's unexplainable events. Are accidents, disasters, and heartbreak the consequences of events that follow moral law, natural law, or divine providence, which is part of God's purpose and will? Or are they simply haphazard, inexplicable bad luck or unpredictable points of collision? Will your answer be more definitive or better discerned by moral self-determination or Holy Scripture?

Daniel 2:21 states that God "removes kings and sets up kings." No king or president comes to power or is removed from power outside of God's ability to control the beginning and ending of each one's time of authority. Individual and presidential decisions and actions have cascading consequences for good or evil. Whether they are simple or extraordinary, God arranges them in a manner that suits his purpose and ultimate outcome. The God who created the universe knows your inner fears, events that will happen in your lifetime, and the day you were born and the day you will die. That may be cause for concern or comfort, depending how you look at it, in that much of your life is out of your control and under God's.

In the following analysis from chapter 3 of the *Westminster Confession of Faith*, we have an explanation how various causes listed below are each distinctive in their origin but legitimately conducted. The following confession extrapolates that God accomplishes his purposes through human free choice and other secondary influences in conjunction with his divine providence.

> God, from all eternity, did, by the most wise and holy counsel of his own will, freely, and unchangeably ordain whatsoever comes to pass: yet so, as thereby neither is God the author of sin, nor is violence offered to the will of the creatures; nor is the liberty or contingency of second causes taken away, but rather established. (WCF 3.1)[1]

One of the most authoritative and insightful pronouncements interpreting the above comes from the *Westminster Confession of Faith*, chapter 5, which deals with the providence of God in all things:

> God the great Creator of all things doth uphold, direct, dispose and govern all creatures, actions, and things, from the greatest even to the least, by his most wise and holy providence, according to his infallible foreknowledge, and the free and immutable counsel of his own will, to the praise of the glory of his wisdom, power, justice, goodness and mercy. (WCF 5.1)[2]

The following section explains distinctions between the first cause and secondary causes in which God weaves his tapestry, ordaining all that comes to pass, according to his purposes.

> Although, in relation to the foreknowledge and decree of God, the first cause, all things come to pass immutably and infallibly; yet, by the same providence, he ordereth them to fall out, according to the nature of second causes, either necessarily, freely, or contingently. (WCF 5.2)[3]

The difference between Christian understanding of righteousness and justice and human understanding of righteousness and justice is that Christian discernment is derived from the Spirit of God, and the human understanding is a product of compromise and human nature, evolved from the sin of man. That sin, inherent in each of us, precludes humanity from ever coming together peacefully or in good will toward one another on its own volition. Suppressing the knowledge, truth, and holiness of God prevents every person and historical age from rising above our nature and becoming the children God intended us to be. It is only through the Spirit that the Son is made known, and it is only because God's grace sends the Spirit to his chosen that anyone can be forgiven and receive God's blessing of spending eternity with him.

Without the renewal of our minds—brought about by the revelation of the Holy Spirit and all that our baptism by the Spirit entails—there can be no lasting peace or reconciliation among men or nations. Man is incapable of self-restoration or self-reconciliation, and he cannot save himself by his works or good-faith efforts. Yet many Christians and multitudes of non-Christians believe that a good person (by human definition), regardless of their religious or ideological beliefs, deserves God's blessing and will be rewarded accordingly. This false confidence is refuted in scripture quite clearly, but for those of the world who live according to the world's standards, the spirit of the world has deceived them. Jesus spoke these explicit words, which represent the gold standard of the Trinity: "I am the way, the truth, and the life. No one comes to the Father, except through me" (John 14:6). We are either children of God or children of wrath.

Two glorious Bible verses transcend and relieve our fears and doubts about what God will do for those who love him: "If God is for us, who can be against us?" (Romans 8: 31), and "Those who are with us are more than those who are with them." (2 Kings 6:16).

The message intended is that when God is on your side, guarding you and upholding you, it does not matter who or what is against you. It is not a matter of greater numbers but of God's omnipotence and absolute power over all things.

"Everyone to whom much was given, of him, much will be required" (Luke 12:48) should give everyone pause. Whatever your personal gifts, resources, or capabilities, if you neglect or excuse your lack of due diligence in developing and using them—for others' good and God's glory—you will find yourself at odds with your Creator and fellow man. Each of us must decide whether to be at odds with God's authority or man's authority.

What happens when nations reject or abuse their individual and collective blessings? Israel, God's chosen people, knew God's response to their disobedience and arrogance. You see, God requires every nation to recognize his sovereignty over individuals and nations. "Truth or consequences" or the law of retribution for evil, comes in many forms. God's quiver contains many arrows that are directed at all individuals and nations that disregard or challenge his right to rule over us.

Hundreds of years ago, American political leader Daniel Webster warned our nation of the disasters that follow national rebellion when he said,

> If the power of the Gospel is not felt throughout the length and breadth of the land, anarchy and misrule, degradation and misery, corruption and darkness will reign without mitigation or end.[4]

It is vital that you know, understand, and practice what God expects of you. In Micah 6: 8, three requirements are required:

> He has told you, O man, what is good; and what does the Lord require of you but to do justice, and to love kindness and to walk humbly with your God.

That directive was made known thousands of years ago, but it equally applies to today's self-righteous, who see themselves as above reproach as they exercise politically correct moral autonomy as a right. Leave out any of the three requirements and you will discover soon enough that stress and conflict will inflict a heavy cost on your day-to-day comings and goings.

The difference between righteous and self-righteous is *self.* Anytime you lead with self-diagnosis, self-serving, or self-judging, you are heading for deep ruts and many potholes. The saying, "Everyone learns the hard way," applies when we insist on doing it our way, regardless of warnings to the contrary. The problem is that sometimes the *hard way* consequences can never be overcome or taken back, and the ripples of our mistakes and errors in judgment go on for years or generations.

This is a good place to remember the importance of getting our priorities right. "Hallowed be thy name; thy kingdom come; thy will be done on earth as it is in heaven." These words from the Lord's Prayer are always relevant and always a command that requires our faith and obedience to commit to serving and honoring God first—and everything else that follows with that in mind.

The Christian doxology speaks to our place in the divine scheme of things and states how we are to relate to God and acknowledge his sovereignty over all things:

> Praise God from whom all blessings flow,
> Praise him all creatures here below,
> Praise him above ye heavenly hosts,
> Praise Father, Son, and Holy Ghost

My point is that questions require you to listen and respond to the questioner; the questioner can use it as a tool to get information or give feedback, depending on the answers and attitude conveyed in the response. The tone of the question and answer either will reveal or generate hostility or a degree of understanding or agreement. In hindsight, it is always prudent to be careful and, as much as possible, be prepared to ask the question (or answer it) with respect and civility. Relationships and associations can blossom or sour, depending on your attitude.

"A soft answer turns away wrath, but a harsh word stirs up anger" (Proverbs 15:1)—this remains good advice today. Further, a good reminder for everyone is found in Proverbs 15:3 "The eyes of the Lord are in every place, keeping watch on the evil and the good."

Hopefully, the above scripture sets the stage for the ultimate questioner, God, as everybody who ever lived will answer, in one way or the other, God's question: "Who do you think you are?" There are numerous situations in the Old and New Testaments where God questions individuals as a test or reminder that he is the Creator, and we are the created. God holds all the cards and is in complete control of everything that happens. Since he holds the keys to life and death for every individual, we might think we would be better prepared to give a wise or prudent answer his questions.

Unfortunately, many of us are hostile or indifferent as to how we would answer or the attitude we might convey.

Another theme throughout this book is to question and challenge the assumptive integrity granted high-profile political, religious, and social movers and shakers, as well as their motivations and intentions in connection with innumerable "progressive" identity groups that contribute to our politically correct moral autonomy ideology. From a Christian perspective, the importance of what the scripture says about their positions or conduct is a relevant concern that we should civilly address. When challenging or questioning, we should respectfully point out that we are not condemning them but are concerned about the consequences their deviation from historically accepted, orthodox standards foretell. A truth unto itself—self-determined, self-defined, and self-approved (mortal autonomy, politically correct, identity politics, self-appraisal)—is always a source of concern, regardless of who or where it comes from.

Often, alternative, or compromised beliefs and truths are potentially dangerous to all who are impacted by their subjective bearings and forced imposition. If you must force or intimidate someone to follow your lead, a logical person would question the validity or integrity of a belief or conduct which is incompatible with scripture. Any ideology—political or religious—that inherently favors one group over another, simply because it is currently politically correct or socially acceptable, which does not consider whether its favorable status has been scripturally merited, deserves to be questioned and debated.

From God's perspective, when his "who do you think you are" is put into play, prudent individuals should remember that every breath they take and all that they have is a result of God's creation and grace. The arrogance and indifference displayed by numerous politically correct actions and moral autonomy assertions are an affront to that grace and will put those individuals in God's crosshairs. How does anyone get to the point where they consider themselves godlike or free from scriptural instructions and deserve the right or have the authority to be morally or ethically independent? Everybody has free will and the right to choose, but no one has the right to be wrong about godly truth, Spirit discernment, and divine wisdom.

You can take this to the bank: any so-called truth or right that circumvents or undercuts the required sacrifices, disciplines, and self-denial demanded by God, in any given social or moral issue, ceases to be truth and ceases to be right the moment it becomes a force unto itself, outside of or independent of the scripturally required obedience. If an ideology or position is not Christ-centered, Spirit-inspired, and empowered, and it cannot validly be corroborated by scripture, it will not receive God's blessing. In fact, it will be at war with him.

In our finite world, where weaponizing identity politics is the current rage, many forget that open-ended morality or moral autonomy means that anyone who does not hold that view has boundaries and exclusions that inevitably preclude their moral standing as correct. When blame and shame are the primary drivers of rights and political correctness, those espousing that progressive ideology cannot look to scripture as a guide; they know scripture preludes blame and shame as a motivator to bring about civility, harmony, and justice. Hypocrisy is rampant when equality or equity is contrived, so those validating non-scriptural, liberal ways and means to justify their ends, are rejecting God's authority.

All corruption or sin, whether private or public, has social ramifications. What you do in private may not be seen others, but God sees the heart and the deceit in private just as well as in the public eye. What is done in public that fits the scriptural definition of sin but is condoned or encouraged, reverberates beyond the immediate impact on an even broader scale. This scriptural reminder should cause us hesitation and regret, when God tells us the consequences of sin:

> But who will by no means clear the guilty, visiting the iniquity of the fathers on the children and the children's children, to the third and fourth generation? (Exodus 34:7)

The sin you and I are committing now has the potential to affect four generations. Think about that the next time you think you are hiding something from others that God sees and might result in future hardships and misery to your children and grandchildren.

One additional fundamental we need to know and acknowledge is that our human nature defaults to what it wants, what it thinks it can get away with, and blaming others for our mistakes and negative consequences. Scripture paints all humans as fundamentally broken—that we are rebellious and hypocritical because we are at enmity with God. Our relationships are so far off base that we have no ability on our own to reconcile our rebellion against God. We are sinful because our broken relationship with God compels us to find other idols to grasp or worship and, in the process, to de-god God.

In every age and stage of human history, power corrupts. We have a bit of wisdom in our saying, "Absolute power corrupts absolutely." On the other hand, the power of the gospel has the inspired ability to turn people away from their lust for power and control over others. However you want to perceive where you are in your human journey, the road less traveled (submission and humility before God) is less traveled because it is not normal to humble yourself or ask forgiveness in a world where politically correct moral autonomy tells you to go your own way and do what seems right to you.

Discrimination is both a word and a function that contains divine and human attributes. In our time, it has the equivalency of a four-letter profanity. Yet a case can be made that the divine nature of God discriminates every second of every day, as he separates the wheat from the chaff and the righteous from the unrighteous. On the other hand, humans recently have determined that almost any form of discrimination is wrong or evil. God reminds us through scripture that honor, integrity, and justice require Spirit-discerned and applied righteous discrimination every time we are confronted with unrighteous ideology that humans incorporate into their callous, moral, and legal definitions of good and evil.

The greater the pride, ignorance, and arrogance associated with politically correct self-righteous indignation, the more sinister the evil divide it creates between righteous Christian convictions. Moral autonomy granted by any authority or entity is a core contributor to the malaise and division that is roiling every aspect of our daily living. Unaddressed from a scriptural point of view, the world will continue to decline and slide toward anarchy. All you need to reinforce that position is to look around our nation and world as it self-destructs.

The sexual and moral revolutions promoted and condoned by progressive liberal ideologies have attempted to cover their backs by incorporating blame-and-shame tactics. That strategy demonstrates that humans, left to their own devices and by adopting an alternative truth, become dysfunctional. Without a spiritual revival, viral humanism will continue to destroy marriages, exacerbate the dissolution of families, and broaden our downward spiral regarding our human and divine relationships.

There will always be numerous sides to every important moral pronouncement concerning major social issues of our day. Conservative and liberal positions will be defended by both Christians and the state. Many Christians would agree that they feel besieged by an ever-expanding moral melting pot that is being stirred to the boiling point by forces opposed to orthodox or Reformed Christian theology, practice, and authority. Many politically correct moral autonomists regard Christian apologetics as unduly infringing on their rights and freedoms, as they believe that everyone is entitled to their opinion and beliefs, and no one should be judged by their understanding of morally acceptable and unacceptable behaviors or attitudes.

Separating the church from the state has always been a matter of individual moral interpretation of where one institutional function supersedes or denies another's. Where you come down on that juxtaposition will require a strong objective argument to convince others that your convictions and positions can stand on their own merit, with or without God. Every human position can only be subjective because we are limited by our moral nature, personal experience, and lack of complete understanding of all relationships of a human and divine nature, to which only God is privy.

"Be still and know that I am God. I will be exalted among the nations, I will be exalted in the earth" is both a declaration and command given from God to David in Psalm 46:10. In this affirmation of sovereignty, God speaks to every generation, demanding obedience, and reverence. He reveals his nature, attributes, and purposes, sometimes quietly and sometimes dramatically, through Christians, human events, nature, and a still, small voice.

One of the most dramatic scenes in scripture is found in 1 Kings 19:11–12, as God demonstrates his power and control over everything to his prophet Elijah:

> Go out and stand on the mount before the Lord. And behold the Lord passed by, and a great and strong wind tore the mountains and broke in pieces the rocks before the Lord, but the Lord was not in the wind. And after the wind an earthquake, but the Lord was not in the earthquake. And after the earthquake a fire, but the Lord was not in the fire. And after the fire, *the sound of a low whisper.* (italics added)

Each of us is responsible for our responses to God's calling in whatever form he speaks to us. While in most cases, his revelation is not so profound as in Elijah's case, we are held accountable nonetheless for failing to see, hear, or understand what he is trying to convey.

Jesus articulates to Christians what he expects of them, as he commands his disciples:

> Go therefore and make disciples of all nations, baptizing them in the name of the Father and of the Son and of the Holy Spirit, teaching them to observe all that I have commanded you. (Matthew 28:19-20)

Prerequisites for being in God's good graces are reverence, gratitude, and humility. Leave out any of these, and all your good works or good intentions are rejected because of your disrespect and ingratitude. With the Spirit guiding you to faithfully obey his instruction, your efforts will be received and accepted by God. Everything outside the Spirit's prompting falls short of God's standards and will not be blessed when you take it upon yourself, to act in an ignorant or arrogant attitude of self-righteousness. Nothing lasting or great comes from self-will or self-guided motivation and intention.

Ecclesiastes 2:26 gives Christians the heart and soul to faithfully abide by God's instruction and counsel regarding how we are to follow his lead:

> For to the one who pleases him, God has given wisdom, knowledge, and joy, but to the sinner, he has given the business of gathering and collecting, only to give to one who pleases God.

Subjective secular values, politically customized to justify their implementation, are used by institutional identity politics to intimidate and discriminate against Christians. We normally associate values such as honor, integrity, demanding work, merit, accountability, and responsibility as good or positive. Negative values, however, can be masqueraded as positive intentions just as effectively in rallying the troops to follow your defiant lead. Self-righteous indignation, self-determination, and self-justification flowing from situational ethics are the core attributes and requirements used by identity politics to attract and empower politically tailored social and moral repudiation of scriptural restraints. Christians are enduring most of this onslaught, as the "correct" people arrogantly brush aside scriptural admonitions that refute their ideological and moral values.

Whenever one dominant political party controls the legislature and the executive branch of government, favoritism is a given. You might say it is the right of the majority to govern according to the principles they ran on and won on. Our checks-and-balances system is designed to prevent a complete takeover by one political ideology. But when that same political party dominates the educational system, the media, and the largest corporate entities and panders to myriad identity groups, granting them unearned merit and validation, you begin to approach anarchy.

If several generations are brought up on the biased ideological positions being promoted by the dominant party, with the media and educational system parroting their sound bites, people are made to believe and told to accept that everything said and done is for their good and in the country's best interests. That is when things get dangerous.

Let me control the textbooks and I will control the state.

—Adolf Hitler[5]

Give me four years to teach the children, and the seed I have sown will never be uprooted.

—Vladimir Lenin[6]

Christians are among the most targeted religious groups that face persecution and discrimination for their refusal to support or validate the ever-expanding ideology commonly referred to as *politically correct moral autonomy*. It sees identity politics as its ticket to overwhelm Christian opposition to abortion, same-sex activity, and excessive entitlements and uses state supremacy to decide what is moral and legal, scripture be damned. Christian values are set in stone; they are not malleable. We have no choice as we are inspired and empowered by the truth revealed by the Holy Spirit, using sacred scripture as both our security and power to obediently address social and moral issues that emanate from human lust, corruption, self-serving behavior, and self-aggrandizement.

In September 2020, the Pew Research Center pointed out that Christians are the most persecuted religious group in the world. It makes the point that various Supreme Court decisions, based on human institutions and documents, have determined Christian influence in schools, businesses, the military, and society in general cannot freely and openly discuss their faith, practice, or prayers because it might offend or put off some groups.

Moral-autonomy and identity-politics ideologies are free to select whatever they determine is normal moral or acceptable human behavior, based on their politics or their subjective take on acceptable and unacceptable beliefs and personal actions regarding any issue. It is hard to be morally or legally wrong or negative if you make the rules fluid enough to accommodate each request for validation, regardless of something's lack of inherent merit or value regarding scriptural instruction.

Approving something because identity groups insist, they have the right or moral acuity to justify its acceptance is not morally or ethically prudent as *every group* has a distinct set of rules or standards that it self-designs. If you make the rules, referee the game, and control what is written or said about the conduct of the players, are you likely to get an objective storyline or a biased, often-false impression that the participants are all first-class citizens with everybody's best interests at heart?

We have become a nation where *more* is a given; it is a politically enshrined, socially radicalized daily quest. Individuals, institutions, and identity groups seem to perpetually seek, by degrees, more legal rights, more identity freedoms, more government entitlements, more something-for-everyone handouts, more sexual validations, more taxes to offset excessive spending and debt, and more anything-goes politically correct moral autonomy!

"More" rights and tolerance excesses have become so indoctrinated into our culture that shame and guilt are laughed off, as if they were old-fashioned, Christian-associated emotions, rather than normal moral responses to sin and evil. We now see evil, hear evil, and speak evil as common, everyday accepted activity. Humility and remorse have gone the way of the dodo bird. God has become an afterthought, and Christians are seen as an impediment.

We each have problems and concerns. We prioritize according to what we regard as our most pressing and immediate needs. Governments and institutions want you to believe that they have the answers to our social divisions and moral issues. Depending on to what they subscribe, we tend to take them at their word and follow their lead as we look for solutions and answers that will resolve our current problems or help us get through them most efficiently or effectively.

One of our biggest mistakes is not identifying the root causes for our national and individual malaise; rather, we look for quick and easy fixes that may get temporary immediate results but have no lasting positive solutions or permanent ethical improvements. A major problem today is the ideology that immediate gratification, by whatever pragmatism works, should be incorporated into our system of governing as much as possible, without carefully considering the probable future detriments that have not been well thought out. Often because of the lack of due diligence, we fail to learn the lessons of history. Due to self-righteous attitudes, history repeats itself causing harm and division.

It has been determined that doling out money for "correct" projects and granting unmerited entitlements and rights to favored political party blocks of voters is the correct way to proceed. *Correct* is subjective interpretation, not a science; *autonomy* is open-ended, with no consistent objective core. Neither is definitive, and each is influenced by the subjective character, interests, and moral makeup of political decision-makers towing the party line or seeking reelection.

That to which you commit will determine that to which you will submit. All of us are loyal to someone or something. How you prioritize that reveals where your heart is and the degree to which you will submit to the requirements of that authority. When you put your money where your mouth is, and your actions speak to where your heart is, you reveal what is most important to you. The question is, what will it reveal? Are you on board with an ideological golden calf presented by the politically correct or by trusting God's divine authority? Many Christians see those who falsely promote unequal, ungodly values as equally viable, as lost souls grasping for meaning and purpose but looking in all the wrong places for the answers. Political arrogance, which emanates from self-righteous rejection of Christian theology, practice, and values, can be found in an ideology that worships the human body and mind, while it goes about "correcting" what God has instituted.

The dominant force in reshaping our social and moral political landscape is the unprecedented amount of self-righteous indignation being displayed, which results in an across-the-board rise in indiscriminate tolerance. It is used as a political weapon by progressive, liberal philosophers and politicians to browbeat and intimidate Christians into "correct" moral submission. Discrimination, real or imagined, is the primary excuse to put into place a system of governing by indeterminate checks and balances. The manner of determining what is real or imagined or what is scripturally true or false (political fiat) is the chink in the armor of the politically correct that frequently reveals their hypocrisy, arrogance, and fox-in-the-henhouse opportunism.

Ecclesiastes may not be a well-known Old Testament book, but it is full of wisdom. A few examples will corroborate that claim.

> I perceive that whatever God does *endures forever; nothing can be added to it, nor anything taken from it.* God has done it, so that people fear before him. That which is, already has been that which is to be, already has been and God seeks what has been driven away. Ecclesiastes 3:14–15, (italics added)

> Wisdom is better than weapons of war, but one sinner destroys much good. (Ecclesiastes 9:18)

This last example should bring both pause and alarm to every living being:

> The end of the matter; all has been heard. Fear God and keep his commandments, for this is the whole duty of man. For God will bring every deed into judgment, with every secret thing, whether good or evil. (Ecclesiastes 12:13)

Anti-Christian, customized moral values that are associated with identity politics are designed to justify the promotion of different strokes for different folks. It acts as a cover for indiscriminate tolerance. By legislating decreed identity rights to validate "correct" values, a *false sense of legitimacy is established.* If an identity-politics issue cannot show it is true to both the letter and spirit of historically accepted orthodox Christian apologetics, it should not be granted ethical merit that it has not demonstrated. The state has no business giving any group a free pass, based primarily on contrived moral values built from mass emotional consent. The consequences of approving and incorporating non scriptural values into our ethical and legal considerations as equally viable, with proven scriptural mandates, is more costly than standing firm and asserting that they are not compatible with Christian teaching.

If we lived during biblical times, scripture might well include a reference to or denunciation of our various right's addictions and sanctimonious choice predilections; *it might read as follows:*

And God gave them over to their excuses, exceptions, exemptions, and excesses. In those days, self-righteousness seduced the people into believing everyone has the right to do what is right in their sight. Thus, evil became good, and good was called discriminatory. Great chaos ensued; the undisciplined sacrificed virtue, integrity, and honor for pragmatism and self-indulgence, yet the people continued to bow and pray to the idols they had made. Widespread violence and destructive lifestyles became a way of life. There was no repentance; therefore, the Lord brought them low with perpetual anxiety and fear, resulting in continuous internal and external conflicts. Rulers hardened their hearts, and the powerful hid behind their walls, trusting that their money and power would protect them, attacking all who held them accountable for their rebellion against God's truth and required sacrificial living. The people suffered day and night. Many lost hope. But God saved a remnant of faithful Christians who trusted in the Lord, knowing he would equip and sustain them during these times of tribulation by sending the Holy Spirit to empower them.

An article in the *Washington Post*, April 28, 2018, had a Pew Research survey of 4,729 participants. It helped to give an idea of the increasing number of Americans who, in one form or another, were rejecting the God of the Old and New Testaments. Previous polls in 2007 and 2014 showed belief in God was declining, from 92 percent to 89 percent to the 2018 number of 80 percent. The two earlier polls were telephone contacts, while the latest poll was online. Only 45 percent of college graduates believe in the God of the Bible. *Seventy percent of Republicans believe in the God of the Bible, while only 45 percent of Democrats do.* In general, people under age fifty viewed God as less powerful and less involved than did older Americans. That downward trend bodes greater friction and hostility toward Christians, as well as increasing the numbers of competing social truths and identity-group politics.

Moral autonomy or independence is a mockery of natural law and truth. Galatians 6:7–8 warns of the consequences: "Do not be deceived; God is not mocked, for whatever one sows, that will he also reap. For the one who sows to his own flesh will from the flesh, reap corruption." Every human, whether he or she knows it or not, participates in a warfare where their flesh and spirit contest for supremacy of their beings.

Ephesians 6:12 reminds us, "For we do not wrestle against flesh and blood, but against the rulers, against the authorities, against the cosmic powers over this present darkness, against the spiritual forces of evil in the heavenly places." Those who disregard this warning are at the mercy of unseen malevolent forces, whose greatest pleasure is seeing us destroy ourselves and others in the act of denying its veracity, while clinging to the promises of politically correct moral autonomy.

Humanism and secularism are the driving forces in our political and social mainstream agendas today. Reverend Burk Parsons of Ligonier Ministries, writing in their *Tabletalk* magazine, describes the disaster that has followed because of the politically correct endorsing *secularism*:

> They are an authority unto themselves, and the foundation for their self-appointed authority is as unstable as the emotions of their ever-changing hearts. Whether or not they know it, they have succumbed to secularism, which begins in the heart and ends in death. Secularism is the belief that man does not need God or God's laws in man's social, governmental, or economic affairs. Ironically, secularism rejects religion, yet is itself a religion. In these United States of America, many of our politicians, courts, schools, and businesses embrace and promote the religion of secularism under the rubric of freedom from religion and by the advancement of human autonomy, which inevitably leads to anarchy.[7]

William Voegeli, senior editor of *Claremont Review of Books*, takes us back fifty years to *The Public Interest*, which, early on, grasped the following:

The intended beneficial consequences of social policies are routinely overwhelmed by the unintended harmful consequences they trigger. It may also be, as conservatives have long argued, that achieving liberal goals, no matter how humane they sound, requires kinds and degrees of government coercion fundamentally incompatible with a government created to secure citizens' inalienable rights deriving it's just powers from the consent of the governed.[6]

The question of "politically correct" and "Christian correct" is not a question of which view is right or correct; rather, it is a question of where your marching orders come from (US Constitution, Bill of Rights, Supreme Court, scripture) and to which authority or institution (human or divine) you will submit. Paraphrasing the first commandment of the Ten Commandments, "You shall have no other gods, idols, interests, relationships or *authorities* before me." However you want to interpret that commandment, it is quite clear that anything you put before or above God's sovereignty is an affront to him and carries dire consequences for the individuals and nations that function as if it does not apply to them. Being the first commandment and the priority of the God, who created all things, it conveys an absolute condition that has no acceptable alternative. The attempt to associate "politically correct" with "Christian correct" may be more destructive than obvious non-Christian practices and principles. An open mind or pragmatic rationalization that portrays the two as essentially equal has led to good intentions becoming personal and national ethical disasters.

Bruce Bawer writes the following in *The Victims' Revolution: The Rise of Identity Politics and the Closing of the Liberal Mind*:

The point (became) simply to "prove"—respectively, endlessly—certain facile, reductive, and invariably left-wing points about the nature of power and oppression. In this updated version of the humanities, all Western civilization is not analyzed through the use of reason or judged according to aesthetic standards that have been developed over centuries; rather, *it is viewed through prisms*

29

> *of race, class, and gender and is hailed or condemned in*
> *accordance with certain political checklists.*[7] (Italics added)

Columbia humanities professor Mark Lilla writes:

> Identity politics on the left was at first about large classes
> of people ... seeking to redress major historical wrongs
> by mobilizing and then working through our political
> institutions to secure their rights. But by the 1980's, it
> had given way to a pseudo-politics of self-regard and
> increasingly narrow and exclusionary self-definition that
> is now cultivated in our colleges and universities. The
> main result has been to turn people back onto themselves
> rather than turning them outward towards the wider
> world they share with others. *It has left them unprepared*
> *to think about common good in non-identity terms and what*
> *must be done practically to secure it—especially the hard and*
> *unglamorous task of persuading people very different from*
> *themselves to join a common effort.*[8] (Italics added)

CHAPTER 2

Human Nature, the Cause of All Social Issues

The conundrum for moral autonomists that arises in many moral or social issues is the appropriate way to counter a Christian moral position that is scripturally factual. Do you mince words; try to mollify or placate the Christian side by compromising "correct" values; and assertively reconcile what scripture instructs cannot be reconciled, or do you let Christian theology and practice speak for itself? Do you dare give Christians a platform of equal opportunity in the marketplace, allowing them to corroborate their validity and veracity with specific, explicit divine instructions from scripture? Should moral autonomists face the music and let the chips fly? Should Christians give a little to get a little?

Compromise is the political way of coming to an agreement when there are liberal and conservative differences. Christians do not have that option. Jesus never compromised anything of an ethical or spiritual nature to get people to like him or agree with him. Attaining peace or harmony by compromise is human nature, not divine nurture. Christians are tasked to seek reconciliation that does not compromise anything outside of our authority and scriptural instruction. How and when we attempt to reconcile is key to being obedient.

In 2 Timothy 4:2, we read, "Preach the word; be ready in season and out of season; reprove, rebuke and exhort, with complete patience and teaching."

The intention is not to condemn but to point out the error, the sin, or the wrong perspective. It is to point them in the intended scriptural direction and assertively encourage them to repent and change their ways, to be in compliance and agreement with mandated scriptural instructions. The reconciling is always for people to change or turn away from their present sinful course, not to give the impression that scripture will condone or allow them to continue to sin or err. Reconciliation true to scripture does not accommodate or compromise unfaithful beliefs or actions, regardless of someone's insistence that it is acceptable. Always point to scripture as the one and only true godly instruction, the foundation of all truth, not today's morality or social considerations of what is acceptable.

Liberty or license and the wisdom to know the difference is not the question but an argument or exercise of definition. In our attempts to arrive at an equitable definition that neither stifles one nor exaggerates the other, majority rule or minority dissent at either end of the spectrum should be the primary reason for selecting one over the other. The majority is not always objective, but it is often subjectively driven by the sheer force of the power of its numbers to overwhelm or subdue those who dissent. Likewise, those dissenting tend to congregate around a position that advances their standards, which may or may not be superior to the majority's.

The rule of moral law, within itself, has the potential seeds of destruction, as human morality is in the eye of the beholder, or ruling authority. The rule of God, within itself, has the necessary seeds of scriptural instruction that God parleys into harmony when it is faithfully embraced. Teddy Roosevelt's secretary of state, Elihu Root, hit the nail on the head when he said, "There must be a reconciliation of liberty and self-discipline; discipline conscious of freedom and liberty capable of discipline."[1] When the degree of liberty or license is determined by the degree of or lack of self-discipline supported by the majority party's authority, it will mimic the morality or immorality of its core constituency. Every human form of government is like that proverbial box of chocolates—you never know what you might get. To compound the dilemma, a new cast of characters and circumstances constantly roils the muddy waters, often to a froth, with moral changes that undermine previously validated standards.

Using politically guided legalism as a guide to redirect us to human laws and legal authorities, the "politically correct" attempt to subtlety encourage Christians to think that civil religion and Christianity are similar in enough ways that we should not sweat the differences. The evil in this attitude is that it tries to convince Christians that they can overcome obstacles by adhering to civil laws and obeying civil authorities, in lieu of Christian doctrine, and practice. They are encouraged to use their own insights and wisdom, apart from obeying the specific requirements of the gospel. The emphasis in this philosophy is that our "good works" and "good will" should become primary and our faithfulness to scripture secondary. Furthermore, this evil deceit tempts us to believe we have earned God's blessings because of our good works, and we thus merit his grace. But here is the real kicker: whenever we turn to civil morality and make it a part of Christian ethics, civil laws over time, will replace the true gospel and become a new accepted social and moral gospel that allows what scripture abhors.

The Enlightenment or "Age of Reason" in the seventeenth and eighteenth centuries set the stage and laid the foundation for today's theological liberalism. It is that "reasoned" liberalism, in some Christian communities, that I address in this writing. Using *Christianity and Liberalism* by J. Gresham Machen as an articulate representation of that theology, he writes:

> What is the relationship between Christianity and modern culture; may Christianity be maintained in a scientific age? It is this problem which modern liberalism attempts to solve. Theological liberalism takes its cues from the world. It is driven by what man must do, what man must attain and what man must determine—not what God has done, what God has accomplished and what God has revealed. The motto of theological liberalism, then and now, is "Christianity must adapt or die." At its core, theological liberalism possesses a deep craving to be relevant to the culture, adored by the world and respected among the intellectual elite. And although its adherents would never admit it, the warp and woof of theological liberalism is, "Truth, if possible, but peace, relevance and worldly influence at all costs."[2]

Every choice is seen as the best choice at that moment. Humans are fickle; choice is often inconsistent due to different pressures and changing priorities. What was right at one time may not be the next time, depending on your demeanor or the political party's current leaning. When you diagnose and dissect politically correct moral autonomy, it becomes obvious to most rational people that different moral strokes for different people, functioning at various stages of moral maturity and comity, is a philosophy that legitimizes opposing truths that are inconsistent with normative or standard ethics underpinned by scripture.

"Political correctness" harkens back to another time, when contrived corruption and its quid pro quo relationships with corporate power took place in Italy. Benito Mussolini, the fascist dictator in Italy in World War II, coined the word *corporatism*. According to him, "Fascism should more appropriately be called corporatism because it is the merger of state and corporate power."[3]

Edmond Phelps, professor of economics at Columbia University, in his book, *Mass Flourishing: How Grassroots Innovation Created Jobs, Challenge and Change*, says it might be more encompassing than Mussolini thought. He writes,

> *The new thinking sees the state as undertaking to protect everyone from everyone else—or as close as is practicable.* Social protection for all is the motto of new corporatism. Government grants of unlimited scope may be made to regions and cities, even if their latent function (in Robert Merton's term) is to *dispense patronage in return for support, political or financial.* Lobbyists are welcome to submit requests for legislation, regulations, and interpretive rulings, especially if they come with bribes.[4] (italics added)

Left to their own devices, without enforced, fixed rules and standards applicable to everyone and only limited by limits they set for themselves, people gravitate toward moral relativity and rationalization to justify their positions and actions. Human nature tells us to look out for number one first, as much as possible. When push comes to shove, shove back harder; do whatever it takes to get what you want or feel you deserve. Excuses and exceptions are the common currency used to get away with questionable or illicit behavior.

Social passions or angst that drive political reforms are often unpredictable or unaccountable, yet they are bandied about in every election as if they were a sure thing. The one constant is the view that the current ruling party is not doing enough or is incompetent in what it is doing; therefore, the bums should be thrown out of power. The mistake of every government—seen as preventable if greater attention to due diligence had been properly vetted—is its too-great dependence on its own abilities, resources, and wisdom and too little dependence on scripture, past experiences or performance, and the necessity of both individuals and organizations involved to exercise greater self-control and personal accountability.

Because the church, increasingly, is being forcibly prevented from exercising its authority as God's designated check and balance on ethical issues, the "politically correct" majority or liberal party tends to be indiscriminately inclusive to appeal to the lowest common moral denominator to satisfy its numerous voting blocks. It feeds off pragmatism, expedience, pluralism, and implied goodwill within identity-group momentum. Truth by degrees and rights by decrees are often pandered as the most effective political and moral mechanisms for attracting new adherents and holding on to an existing base.

Two scales of justice are posited as the rightful or superior manner of determination. One primarily is centered around the federal government and civil institution's moral authority, and the other is grounded in Christian theology and practice. The separation of church and state has progressed to the point where any fundamental disagreements are settled by the state, removing, as much as possible, any influence by the church, as it examines the merits of the state's position. The church, God's instrument on earth, is tasked to look at the state's description of equality and equity and compares it to scriptural instructions and requirements. A good case can be made that the state frequently sidesteps church accountability, as pointed out in scripture, and makes its case by its might, not to its obligation to be a faithful representative of God's plan for all earthly authorities; to administer its civil, legal, and ethical obligations according to his divine authority, as stated in scripture and proclaimed by Christ.

What happens when unequal moral equivalencies are institutionalized as equal? Can anyone be set free by "doing the right thing," according to politically correct reasoning? If not, why are so many unable to comprehend that they are in bondage to someone's lies or authority's deception, as far as they live and die by what other people say, do, or believe? The spirit of psychology within our human nature is limited and handicapped, as it can only see and do what it is privy to and prepared for. It cannot escape God's assigned human limitations; it can only be set free by the Holy Spirit's divine intervention.

Charles Spurgeon, the great nineteenth-century preacher, and theologian known as "the Prince of Preachers," expounds on the necessity of having faith alone in Jesus:

> But if you have no faith, no matter the zeal, no matter what works, no matter what knowledge, no matter what pretensions to holiness you may possess, you are nothing, and your religion is in vain. No faith is genuine that does not bear the seal of the Spirit. No love, no hope can ever save us, unless it is sealed with the Spirit of God, for whatever does not have His seal upon it, is false. The Holy Spirit does not reveal in these last times any fresh laws or any novel doctrines or any new evolutions.[5]

Whew! Talk about not mincing words. He also weighs in on how the church shows its true colors and how the condition of the church impacts its ability to draw individuals to Christ: "In proportion as a church is holy, in that proportion will its testimony for Christ be powerful." That would seem to indicate that the church is not practicing what it preaches to the degree it could be called faithful.

When scriptural discrepancies are politically sanitized, ungodly people, who consider themselves good, rally around the deception and declare it as progressive, inclusive morality. Remember the golden calf that was created and worshipped by the Israelites in the book of Exodus? Today's progressive, inclusive morality is fashioned around the idolatry of self-aggrandizement and moral autonomy. We worship the creature, not Creator. Instead of worshipping a calf, we have "progressed" to worshipping ourselves, our bodies, our minds, and endless identity political rights. Claimed civil or moral rights that are not spelled out in scripture are susceptible to misinterpretation as implied rights by the interest group seeking them. The intent is to proffer that these new rights have been decoded recently, according to the politically correct, progressive interpretation.

Identity politics is very much like the whack-a-mole game at a fair. The unpredictability makes it hard to consistently hit your target. The political weaponizing of favored groups creates more friction than unity. Showing favoritism where merit or responsible behavior is lacking is neither moral nor correct. There will never be unity when demanding work and self-discipline are penalized in favor of squeaky wheels that spin violently and do nothing more than complain about those who showed integrity and grit in achieving their goals.

Anything that takes God's place—anything which is put above or before him, that refutes or subordinates his ultimate authority, which distorts scripture for any purpose—becomes a form of idolatry. All current morality is a set standard, an ideology or accepted mindset agreed upon by individuals, groups, or organizations that spell out or dictate their commonly adopted beliefs and practices. Moral autonomy is the consensus standard, as seen or authorized by progressive ideology. It is a prerogative given to those who agree with or who favor their political point of view, concerning major social issues or state authority, over church viewpoints.

The political and social world are turning inward, away from Christian theological truth and practices and toward self-determined, free-standing social morality—one where individual authority divides us and drives us toward polarizing identity groups, where each one establishes its own pecking order of standards for morality and acceptable practices. Every day, we see groups and organizations, with large and small factions, dueling for attention, power, and influence, insisting that other identity groups— or even forcing them to—kowtow to their rightful place in the political smorgasbord or to assimilate specific identity tenets into their moral, normal view of our political and social institutions. Increasingly, past traditionally honored ethical standards and theological positions have been reduced to being quaint, old-fashioned, out-of-date tripe.

Free will does not come with a get-out-of-jail-free pass. You can choose whatever you want, but every choice is subject to consequences associated with the choice. Free will that breaks boundaries or ethical standards set by scripture comes with a prohibitive cost—God's wrath. When your will is not God's will, the negative consequences that ensue, in one way or the other, will be God-ordained, not by chance or bad luck. Known truth will have known consequences that are consistent with it. God's truth, as exercised and obeyed by faithful Christians, in the end will triumph over any human opposition.

Moral autonomy is a portal to indulge our baser desires. We have made a permissive, perverted gay union legally and morally equal to a pure, faithful Christian marriage between a man and a woman. Without the discipline and accountability required in scripture, morality and truth become conditional to criteria subjectively assigned to them by each authority's or group's prerequisite conditions. The question every person and every group must ask, and answer is, "Are you guiding and directing people to sanctify and obey God's laws first or are you adjusting God's standards to fit yours?"

Rights activists, pluralists, and pragmatists believe that what they consider acceptable behavior is practical, rational human nature. Unfortunately, in the process of persuasion and argument, feelings and passions often overwhelm any spiritual grounding they may have, to the point that winning "ugly" (whatever it takes) means that if they lose any godly integrity in the battle, so be it.

We have arrived at a point where the truth—God-inspired scripture passed down for thousands of years by the work of the Spirit; God's very words—is being suppressed, distorted, and fabricated by millions in the name of rights, tolerance, and personal freedoms.

One consideration must be that *everyone* involved or affected by the hoped-for outcome, either directly or indirectly, would they benefit by its imposition? If God is for it, he empowers the faithful by giving them discernment to determine the ways and means to bring it about in his appointed time. God is always capable of finding a way, using both the faithful and unfaithful in such a manner that his intent and his standards overcome any human opposition. Truth or consequences are inevitable. If God is against it, no human intent, goodwill, or effort can prevent his opposition to it.

All scripture is divine and inerrant, breathed out through the voice of the Spirit, speaking out through the writer's pen. Explicit statements, commands, and instructions—the very voice of God—are constantly attacked by those who see them as impediments, singling out certain acts or lifestyles as incompatible with scripture. Because they are not willing to conform or they vehemently disagree, they will find reasons or rational excuses not to obey. Reading between the lines, they see implied—but not specifically spelled out—unwritten acceptance under certain circumstances or "correct" conditions that they believe is enlightened theology. Much of that flows from God's unconditional love, which is better understood in modern times as being more inclusive than it was at the time the scripture was written.

One huge concern in Reformed Christianity is that any form of "love" that operates independently of scriptural obedience is not, in fact, love. God's *unconditional love* comes with *conditional consequences*. While everyone may be loved by God, everyone is also held accountable by God, in some form, when they are disobedient, indifferent, ungrateful, or defiant. The love by God and from God is tempered by his holiness and justice. Every sin, regardless of its origin or intention, is an affront to a holy God, an act of disobedience. As God is equally as just as he is loving, discipline and/or punishment is equally meted out as both a correction and warning. If God did not punish because of his unconditional love, he would not be a just God or a holy God. Justice requires equity; good is rewarded; evil is punished. Holiness requires purity of body and soul, a being without blemish or imperfection. No one is righteous in the eyes of God, and those who tell you they are do not know scripture—or they are arrogant.

Contradictory scriptural interpretations cannot be equally divine or equally true. For example, the Old Testament and New Testament both point out that same-sex activity is a grievous sin, worthy of capital punishment in the Old Testament. For two thousand years, the church embraced the divine construct that homosexuality was unacceptable and incompatible with Christian apologetics. If it was worthy of severe punishment in all ages, and today, liberals and progressives say the circumstances and understanding are more enlightened, then the Spirit misled millions of Jews and Christians over the centuries. Or all the saints and followers in the Old and New Testaments got it wrong, according to the thinking of millions of today's proponents. If, in fact, homosexuality is good or acceptable, how could so many, for so long, get it wrong, both in scripture and secular history? Does it make divine sense that all the writers condemned homosexuality and all the historically accepted Christian traditions considered it sinful from the very beginning? What changed today to make it "correct"?

Again, why wouldn't God send the Spirit to correct all the people who believed what was explicitly instructed in scripture, if everyone got it wrong? They did not get it wrong for two thousand years; the church did not get it wrong for two thousand years, or else God is at fault for not correcting it. Do you think God would wait two thousand years, from the beginning of Christian tradition until today, to inform the current church that we got it wrong, even though the apostles, saints, and great theologians believed it too? How could everybody in the past have gotten it wrong, and today, the Spirit reverses the letter and spirit of scripture concerning same-sex activity and tells us that it is acceptable under the conditions that homosexuals insist are correct? The bottom line—either God changed the Spirit's instruction and our understanding, or Satan has deceived so many that those who faithfully believe God's explicit labeling of homosexuality as an abomination are now the bad guys, and the evil the Spirit described in past scriptures no longer applies.

We all want solutions to our individual and corporate problems. We all want greater control over our lives and surrounding conditions. Validation, respect, and fulfilling lives are lifelong quests. One problem with political correctness is in defining what it includes within that definition. Is it primarily political, social, moral, or philosophical? Which predominates? Who do you ask to answer that question? Where is it spelled out, and what authority determines legal and moral standards? How can political, social, moral, or philosophical viewpoints from numerous sources and authorities be equally just and equitable to all people in all places, when only the predominate elite from each category make decisions that designate that people or groups are acceptable or incorrect?

What does "moral autonomy" include or exclude? Should a political party, a right's group, most people, or so-called national values determine what is correct autonomy? Does voting to decide what social position is correct make it any more valid because of majority rule? No! Should God be excluded or included across the board or only as determined by those making decisions, based on their philosophy of right and wrong, acceptable, or unacceptable? Finally, autonomy is not tied to a particular standard or core conduct; it is independent by its definition. If something is independent from governing principles, how can it be correct, with no basis of comparison?

Human history has shown over the millennia that when political license is put into play and attempts to subvert, deny, or attack Christian theology and practice, moral breakdowns and social, self-righteous mentality become tools to impose new legally backed social requirements that adhere to the governing stipulations. When the letter and spirit of God's laws are not obeyed, the truth becomes abused, nations become confused, and people are used.

Many of our political and social moral issues are rooted in the misplaced belief that tolerance, inclusion, equality by fiat, and equal respect for unequal truths will bring about greater peace and prosperity for the haves and have-nots in our country. A compelling case can be made that there is more tension, animosity, and division now, because of the recent impositions of politically driven moral standards, than there was in past generations, due to political obfuscation and intimidation.

Morality is not a good guide of what is right, good, or acceptable. It is always a manipulated platform by various vying powers to direct and control as much of the population as possible to follow their instructions. Morality is not the same as ethics. Morality is more a combination of legal, social, and current authorities—guidelines of what is acceptable to them and then implemented into the general population. Ethics, however, are derived from what should be mandatory behavior, as instructed by God's truth, inspired by the Spirit, and written in Holy Scripture.

Truth is not a matter of what *you* believe to be true; it is a matter of what God says is true. It does not rely on past or present human arguments for its veracity because of what scholars or moralists determine is true; it is based on what Jesus says is true.

Truth does not originate from human authority or institutions, nor is it objectively defined by any human authority or institution. It cannot be contained by dissenters who seek a separate, more pragmatic version that allows them greater freedom to go their own way. Paul reminds us of the consequences that result from tampering with God's truth: "For the wrath of God is revealed from heaven against all ungodliness and unrighteousness of men, who suppress the truth in unrighteousness" (Romans 1:18).

Truth's power and order inevitably manifests itself under the direction and timing of God's Word and will. Its consequences, good or bad, depending on what choices are made, are applied to everyone, regardless of whether you accept it or reject it. No one escapes God's "truth or consequences." Those who get away with it on earth do not escape God's judgment. As William Barclay so eloquently puts it, "The judgments of eternity will correct the judgments of time."[6]

Ethical truth is only accurately conveyed and discerned through the power and revelation of the Holy Spirit. Human inspiration or wisdom has no ability to create it or to declare that it has a newly discovered or discerned truth that was not previously known. There may be a new understanding of existing truth that provides additional enlightenment of that existing truth, but it is only the inspiration and power of the Holy Spirit that enables us to better understand a truth that God declared from the beginning of time. God's truth, as revealed in scripture over the ages, never is outdated or invalidated by human traditions or institutions.

Jesus speaks to the issues of authority and truth, when he assertively states, "The one who speaks on his own authority seeks his own glory but the who seeks the glory of him who sent him is true and in him there is no falsehood" (John 7:18).

All human authority and its claim of truth has a chain of command attached to it, and human institutions claiming a truth have a document associated with it. Both individual and institutional authority have a paper trail that determines the source and degree of that authority. All foundation documents that attempt to validate their truth are tied to human ambitions, traditions, loyalties, political dynamics, and personal biases. Every political party and government in the past and present are influenced by human frailties and self-aggrandizement in varying degrees. Let us face it; our race relations, sexual relationships, business ethics, and religious affiliations are always simmering under the radar until someone, or some event opens a wound or draws out our self-righteous indignation.

"These are the times that try men's souls" was written over two hundred years ago by Thomas Paine. You might agree that it rings true today. The problem is that most of us would disagree on who or what is the root cause of the problems. Equally true and vexing is the saying, "One man's trash is another man's treasure." Again, there is a radical disagreement as to what is trash and what should be treasured. Morality and situational ethics are ever-present points of contention that eternally create conflict whenever humans believe they are in control and become more enlightened as we progress to a higher form of being.

What we are experiencing today is a secular false starting point of accepted morality, which believes the best of human nature, combined with progressive liberal theology, leads us to erroneously believe we are better than we really are and that, in most cases, our better nature will do the right thing. This book takes the view that orthodox Christian truth is the only venue that has all the answers to our social issues. Further, there are not two opposing or equal answers within or outside Christianity that are equally valid or acceptable to God.

The biggest obstacle to Christianity today is the undisciplined, misinformed, and unfaithful lifestyles of professing Christians. The church has become so indoctrinated in its aversion to any form of discrimination that it has placed a higher priority on keeping church peace and social harmony by compromising, rather than by keeping God's truth by discriminating. In accepting a false morality, which begets a false peace, and rejecting a historical scriptural truth that resists compromise, we fail to achieve either peace or truth, regardless of our passion or efforts to bring about their fruition.

Reverend Jason Stellman of Exile Presbyterian Church, in an article for Ligonier Ministries monthly magazine, *Tabletalk*, wrote from the perspective of Satan as to how best deceive Christians. Satan believed that by using secular civil morality as an entry point, it would gradually introduce apostasy as accepted theology within the church. The following represents the first and last paragraphs of his writing:

> Concerning our mission to bring about the most widespread apostasy possible, we cannot stress enough the need for subtlety. While our aim is indeed great, it must

be achieved by small and incremental steps. If we wish to destroy, we must first distract. The reason, dear protégé, that the confusing of the civil and spiritual kingdoms is so crucial to our agenda is that regardless of which side of the political aisle wins or loses, the victory remains ours. To borrow the language of those despicable theologians who are truly a threat to our designs, the sooner civil morality becomes the task of Christ's spiritual kingdom, the sooner will "law" become "gospel" in the minds of its citizens. And once that exchange has been made, the American church is ours.[7]

Any so-called truth or "right" that circumvents or undercuts the required sacrifices, disciplines, and self-denial demanded by God in any given social or moral issue ceases to be true; it ceases to be right the moment it becomes a force unto itself, outside of or independent of the scripturally required obedience.

Christians are in a battle with identity politics, the cancel culture, progressive liberalism, pick-and-choose secular and religious organizations, and the rejection of scriptural instruction that points out the sins of abortion, same-sex activity, and compromise to avoid offending various moral autonomy positions. Comprehensive Christianity does not shrink from defending all tenets of orthodox apologetics; rather, it promotes the fullness of the entire Word of God. "Thus says the Lord" should be our clarion call to point offenders and believers to God's inerrant authority, as revealed in the entirety of his Word. John Calvin spoke to that when he said, "A soul, therefore when deprived of the Word of God, is given up unnamed to the devil for destruction."[8] We should have the unapologetic conviction that the Word of God is both our sword and our defense as we present his truth and authority as binding on all. The inerrancy of the Bible must be defended as a cornerstone of our witness.

James Allen writes in his book, *As a Man Thinketh*:

> Every man is where he is by the law of his being. The thoughts which he has built into his character have brought him there and in the arrangement of his life there

is no element of chance. All is the result of a law which cannot err. This is just as true of those who feel "out of harmony" with their surroundings as of those who are contented with them. Man is buffeted by circumstances so long as he believes himself to be the pawn of outside conditions. Man does not come to poverty or go to jail through the tyranny of fate or circumstance but by the pathway of base thoughts and desires.[9]

CHAPTER 3

❦

Progressive Morality Creating
Regressive Integrity

Social progress is a matter of interpretation. It depends on who you ask and what standards or attitudes they incorporate into their process of evaluation. What criteria should be included to objectively measure improvement or gain? Who or what determines the criteria used? What authority represents the will of the people? If the authority is a person, organization, historic document, or God, how and why did the people determine that authority best represented their interests? The ultimate choice of authority will reveal the nature, character, and moral disposition of the people. Every authority chosen, outside of God, becomes a demigod unto itself. In today's moral climate, demigods have determined that they are the ultimate authority.

Society today looks at sensitivity, inclusion, tolerance, equality, and rights as its primary criteria defaults. Indoctrinating those aspects of evaluation as their core values, moral autonomists embrace situational ethics as a vehicle to progressively promote and implement their agenda. Their false belief that humankind is progressively moving forward toward greater harmony and respect for others—because we are moving away from past rigid, more cut-and-dried ethical standards that past generations used to measure social progress—is riddled with riots, animosity, political arrogance, social intimidation, and anti-Christian vitriol.

We are, in many ways, more divided than united. Demigods are prone to arrogance and self-aggrandizement. When subjective criteria and standards are used as the basis for interpreting social progress and implementing any required changes, look out for the use of force and intimidation as the primary ways and means to control the people and eliminate dissent.

On the other hand, a Reformed or scripturally faithful Christian looks at social progress through classic, orthodox standards of conduct and belief based strictly on scriptural commandments, instruction, principles, and spiritual concepts, as written in the Old and New Testaments, and demonstrated by Christ.

Politically correct emphasis on feelings and emotions, coupled with the belief that what is new and modern is superior to previous Christian theology and practice, predominates much of today's moral conditioning. Simply because a historic tradition, theology, or standard is old, according to modern social gurus and charismatic personalities, which makes it suspect or inferior to today's scientific progress and progressive morality advancements. By claiming we are achieving social progress without providing systemic evidence of merit, combined with no enforcement or requirement for personal integrity and honor in all relationships and ever-increasing lack of discipline and civil respect for differing opinions, the increasing problems and negative consequences that result from those shortcomings should be more objectively identified with decline, not progress!

A persuasive case can be made that the ordinary people of American society are living in a false comfort zone, based on our social and moral misreading of what is good, who is good, or what is correct. We have allowed unelected judges and elected politicians to steer us away from Christian ethical requirements and scriptural truth to pragmatically resolve systemic social and moral issues along party lines and interest-group pressure.

Revisionism is the word that accurately describes politically correct moral autonomy and situational ethics. It is always associated with negative connotations, where a new government or political philosophy attempts to improvise and revise existing, accepted historic beliefs, standards, and practices to justify changes that subvert or nullify past orthodox moral or religious positions. Revisionism raises its ugly head whenever inconvenient truths deny a government or political party their subjective, preconceived reality goals that deny their implementation. What they are doing is customizing goals and moral guidelines to suit their pragmatic, self-determined ways and means of reaching their ends.

Christians know that sometimes you need to wait for God to clear a path or set the stage before you commit to an action. Other times, you need to take a leap of faith and act immediately when a crisis or opportunity comes into focus. God's timing is always right, whereas our timing is often too little too late, or too much too soon. The best way to improve your odds of getting it right is to know scripture, follow the lead of the Spirit, and pray for discernment that praises God or glorifies Christ. Every Christian is tasked to awaken people to God's holiness and our sinfulness. Trusting in Jesus alone glorifies God and, in the process, helps you find and embrace the peace that follows from knowing that truth.

Politically correct may be many things, but it cannot be all things to all people. Like all other human ideologies or subjective political mindsets, it will not save our society from self-destruction. Repetitively invoking moral autonomy or dependence based on a biased political authority will not increase the degree of our individual or corporate honor or integrity, nor can it provide a way out of the morass it has introduced into our system of government.

From the mind and pen of Albert Einstein:

> No problem can be solved from the same level of consciousness that created it. The world will not evolve past its current state of crisis by using the same level of thinking that created the situation.[1]

A biased, self-serving, politically correct moral autonomy agenda that favors one group over another for political purposes rarely results in a win/win solution to any physical, economic, or moral problems.

"The trustworthiness of the messenger affects the trustworthiness of the message."[2] Those words from William Barclay, a twentieth-century Presbyterian minister and theologian, describe just how crucial trust is for every human, every human institution, and all individual and corporate relationships. Think about it. Trust is the key that cements or destroys every aspect of human endeavors. Love without trust is shaky. Business without trust is a step away from taking advantage of another. Government without trust is temporary and chaotic. Individual and group relationships depend on trust.

All great achievements and undertakings revolve around trusting someone or something to be true to themselves and others with whom they are interacting. Truth of a moral or ethical nature is fundamental to order, harmony, and goodwill. All ethical truth is objective, not subject to time, place, or context. Faith based on God's truth is always superior to a truth that is based on human faith grounded in human nature or human wisdom. God's truth has been proven and validated, whereas human faith is belief or acceptance of something posited or unproven. The eternal problem for all humankind is separating fact from fiction and proven truth from claimed truth.

Throughout the New Testament, Jesus stresses fundamental points and requirements that are essential for each of us to grasp and fulfill. Among those was the Fatherhood of God, unceasingly reaching out to his wayward children. In Matthew 6:9–13, Jesus teaches his disciples the Lord's Prayer, as he said,

> Pray then like this: Our Father in heaven, hallowed be your name. Your kingdom come, your will be done, on earth as it is in heaven, give us this day our daily bread, and forgive us our depts as we also have forgiven our debtors, and lead us not into temptation but deliver us from evil.

His further instructions convey a warning and consequence for all who fail to fulfill the above requirements, as he said,

> For if you forgive others their trespasses, your heavenly Father will also forgive you, but if you do not forgive others their trespasses, neither will your Father forgive your trespasses. (Matthew 6:14–15)

We all must grasp and incorporate into our physical and spiritual well-being the importance of understanding that God is our divine Father, which Jesus emphasizes throughout scripture. Again, William Barclay puts it into the proper perspective as he states, "The Fatherhood of God is the only possible basis for the brotherhood of man."[3]

The Fatherhood of God and Jesus, his Son, revealed by the inspiration or revelation from the Holy Spirit, is the key to understanding the necessity for getting your source of authority right. Every moral value or ethical position you take comes from a source of authority. Every source of authority sends out messengers to represent its motivations and intentions, which are to be followed by all those under that authority. As previously mentioned, the quality of the messenger and his message are dependent on the source of authority—so much so that the character or nature of the authority will either skew the truth or verify its veracity by the instructions that are put into play by force of law or force of public promotion.

In Leviticus 19:15–16, 18, God instructs the Israelites, stressing directly what is required of them concerning their "correct" attitudes and "right" relationships with each other and him:

> You shall do no injustice in court. You shall not be partial to the poor or defer to the great, but in righteousness shall you judge your neighbor. You shall not go around as a slanderer among your people, and you shall not stand up against the life of your neighbor; I am the Lord. You shall not take vengeance or bear a grudge against the sons of your own people, but you shall love your neighbor as yourself: I am the Lord.

In Isaiah 55:8–9, 11, the Lord speaks to his people, reminding them that he alone is eternal and forever in control. His will and purpose always succeeds, regardless of our responses to him:

> For my thoughts are not your thoughts, neither are your ways my ways, declares the Lord. For as the heavens are higher than the earth, so are my ways higher than your ways and my thoughts than your thoughts. So shall my word be that goes out of my mouth; it shall not return to

me empty, but it shall accomplish that which I purpose,
and shall succeed in the thing for which I sent it.

Scripture guides us, explicitly and implicitly, regarding the validity or
fallacy of our words, beliefs, and actions. A good example is Philippians
4:8, as we read:

> Whatever is true, whatever is honorable, whatever is
> just, whatever is pure, whatever is lovely, whatever is
> commendable, if there is any excellence, if there is anything
> worthy of praise, think about these things. What you have
> learned, received, and heard and seen in me—practice
> these things and the God of peace will be with you.

Paul was pointing out that before you speak, act, or profess and process
a belief, cross-reference each of the eight conditions listed in the scripture
verse when taking an ethical position, a judgement of good and evil, or
evaluating the pluses and minuses of your subject or actions with his
example. Is what you propose coordinated with the divine, requisite "trust
and obey"? Further, God blesses or gives you and others his peace when
you follow Jesus's lead and bring honor and glory to him in the process.

Charles Stanley, pastor emeritus of the First Baptist Church in Atlanta,
Georgia, succinctly puts it this way: "We are either in the process of
resisting God's truth or in the process of being shaped and molded by his
truth."[4]

A. J. Tozer, an American pastor and author, adds to that wisdom with
his summation:

> It is not what a man does that determines whether his
> work is sacred or secular, it is why he does it. The motive is
> everything. Let a man sanctify the Lord God in his heart
> and he can thereafter do no common act.[5]

Scripture indicates it is mandatory that God be present in any search
for or question regarding a truth. It is the foundation for understanding
the requirements with which God has tasked each Christian, as well as the
ways and means to implement them obediently.

> All scripture is breathed out by God and is profitable for teaching, for reproof, for correction and for training in righteousness. (2 Timothy 3:16)

> Knowing this first of all, that no prophecy of scripture from someone's own interpretation. For no prophecy was ever produced by the will of man but men spoke from God spoke as they were carried along by the Holy Spirit. (2 Peter 1:20–21)

C. S. Lewis summed it up nicely when he said, "If Christianity should happen to be true then it is quite impossible that those who know this truth and those who don't should be equally equipped to lead a good life."[6] Think about the implications of that assertion. If God is real and our Creator, and Jesus is who he said he is, then Christians are better prepared and empowered to be blessed and forgiven, as well as to enjoy a more fulfilling and fruitful living experience. If there is no God or Christ, then everyone is on their own, as nothing is set in stone, and everything is open to individual interpretation as to good and evil, right, and wrong. If Christians are right, eternity is their reward. If non-Christians are right, there is no heaven or eternity, as that is God's bailiwick, and death is the end for everyone. If there is no God, nothing is sacred, and everything is either common or subject to interpretation.

Unequivocally, no human can rightly interpret scripture of his own accord. The Holy Spirit is the only possible divine inspiration that can guide us to faithfully interpret, understand, and obey that which is holy, divine scripture. Paul, writing to fellow Christians in Corinth, states:

> The natural person does not accept the things of The Spirit of God, for they are folly to him, and he is not able to understand them because they are spiritually discerned. The spiritual person judges all things but is himself to be judged by no one. For who has understood the mind of the Lord so as to instruct Him? But we have the mind of Christ. (1 Corinthians 2:14–15)

The nature of your authority, messengers, and messages will vary, depending on your choice of one or more entities. All human sources will convey, by varying degrees, a mixture of good, bad, or indifferent qualities and attributes, subject to their physical, spiritual, emotional, and relational maturity. Thus, any individual or right's group has within its different group dynamics, which means every authority, messenger, and message is subject to deceit, hypocrisy, bias, and educational and environmental conditioning. All human authority, living or historic, be it a person, construct, legal system, or form of government, is always conditioned by human ways and means of doing things. Unless they have been granted the grace of God through the life of Jesus and the inspiration of the Holy Spirit, everything attempted will either fall short or fade away, due to human error and inconsistencies.

If no absolutes that are God ordained and empowered stand the test of time, then nothing is sacred. If nothing is sacred, neither is truth. If God's truth is not sacred, trusting in anyone or anything else is a losing proposition, where it can be bought and sold to the highest bidder, dominant human force, or most persuasive philosophy or mantra. When you have nothing to gain by being truthful, human nature finds an opening to persuade you to do what you want to get the quickest results or biggest bang for your buck. Everything of importance that has intrinsic value, depends on trust and truthfulness. Nothing of lasting value and worth can be built on relationships or group dynamics that do not place a high value on both truth and trust.

What has become evident over time, regarding politically correct moral dynamics, is the systemic hypocrisy and inconsistency of their moral and ethical gyrations. Presidents and judges add or subtract in every generation, regarding social issues. Changes, additions, or subtractions are incorporated into the political party platforms that were not there ten or twenty years ago. This means that what is true or acceptable today is subject to reinterpretation in every generation.

Taking a divine stand that there are absolute truths, in John 8: 31–32, Jesus makes the point of what is required to know the truth, and he describes the gift it brings to those who obey it: "*If you abide in my word*, you are truly my disciples and you will know the truth; and the truth will set you free." (Italics added)

In God's scheme of things, as presented and ordained in scripture, there is a cost that must be paid for embracing evil and distancing yourself from the divine. Attempts to redefine truth to suit your preferences do not sit well with God. In 2 Thessalonians 2:9–12, the Spirit speaks through Paul and admonishes those who make biblical standards optional or irrelevant when he says,

'The coming of the lawless one is by the activity of Satan with all power and false signs and wonders, and with all wicked deception for those who are perishing because they refused to lover the truth and so be saved. Therefore God sends them a strong delusion, so that they may believe what is false, in order that all may be condemned who did not believe the truth but had pleasure in unrighteousness."

Proverbs 1:7, succinctly and to the point, expounds that "The fear of the Lord is the beginning of knowledge; fools despise wisdom and instruction."

Moral autonomy proponents—those who default to morally justified, self-righteous situational ethics—would have you believe that individuals are free to actuate a moral evaluation within a situational context they construct, rather than applying a historically accepted moral absolute that many view and trust as valid. Morality is the accepted standard within a group or nation that is considered right or just, based on their teaching and the implementation of what is acceptable or unacceptable conduct or behavior. Moral autonomy gives you permission to decide for yourself whether an act fits your standards of decency, based on your principles or conscience's interpretation of right and wrong, irrespective of any ethical absolute.

Politically correct moral autonomy combines situational ethics within a political context. The political party decides what is moral normal in conjunction with an acceptable standard of conduct that they can support. It is based on subjective convictions pragmatic enough to attract a wider, more compliant audience.

Absolutes, on the other hand, are not subject to any moral context. They are fixed and uniformly applied in every ethical context. Correct moralists see which way the wind is blowing and incorporate as many of the fluid standards of conduct to which most of the people are willing to submit and commit. To them, it is not so much about the truth or validity of an act or behavior as it is to what the lowest common moral denominator most people will accept, per the guidance of a political party's platform.

Christians worth their salt do not put much stock in either moral autonomy or political correctness, as both are subject to and influenced by trends, environments, and human error. Situational ethics is no better. Both defy and deny God's truths and eternal, divine authority, using human norms and standards. You cannot have it both ways. If you commit to one, you disavow the other. When you incorporate varying degrees of each, you reveal your weakness or uncertainty, which shows your lack of conviction and resolution. A quick analysis would indicate those who straddle opposing positions to satisfy both camps are deceiving each. Choice is often a cover to hide a lack of ethical integrity. Who wants a team member who is just as supportive of your opponent's opposite position as of yours?

Each of us must decide which camp we are in and then make the commitment to be all in. Three scripture verses come to mind that might help in making a more complete commitment to genuine Christian theology and practice.

> What then shall we say to these things? If God is for us, who can be against us? (Romans 8:31)

As God has equipped us for the purpose of better serving him, 1 Peter 4:10 reminds us, "As each has received a gift, use it to serve one another, as good stewards of God's varied grace."

Once you have received the power of the Spirit to assertively act on behalf of your full commitment, these words from Romans 8:28 will bring comfort and confidence as you go forward:

> And we know that for those who love God, all things work together for good, for those who are called according to his purpose.

Inconvenient truths and historically accepted facts present the biggest hurdles for party-aligned positions and politically correct dogma. Politics, in many ways, is a game or puzzle that constantly adapts to contemporary, evolving standards and conditions. They must overcome or reinterpret morality or ethics that are counter to the party positions promoted by their elite power brokers. The trick is to convince the public and special-interest groups that their new and improved versions of truths and facts are, in and of themselves, superior to what is currently in vogue.

In the case of politically correct moral autonomy, from a Christian perspective, self-righteous disavowal of Christian standards and authority are the primary focus and effort, using whatever means possible to overcome their influence and opposition regarding party directives. To do so, they must refocus attention away from scripture and Christian traditions that are God-ordained to a more fluid, pragmatic set of rules and standards that appeal to everyone's inherent human nature and are more attuned to emotions, rights, and majority groupthink. Herd mentality can be bought or orchestrated by continually sweetening the pot with entitlements, freedoms, and fewer restraints. Playing one faction against the other, if done correctly, can turn the tide to the point where opposing those who are politically correct constitutes a threat to your life and livelihood. We are approaching what some might call ideological totalitarianism.

We each embody what our choices require us to defend. We choose what we believe is right morally, is in our best interest, or what society accepts as valid, normal human behavior. The human conundrum is our inability to agree on what is ethically right and what is human normal. Your rights and others' best interests require your considering the emotional or physical harm it may cause if each is not equally and equitably applied.

If what we believe or do conflicts with others, how do we respectfully consider which is the superior moral or ethical choice? What should be incorporated to ensure justice prevails over self-righteous indignation? Does "different strokes for different folks" hold everyone equally accountable? If not, why not? Is it right to favor one group over another, without their having earned the ethical justification required to grant their favored status?

The endless argument and questions that need to be asked and answered, which can settle each of the above, is their one universal source of authority that equally applies to all people in every generation. Or does human free will inherently include moral autonomy to the degree it rivals or is equal to any other source of authority, divine or human? What do you think? How did you arrive at your eventual answer?

We choose what the mind wills and thinks is best for us the moment we make the choice. There are obviously all kinds of factors and environments that influence how and what we think. What a person thinks about, we put into motion using various plans and actions that will satisfy our desire to attain it.

Your lifestyle and living principles reveal what is important to you; they represent what your core values are and what you stand for. It is not so much what you say that gives you away or validates you; it is what you do and act upon that reveals who you truly are, where your heart is invested, and what you choose as your ultimate authority.

In most cases, our moral preferences look at various attractive options, sift through them, and then prioritize them. Deference or equal consideration for others' positions, in most cases, is not as appealing, as it denies or prevents our own hearts' desires. In this book, I will try to clarify the importance of getting right who or what is the ultimate authority in our lives. Should our choices and lifestyles be ruled by human nature's predilections, which frequently incorporate situational ethics? Or should they equally incorporate divine or objectively equitable thoughts and actions, as instructed in scripture, to reach equal justice for all?

Many claim to be morally enlightened. Everywhere you look, there are charismatic politicians, rights leaders, and even religious authorities who see themselves as purveyors of wisdom that were unknown or unacceptable to past generations. They teach a modified or new understanding of what is morally or ethically acceptable by most open-minded, correct thinkers. But scripture warns us of wolves or evil people who masquerade as enlightened people claiming new truths have been revealed to them.

Christians put Christ first. They defend scripture by honoring and obeying his instructed Word and will in their witness and their lifestyles. Human nature, on the other hand, defends its choices that conflict with Christian apologetics and witness by either exonerating them as human rights or moral normal, socially acceptable behavior, which combines free will and/or moral autonomy. The problem with humanism is that it is so deeply ingrained in our psyches that it will do whatever it takes to prevent God from overriding its default mechanisms, which defy God's authority without making us feel guilty in the process. Its combination of defying and denying can only be broken by outside intervention; namely, the Holy Spirit.

C. S. Lewis hit the nail on the head regarding happiness, peace, or personal integrity when he said, "God cannot give us happiness and peace apart from himself, because it is not there. There is no such thing."[7] The long and short of that critique of wisdom is that you cannot give something that others seek or want if you do not have it within yourself to give. You cannot assign it either. If you believe you can look to yourself or others to provide what only God can convey, then you are deceiving yourself and others into believing the impossible can be circumvented by using extreme measures. Promoting rights that are not granted by God exacerbates the deceit so that both you, as the giver, and your intended receiver cast yourselves as either arrogant or ignorant by disregarding God's natural law and order.

When there is a conflict of philosophies or religious codes of conduct, the various positions must be clearly identified and evaluated, using the known, historically accepted facts and evidence that support them and viewing them through an objective lens, as much as possible, to prove the superiority of one over the other. Too often, force or legal intimidation, rather than debate, is the manner chosen to bring the opposition into line. Another is to promote false perceptions or half truths about the character or nature of the opposing religion. The better way—the Christian way—to determine the true nature of an ethical or moral position is to prove that the benefits of living a scriptural, faithful lifestyle or code of conduct, which results in producing superior families, individuals, and honorable relationships with God and country, is the ultimate right venue.

Which of the three you choose will reveal the strength or weakness of the posited position taken. The weakest case will use force or intimidation because it knows it has the weakest claim; otherwise, it would allow competition to prove its validity or reveal its shortcomings. The use of character attacks or intentional misrepresentation is typically put into play at the first sight of resistance from an opposing party. That is the default tact of politically correct moral autonomy.

Once that has been put into motion, there is no reason not to employ false accusations, half-truths, or out and out lies to smear the opponent's ability to defend its case. Arrogantly replacing Christian authority with permissive, moral independence and denigration squarely pits all who identify with moral autonomy as opponents to both the letter and the spirit of Christian theology and practice.

Jesus, then and today, reminds us that God speaks to us and provides a means to understand his motivation and intention through the power of the Holy Spirit. He is saying that those under the influence and power of the Spirit are given discernment that others do not have. Then and today, many see and hear Christ's messages, his invitation, and his warnings, but those outside the Spirit fail to rightly interpret and apply those invitations and warnings written in scripture.

Those who claim that ethical social issues are negotiable and should be considered a matter of individual interpretation do so in good faith; they believe and claim that sincerity, feelings, fairness, good intentions, and tolerance are as viable as discipline, sacrifice, and humble submission to the Word and will of God. Exception and the benefit of the doubt all play into their philosophy, which is that Christians are too negative and anxious about the letter and spirit of scriptural requirements of faithful interpretations regarding social issues, such as abortion or homosexuality, when various lifestyles are not explicitly in line with historic teaching.

Unfaithful Christians and everyone else will no doubt sharply disagree and attempt to build a case that rejects that premise; their premise is that humans are basically good and usually do the right thing most of the time. The unresolvable conundrum for Christians who are "correct" is that there is an acceptable degree of divergence or separation from the authority and justice of God to keep them in his good graces, in the event they are off the mark. Where is the point of no return regarding sins of omission or commission? In James 4:17, we are reminded that it is not only important not to sin but also to do good, when we have the power to do it. He wrote, "Whoever knows the right thing to do and fails to do it, for him it is a sin."

Those who know scriptural truth—who have been exposed to it—and chose to include or exclude more or less than is there, typically have an agenda. Thus, they must manipulate a part of that truth that does not fit in with their agenda. They have been blinded by their political-identity fealty. Many who take the name *Christian* do so according to whatever the moral issue or political agenda requires; they associate their brand of *Christianity* with it to make it more palatable. That increases the prospect that it will be incorporated into the political or rights platform they are promoting.

Christians are tasked and expected to stand firm, rather than seek common ground, to avoid division. Whatever we each commit to as our core moral foundation will determine to what we will submit. For Christians, it is far better to endure the slings and arrows of those opposed to fixed faithful obedience that is committed to the letter and spirit of divine scripture than to submit to political or legal pressure to gain agreement through compromise or intimidation. All individual interpretation outside the guidance of the Holy Spirit is subject to individual bias, self-empowerment, and self-exoneration, ingrained by the counter-truths of those who profess to be politically correct.

Corrie ten Boom, a courageous Christian woman who defied the Nazis during World War II, is estimated to have saved eight hundred Jews by hiding them in her house. She and her family were eventually turned in by a Dutch traitor and sent to prison, where some of her family members died. She survived and wrote an inspiring account of the horrors they endured as Christians living out their faith. She believed that God delivered her, as she testified, "The safest place to be is in the center of God's will."[8] Despite her dire circumstances, her faith and courage to do what she considered as God's will provided her the ultimate salvation she was seeking. She found the strength to empower her, as we all can, from Philippians 4:13, which reads, "I can do things through him that strengthens me."

What happened in Europe before the Nazis started World War II, which made a dire situation worse, was the weakness and indifference of both Christians and Jews who were in denial or disbelief that Hitler would carry out his threats and political rants. He began to attack group after group, saying they were not real Germans or good enough to be tolerated in his nation. Martin Niemoller, a German Lutheran pastor, who was himself imprisoned for four years under the Nazi regime, spoke words of which we too appear guilty. A case can be made that we are repeating, in some ways, what he experienced seventy-five years ago, as he said,

> At first, they came for the Communists, and I did not
> Speak out—because I was not a Communist. Then they
> came for the Catholics, and I did not speak out—because

I was not a Catholic. Then they came for the Jews, and I did not speak out—because I was not a Jew. Then they came for me, there was no one left to speak for me.[9]

Niemoller's summation interestingly came to be known as the "bystander's credo." Are Christians today guilty of allowing our government to dictate what is moral, what is correct, and what is true?

Christ's message and divine truth stands on its own merit. It does not require anyone's endorsement to make it more valid or to be concerned that any moral rejection makes it less valid. The Christian message from a Christian messenger is to point naysayers to the truth of Christ and the need to humble ourselves and believe in him as the Son of God. Those whom God has chosen to become his followers will be inspired by the Spirit to understand and accept the good news within that revelation.

John Calvin's following declaration is Spirit-discerned wisdom that he wants each of us to embrace:

We should never be attentive to God's word were he not to open our ears; and there would be no inclination to obey, were he not to turn our hearts; in a word, both will, and effort would immediately fail in us, were He not to add His gift of perseverance (Holy Spirit).[10]

Submission to the Holy Spirit is a prerequisite for individual and national harmony.

What causes quarrels and what causes fights among you? Is it not this, that your passions are at war within you? You adulterous people! Do you not know that friendship with the world is enmity with God? Therefore, whoever wishes to be a friend of the world makes himself an enemy of God. Submit yourselves therefore to God. Resist the devil and he will flee from you. Humble yourselves before the Lord and he will exalt you.

—James 4:1, 4, 7, 10

CHAPTER 4

❧

Scripture and Today's Sources
of Truth and Authority

Two forces to which we each are subject are human nature and divine nurture. The former position represents the human spirit, the latter, the Holy Spirit. Human truth varies, depending on who defines it and the source of authority that declares it to be true. Divine truth from the past is the same today; it never changes. There is no new truth. There may be a better understanding of an existing divine truth revealed by the Holy Spirit, but it is not a new truth, nor do individuals ever create or discover a truth that was not already in existence. All "new" scientific discoveries are simply people coming to understand or realize that they are advancing their knowledge of what already existed from the beginning of time.

In many of the moral or socially disputed cases over the last forty years, much of the evidence collected and presented as fact suggests that a strong political bias is influencing national legislation and jurisprudence. No doubt a variety of groups and individuals, who have a worldly attitude and a politically correct viewpoint where human nature reigns supreme, will insist it is not the government's function to consider whether it meets Christian standards or God's approval. It is the will of the people, by the people, and for the people that is paramount in moral decision-making, which drives their attempts to be all things to all people.

Paul had to deal with the same problems of false teachers and messages in his time too. Only today's politically correct are more educated, wily, and persuasive. Here are Paul's words:

> And what I am doing I will continue to do, to undermine the claim of those who would like to claim that in their boasted mission they work on the same terms as we do. For such men are false apostles, deceitful workmen, disguising themselves as apostles of Christ. And no wonder, for even *Satan* disguises himself as an "angel of light." *So, it is no surprise if his servants, also disguise themselves as servants of righteousness.* Their end will correspond to their deeds. (2 Corinthians 11:12–15, italics added)

To counteract all human attempts to disregard the physical and spiritual laws that God set in motion from the beginning, he designed automatic, systemic checks and balances to both warn and punish all who defiantly go their own way and refuse to submit. No one nation or individual can escape the consequences of their deceit, defiance, or rejection of God's law and will. If we look at the United States today, we will see a good example of what transpires when we play God and then deny that we are by trotting out the ever-present mantra, "It is the politically correct and right thing to do." Everywhere we look, abortion, homosexuality, and worshipping false gods are the accepted political norm. The politically correct will pull out all the legal and cultural validations and fight tooth and nail to ensure their desires and demands are implemented. They work, day and night, to make sure everyone has the legal and moral right to engage in scripturally condemned activities and to do so in good standing.

Absent God, morality—individual and group—becomes a matter of preference, not deference. *The reality is that those who look to social truth for salvation may have to compromise gospel truth to achieve it.*

You cannot accurately see the truth, understand its vision, or accurately portray its message if your alternative version substitutes tangents for core wisdom. You can only see what you have prepared yourself to see. You can only hear what you have prepared yourself to hear. You can only do faithfully, when the Spirit partners with you, what you are meant to do.

Evil masquerading as enlightenment has become so entrenched in our society that millions do not recognize it when they see it; they have become so indoctrinated to it that, to them, it is normal human behavior. The words, "Let the words of my mouth and the meditation of my heart be acceptable in thy sight, O Lord," have no bearing on their everyday discourse. A pure heart and clean mind, per God's definition, has little or no influence on what they practice and preach. Moral autonomists are attuned to another spirit—human nature.

It is hard to admit this but many who take the name *Christian* believe in God but do not believe God. They do not accept his required strict accountability, as he reveals his Word and will in scripture. They believe in their self-inspired versions or interpretations, which, far too often, are influenced by their political party, religious affiliation, or identity status. In other words, they have created God in their image. God is pictured or understood, based on personal codes of conduct and political persuasion, rather than Spirit-discerned revelation, as inspired in both the Old and New Testaments.

If it takes you two weeks to read this book, approximately forty thousand unborn sons and daughters will have been aborted. One of the pillars of politically correct philosophy is the right to kill those who are inconveniently conceived. It is estimated that over sixty million sons and daughters have been aborted over the last forty years. The Holocaust committed during World War II murdered approximately seven million individuals, mostly Jews. Do you find it an abomination that sixty million future American citizens were killed as a right—not because they were guilty of anything but because they were conceived irresponsibly at inconvenient times? Where is the politically correct compassion, mercy, love, or grace when an innocent life is killed intentionally by its mother?

Dr. Justin Holcomb, a minister in Seattle, in his article "Ethics of Personhood," concludes that "without the biblical understanding of human personhood and dignity as image-bearers of God, society is free to degenerate into violence, oppression and exploitation of the weak by the strong."[1]

You cannot be considered a faithful Christian when you identify more strongly with a label or position that incorporates more or less than scripture advocates and mandates. Sincerity or good intensions that lack core, fundamental discernment are just as harmful as indifference to core truth. Many, without due diligence in scriptural matters, blissfully follow the lead of deceptive pied pipers of political correctness. Differing opinions and positions on social issues and spiritual matters are prone to error whenever they incorporate more or less than is within the confines of faithful Christian theology and practice that is explicitly revealed by the Spirit in scripture.

It is as if the politically correct are bringing Christ before the crowds and declaring Christianity a threat to their kingdom, and he must be silenced. In this case, those who have political authority are the authorities who were appointed by God, who have become the Pharisees of today. It was God who allowed them or appointed them to become his representatives on earth, and they sold him out by betraying Christian discipleship. Jesus would harshly condemn those who have no excuse for not knowing who he is and what he represents. His words to them today *might* be, "You have no authority to change what is already written; no authority over me. Therefore, because you attempted to silence me, to disown my word and will, yours is the greater sin, not those who follow your lead, who were not appointed authorities."

What is astonishing, though, is the extent to which everyday people have been converted into accepting the deceit as being acceptable and then promoting it themselves as new truth. We all hate to admit that it is far more prevalent and far more "in your face" than in previous times. Comparisons are difficult to accurately portray because of time and other variables. Let us not compare our times with previous times but strictly on the historic, unchanging words and wisdom of scripture. Isaiah warned, "Woe unto them that call evil, good and good, evil that put darkness for light and light for darkness" (Isaiah 5:20).

In the inspiring Christmas carol "Joy to the World," the curious words "far as the curse is found" are spoken with little or no thought as to their magnitude or meaning. But they convey a deep insight and understanding to faithful Christians—that all the world's people live under the curse that unconditionally infects each of us; the bent to suppress God's truth; and to evade and deny divine requirements by substituting and replacing its letter and spirit with our preferred, distorted versions. The curse is so embedded in our society that we do not recognize it as evil but as the moral, normal way of conducting business and living our various lifestyles. Human nature may mean normal expected and accepted behavior in the scientific and psychological fields, but it means human evil to God.

Every attempt to inform and convince others of a certain viewpoint should have a key theme that sums up the core value that you believe sets apart one's claim to a superior validity. John 15:5 is the setting that best addresses the attendant core value that I believe is necessary for all to hear and understand: "I am the vine; you are the branches. Whoever abides in me and I in him, he it is that bears much fruit, *for apart from me, you can do nothing*" (italics added).

Jesus addresses the disciples, emphasizing the importance of trusting and obeying him if they are to be effective ambassadors and remain faithful in their relationships with him and others. The message is clear and stark to believers—everything you do through me and in my name will be inspired by the Spirit and blessed by me because it meets God approval. Anything you try to accomplish outside the inspiration of the Spirit will not be blessed by me or approved by God. To all nonbelievers, Jesus lays down the marker that nothing you do will be blessed by him or the Father and whatever "good" you attempt will be minimized or short-lived because of your lack of belief and misplaced faith in yourself and others.

In so many words, Jesus is saying that no matter your passion, conviction, or authoritative power, all attempts to alter or suppress God's truth and a right relationship with him will result in failure; any temporary gain will be short-lived and fall apart because it did not honor or bless the words and will of the Father or the Son. Everything you say and do is scrutinized by God, and all your efforts to accomplish something outside that which meets with his approval is doomed. Nothing succeeds or reaches its fullest potential unless God blesses it. If God, in scripture, declares it will not happen by doing it your way, and it will not last if you do it your way, and you still choose to do it your way, your vanity will overshadow and nullify any good you claim for yourself.

Proverbs 3:5–6 speaks to our bent to go our own way:

> Trust in the Lord with all your heart and do not lean on
> your own understanding. In all your ways acknowledge
> him and he will make straight your paths.

Today, institutions, identity groups, and governments consistently manipulate the truth and redefine evil, attempting to legalize the necessary changes to put it into practice, exonerate excessive indulgences associated with the changes, and morally validate the sin, to the degree that they can make people believe *that rotten eggs smell like bacon*. Unquestioned political ideology and excessive identity-group loyalty creates unbalanced authority that percolates malevolence under the cover of diversity and moral autonomy.

Charles Spurgeon, in his book *The Holy Spirit*, explicitly details what is and is not from the Holy Spirit:

> Always look with great suspicion upon any comfort offered to you, either as a sinner or saint, that does not come from Christ. The ministries that make much of Christ are of the Holy Spirit and the ministries that discredit Him, ignore Him, or put Him in the background in any degree are not of the Spirit of God. Any doctrine that magnifies man, but not man's Redeemer, any doctrine that denies the depth of the Fall and consequently detracts from the greatness of salvation, any doctrine that makes man sinless and therefore makes Christ's work less-away with it, away with it![2]

Despite explicit and implicit warnings and living instructions from the Old and New Testaments (Ten Commandments and Beatitudes) the "correct" people see themselves as moral shining lights, independently operating outside historically accepted Christian theology and practice. They fail to consider, however—or refuse to accept—that in every act of leaving God out of any transactions or relationships and substituting themselves or their identity group as the good guys who are more in touch with today's advanced culture, they attempt to do the impossible. They try to meet the needs of others using human standards of enlightenment and progression that run afoul of divine instruction and revelation. All individuals or organizations who rebel against, deny, or hinder the work of the Spirit are evil, regardless of their position, stature, or influence. Every government or social undertaking that defies scriptural instruction and refuses Spirit inspiration is guilty to the degree it magnifies itself and denigrates the Spirit of truth.

St. Augustine reminds us that knowledge that passes as human wisdom can be skewed by those who pride themselves in their status or authority. How it is presented and supported determines the degree of positivity or negativity that ensues from it. The motivation and intention will be evident in its presentation, as Augustine states, "Knowledge only does good in company with love. Otherwise, it merely puffs a man into pride."[3]

Chronological snobbery is an apt description of most worldviews or schools of thought that embrace modern or current trends of measuring progress. Modern schools of thought, theories, or social and economic doctrines often consider themselves superior to anything from the past, regarding their expertise in any field. G. K. Chesterton, an English writer and Christian theologian from the first half of the twentieth century, emphasizes the value and importance of tradition by describing it as the "democracy of the dead":

> Tradition refuses to submit to the small and arrogant oligarchy of those who merely happen to be walking about (alive). All democrats object to men being disqualified by accident of birth; tradition objects to being disqualified by the accident of death. Democracy tells us not to neglect a good man's opinion, even if he is our groom; tradition asks us not to neglect a good man's opinion, even if he is our father.[4]

Chesterton was keenly aware of the world's penchant to rush to new rights and freedoms, based on emotions and feelings not necessarily based on accepted facts or scriptural scrutiny. He said,

> To have a right to do a thing is not at all the same as to be right in doing it. Fallacies do not cease to be fallacies because they become fashion. The Christian ideal has not been tried and found wanting. It has been found difficult and left untried.[5]

Considering how Christians view a foe or evil force that confronts individuals and nations, he hits the nail on the head with this wise and timely reminder of how Christians with orthodox views describe ethical conflicts: "A true soldier (Christian) fights not because he hates what is in front of him but because he loves what is behind him."[6] Standing firm, representing Christian stalwarts of faith and Spirit-inspired dialogue is essential to effectively and faithfully spread the Word and will of God.

A keen observation for those who know (or should know) that the validity of moral autonomy is frequently nonsense in that the American political and cultural landscape reveals systemic nuance, double-talk, and half-truths, which are orchestrated to satisfy a majority of those caught up in political correctness.

The evidence to support the above is this: by not matching scripture with Spirit revelation as the basis for all ethical conduct, they have made "equal rights and validation of unequal truth and conduct, sacred and inviable." In other words, they have made equality something it is not—always just or ethically right. We frequently have the misconception that equality, in and of itself, is a good thing or fair treatment. But demanding or imposing equality by political fiat across the broad spectrum of American culture that grants equal status, rights, and validation assumes that each group or spectrum is honorable, just, and accountable. It often levels the playing field, where two opposing truths or beliefs are not equally true or equally just. Forced or artificial equality may provide equal legal rights or social approval, but it cannot change established scriptural truths or change historically expected and enforced ethical and moral behaviors.

If something cannot stand on its own merits, it should not be made equal with that which can. A major mistake of the politically correct is that they substitute subjective equality for true equity and make it their "holy grail." Equity in economic matters also has proven, over the years, to provide a sounder economic policy than forced or contrived equality manipulations that rob Peter to pay Paul.

All scripture, from the Old Testament through the New Testament, states that it is essential that God be present and involved in any search or question regarding any truth. Scripture is the foundation for understanding the requirements with which God has tasked each Christian and the ways and means to correctly implement them.

> All scripture is breathed out by God and is profitable for teaching, for reproof, for correction and for training in righteousness. (2 Timothy 3:16)

> Knowing this first of all, that no prophecy of scripture comes from someone's private interpretation. For no prophecy was ever produced by the will of man, but men spoke from God as they were carried along by the Holy Spirit. (2 Peter 1:20–21)

Sin abounds when it is confused with tolerance and human rights, based on personal justification rather than scriptural discernment and justification.

We must worship only one God—the God of the Old and New Testaments. There can be no tolerance for mixing or combining the worship of him with the worship or reverence for other gods, idols, or philosophies. Martin Luther, the catalyst for the Protestant Reformation, put it this way:

> Because of the word of God, zeal and disputes arise. For that is the course, the manifestation, and effect of the Word of God; as Christ says; I came not to bring peace but the sword; for I am come to set man at variance against his father, and so on. *That is why we must bear in mind that God is wonderful and terrible in his counsel, so we will not strive to smooth out differences if by doing so we condemn the word of God. Through this a flood of insufferable evil will most likely pour over us.*[7] (italics added)

Luther's world was a time when spiritual darkness dominated both the Christian and non-Christian communities. The church itself had gotten off track, away from scripture to the point that spiritual darkness both obscured and eclipsed the gospel itself, in the form of human scriptural modifications and explicit doctrinal manipulations. Here are the brave words Luther used to defend himself and his position when he was on trial at the Diet of Worms (the assembly of the major political powers of the Holy Roman Empire) in 1521:

> Unless I am convinced by the testimony of the Holy Scriptures or by evident reason—for I believe neither pope nor councils alone, as it is clear that they have erred repeatedly and contradicted themselves—I consider myself convicted by the testimony of the Holy Scriptures, which is my basis; my conscience is captive to the Word of God. Thus, I cannot and will not recant, because acting against one's conscience is neither safe nor sound. Here is stand; I can do no other. God help me. Amen.[8]

Brave words and tremendous courage in defending himself against the religious and state powers that ruled Europe. His life was in their hands, and he stood fast, refusing to recant, putting his life at risk, even burning at the stake. Would that God raise up more people who are willing to risk everything to be faithful to the Word and will of God!

Paul had to deal with the same problems of false teachers and messages in his time too. Only today's politically correct are more educated, wily, and persuasive. Here are Paul's words to confront their false pretenses:

> And what I am doing I will continue to do, in order to undermine the claim of those who would like to claim that in their boasted mission they work on the same terms as we do. For such men are false apostles, deceitful workmen, disguising themselves as apostles of Christ. And no wonder, for even Satan disguises himself as an "angel of light." So, it is no surprise if his servants, also disguise themselves as servants of righteousness. Their end will correspond to their deeds. (2 Corinthians 11:12–15)

Inalienable rights and divine obligations are God-instituted, inherent from the creation of Adam and Eve and crafted in stone in the form of the Ten Commandments. There is only one original, binding universal declaration of rights and wrongs, which no human authority can amend by adding, subtracting, or modifying that which was defined and ordained by God in scripture. Ever since the Ten Commandments, the people of God have been inspired and commanded to steadfastly commit to them and submit to God's instructions regarding the value of all humans made in his image and what he required for him to bless and keep them under his good grace. We may not agree with or understand God's reasoning or ultimate plans, but we must trust scripture to be true, and our faith must trust God to be faithful and omnipotent.

The essence of politically correct moral autonomy is people's ascendant self-importance and moral self-determination. The essence of politically correct authority is moral self-validation. For the politically correct moral autonomist, the emphasis is defiantly centered on human capabilities and the government's progressive authority and right to determine what is acceptable. Their motto might be, "Rights rule; choice reigns." None is so blind as one who exudes an arrogant attitude of superiority. Politically correct moral autonomy, by its very definition, eschews any degree of scriptural due diligence. *If those who promote and embrace its clarion call made even a small effort, they would not falsely equate political/civil morality with gospel fidelity.* Christian theological differences in motivation and intention that conflict with philosophical differences of liberal government management and goals negate any claims of moral autonomy equality, with past historically interpreted and accepted scriptural mandates and standards.

> In times like these, it is important that we don't find ourselves desiring deliverance more than revelation. Sometimes, when we do not understand what is happening around us, we just want the pain to stop. But wanting our too early simply evades the process that God wants us to go through. It eliminates the growth we will experience if we stay the course. No matter how painful or how terrified we are of the unknown, we must remember that our former lives were not necessarily better. They were simply different. When we find ourselves dwelling on the simpler days, we should remember Isaiah 43:18–19, which says, "Remember not the former things, nor consider the

things of old. Behold, I am doing a new thing; now it springs forth, do you not perceive it? I will make a way in the wilderness and rivers in the desert." Those who stayed during their challenges benefitted from a full restoration of God's promise in their lives. God wants to deliver us unto our purpose, but it is up to us to stay the course.[9]

The above guidance and wisdom are taken from Zim Flores's article "Don't Gut the Fish," taken from *Good News*, a monthly Methodist publication. She used the book of Jonah as a backdrop for the writing.

When you act or make a judgment on someone or something without the required requisite background information and validated facts (due diligence), you are either assumptive or presumptive. All individuals are guilty of and pay a price for moving forward without scriptural scrutiny or Spirit-inspired discernment. Limit your self-inspired actions and judgments and look more to divine instruction. It will save you and others from a lot of pain and insecurity. The judgment of eternity will "correct" the judgments of man. You may get away with some of your errors and harm inflicted on others here on earth, but nothing escapes God's notice and judgment.

Jesus is addressing the disciples, emphasizing the importance of trusting, and obeying him if they (the disciples) are to be effective ambassadors and remain faithful in their relationships with him and others. The message is clear and stark to believers—everything you do through him and in his name will be inspired by the Spirit and blessed by Jesus because it meets God's approval. Anything you try to accomplish outside the inspiration of the Spirit will not be blessed by Jesus or approved by God. To all nonbelievers, Jesus lays down the marker that nothing you do will be blessed by him or the Father and whatever "good" you attempt will be minimized or short-lived because of your lack of belief and misplaced faith in yourself and others.

In so many words, Jesus is saying that no matter your passion, conviction, or authoritative power, all attempts to alter or suppress God's truth and a right relationship with him will result in failure, and any temporary gain will be short-lived and fall apart because it did not honor or bless the words and will of the Father or the Son. Everything you say and do is scrutinized by God, and all your efforts to accomplish something outside that which meets with his approval is doomed. Nothing succeeds or reaches its fullest potential unless God blesses it! God in scripture declares it will not happen by doing it your way; it will not last if you do it your way; and if you still choose to do it your way, your vanity in continuing will overshadow and nullify any good you claim for yourself.

History has shown us there has never been a world without wars, violence, racial issues, sexual divisions, or religious conflicts. Even the most so-called enlightened nations never came close to pleasing all the people all the time. Future prognostication will foretell much of the same. The reason is inherent in human hearts—there is no human solution for selfish choices, lifestyles, or relationships. Blaming others or treating them as inferiors has always been a favorite of those who regard themselves as better or more important because of their power, wealth, or education. The weak and poor across the world are still looked down on and taken advantage of. Class warfare and economic inequality are the result of social and political manipulations and morally callous attitudes regarding equitable distribution of goods and services to all in need. The world has plenty of money and food to go around, yet here we are, like every other generation, with poverty and misery more widespread than ever.

"Do unto others as you would have them do unto you," and "Love your neighbor as yourself" will not happen, no matter how passionately you preach it or promote it. Faith in general humanity to do the right thing will not materialize until God intervenes. In that same vein, those who put their trust in others or trust in a progressive political solution to get us out of this mess are tilting at windmills. That does not mean we should give up or stop trying; it simply means that everyone's reality is that we are incapable of fixing what is inherently wrong with us.

Psalm 2:1–6, 10–12 reveals a powerful and insightful understanding of God's nature and his response to those who see themselves as good, authoritative independent moral agents:

> Why do the nations rage, and the peoples plot in vain? The kings of the earth set themselves, and the rulers take counsel together against the Lord and against His Anointed, saying: "Let us burst their bonds apart and

cast away their cords from us. He who sits in the heavens laughs, the Lord holds them in derision. Then He will speak to them in His wrath and terrify them in His fury saying, "As for me, I have set my King on Zion, my holy hill." Now therefore, O kings, be wise, be warned O rulers of the earth. Serve the Lord with fear and rejoice with trembling. Kiss the Son, lest He be angry, and you perish in the way, for His wrath is quickly kindled. Blessed are all who take refuge in Him.

Dissociation is an accurate description of moral autonomy. Webster's II New College Dictionary defines it as "the separation of a group of related psychological activities into autonomously functioning units."

Today, we embrace about everything except scriptural doctrine and practice. Calling someone or something evil is itself seen by many as evil. And heresy—well, we just have no tolerance for calling anything that drastic a name. Our self-sufficient pride and excessive emphasis on social and sexual rights overshadow anything of a humble, pure, and chaste nature. In 1 Corinthians 3:16–17, however, we are brought to task by Paul, as he admonishes those who hinder church doctrine and practice:

> Do you not know that you are God's temple, and that the God's Spirit dwells in you? If anyone destroys God's temple, God will destroy him. For God's temple is holy, and you are that temple.

Human corruption is both inherent in our nature and inevitable in our discourse. Its correction is beyond our capability. In our day, civil, legal, and political forces devote much time and energy to extrapolating and legislating morally permissive rights (not Spirit-initiated or sanctioned) from various human authorities and institutions. The motivation is to placate diverse identity groups' selfish interests by pandering to their demands. In many ways and forms, both the political pandering and identity-group arrogance is an alignment of pride and prejudice directed at Christian resistance.

Paraphrasing Jesus's conversation with his disciples concerning parables in Matthew 13:13–15, "Some people hear but do not understand; they will indeed see but not perceive; the hearts of these people are closed to my Word; their ears heavy and eyes are blind." This discourse was Jesus weighing in on the arrogance and rebellion of all fallen people who are under the influence and control of their baser earthly nature—all that is a part of our carnal condition that we refer to as our "flesh." What we see on a regular basis is the morality that expresses the emotion of being sorry they were caught or exposed, more than sorrow for embracing or committing the sin. In other words, if they had not been caught, they would have continued to commit the sin. The appeal of the sin was greater than the concern of being sinful.

The old familiar hymns of the church convey words and themes that remind us of who is worshipped, who we serve, and why. In the hymn "Holy, Holy, Holy," we sing,

> Though the darkness hides thee
> Though the eye of sinful man thy glory may not see
> Lord, only thou art holy and there is none beside thee
> Perfect in power, in love and purity.

"How Firm a Foundation" reminds Christians that Jesus's power and authority is ever present and sufficient to see us through in every situation:

> Fear not, I am with thee, O be not dismayed
> For I am thy God and will give thee aid
> I'll strengthen and help thee and cause thee to stand
> Upheld by my righteous, omnipotent hand

"This Is My Father's World"_has a verse that speaks to our current harsh world of politics and social immorality:

> This is my Father's world. O let me never forget
> That though the wrong seems oft so strong,
> God is the ruler yet.
> Why should my heart be sad?

The Lord is King; let the heavens ring!
God reigns; let the earth be glad!

The heart of Christianity is Christ. Everything flows from where one's heart resides. The faithful Christian's heart (where his or her treasure is) proclaims only Christ's divine truth; there is no other divine truth. None. The Christian spirit, energized and motivated by the power of the Holy Spirit, embraces that truth, and receives a full measure of discernment. Spirit discernment is the key to separating the wheat from the chaff. Spirit wisdom is steeled to proclaim God's word; powered to put it into effect. The Spirit alone fine-tunes interpretation, proclamation, and action into one continuous, consistent, step-by-step declaration that rejects outright any human claim of equality or any human effort to redefine Christ's truth.

Moral autonomists want to convince you that they can make a good case that Christian ethics of the past are yesterday's truths and should be discarded; that they are no longer binding or in any way absolute. Today, hard, and fixed standards are an impediment, rather than a guiding light to equitable reward and punishment. This new doctrine and practice first encourages finding "common ground" rather than ultimate truth. In so doing, blending right and wrong into a compromise is seen as a higher priority than separating fact from fiction and truth from speculation.

CHAPTER 5

Church or State

There is not one social issue, one truth, that God considers unresolved or a problem. There is no list of problems for which God must rethink or redo his truths that he set in motion and settled at creation. *To the Trinity, everything is clear, every truth is uncontestable, and every Spirit-inspired revelation testifies to that same divine discernment.*

It is obvious that the trend for greater government control and intervention is accelerating across the world. Here at home, we see government-directed eyes and ears embedded socially and institutionally, tracking, and litigating against those who are brave enough to question and challenge their moral authority. Honor, integrity, and required self-discipline demanded by faithful Christians have become obstacles for the "correct" in their quest for greater control. To a great degree, we now are governed by intimidation and threat as much or more than equal equity for all, which is God-ordained. A state that dictates and coerces its Christian citizens to kowtow to its moral directives, which conflict with scriptural mandates, is both pagan and depraved!

On the other hand, the church or Christian community that incorporates conflicting and opposing positions mandated by scripture into its fellowship and practice has been transformed into a false representation of the valid letter and spirit of faithful Christianity. It will eventually become a pariah more closely aligned to secular society and satanic forces.

Mike Lowry, writing in *Good News*, a conservative Methodist publication writes:

> The death of nominal Christianity or cultural Christendom is a good thing. Ironically, or more accurately providentially, the Christian church grows when persecuted and withers when awash in prosperity. Individually and collectively we are being forced, by the movement of the Holy Spirit, to confront whether we are really Christ followers or not. Put theologically and biblically, is Jesus Lord of your life and your church's collective life or not?[1]

The letter and Spirit of God's truth cannot set you or anyone else free unless you obey it and live accordingly, as directed by the Spirit. "Let no one disregard you" is the Spirit telling all faithful Christians that you have the backing and authority of the authentic, unseen Spirit of the church to broadcast and communicate your commitment and the right to hold all accountable to God's one standard of conduct and his one standard of judgment.

Listen to the words of Peter as he warns against the deceptions of false teachers and prophets:

> *But false prophets also arose among the people, just as there will be false teachers among you, who will secretly bring in destructive heresies,* even denying the Master who bought them, bringing upon themselves swift destruction. And many will follow their sensuality and because of them the way of truth will be blasphemed. And in their greed, they will *exploit you with false words.* Their condemnation from long ago is not idle, and their destruction is not asleep. But these, like irrational animals, creatures of instinct, born to be caught and destroyed, in their destruction, suffering wrong as the wage for their wrongdoing. They count it pleasure to revel in the daytime. They are spots and blemishes, reveling in their deceptions, while they feast with you. They have eyes full of adultery, insatiable

for sin. They entice unsteady souls. They have hearts trained in greed. Accursed children! For, speaking loud boasts of folly, they entice by sensual passions of the flesh those who are barely escaping from those who live in error. *They promise them freedom, but they themselves are slaves of corruption. FoOr whatever overcomes a person, to that he is enslaved.* 2 Peter 2:1–3, 12–15, 18–19, (italics added)

Who can take it upon themself to confer moral equality when it is not theirs to give? By the politically correct assigning moral acceptability to contested behavior, it becomes morally equal. Newly validated rights that were previously historic wrongs, assume the mantle of being equally fair, just, and right in their eyes. Frequently, pride accompanies politically correct authorities, who work to bring about such a transition. Nevertheless, no Christian with scriptural integrity and Spirit indwelling would offer moral equality without requiring moral equity. Equity is synonymous with justice. Morality is synonymous with what is acceptable. Proper discernment and interpretation regarding any scriptural "truth" or "equality issue" that is being debated or argued can only be faithfully resolved by scripture itself, not by a combination of political, social, or religious views!

Christianity, at its best, is the closest to the letter and spirit of God's law. Those with the greatest reverence for God and his truth, revealed in scripture, will exhibit the greatest reverence for all lives, born and unborn. The quality of spiritual life for every human is relational to the degree God's truth is known, embraced, and obeyed.

The right to choose and indulge in your heart's desires is normal; it is near and dear to each of us. Humans have the right to choose their own paths or courses of action. However, when selfish imposition of moral autonomy by various institutions and organizations incorporate ungodly self-exoneration as part of their rights equation, shouldn't it be called out for what it is—evil? What happens when individual indulgences, right's agendas, and opposing moral-autonomy viewpoints conflict with each other and create mass national animosity? Who or what is objectively qualified to identify any moral deficiencies and redirect them to a higher ethical standard that leads to godly approval? The ultimate question that needs to be answered is this: What final authority guides our choices, our feelings, our inclinations, and our personal beliefs, which all are subjective by varying degrees—the Word of God; the authority of God, which alone is objective truth; or the word and authority of subjective human institutions and human psychology?

There is no acceptable way to portray a lesser, humanistic authority as equally correct with the divine authority that established all human authority. One of the wisest men who ever lived, King Solomon, closed out the book of Ecclesiastes with words of wisdom and warning:

> The end of the matter, all has been heard. Fear God and keep his commandments, for this is the whole duty of man. For God will bring every deed into judgement, with every secret thing, whether good or evil. (Ecclesiastes 12:13–14)

In today's modern vernacular, paraphrasing William Barclay, a Presbyterian theologian in the twentieth century, the justice and judgement of eternity (God) will correct the injustice and misjudgment of time and human morality.

If the goal of our nation is to achieve social harmony, based primarily on social and legal equality, and we achieve it, our nation will fail. We are failing now, individually, and nationally because our emphasis is misguided. Good intentions notwithstanding, it is getting worse! Why? Because in our haste to make sure every person and interest group is equal in social stature and civil law, we have thrown out the necessary ingredients required for our ultimate success—personal integrity and accountability, based on scriptural instructions.

When the emphasis on equality or rights does not include required conditions of earned merit or valid minimum conditions of accountability to earn the status of equality, you get the lowest possible accepted moral denominator—everyone for themselves! There cannot be any true, ongoing, consistent national or social unity when forced group equality is more valued than individual integrity or honoring the required conditions of scripture. Neither harmony or integrity will be achieved, regardless of how much a liberal president or Democratic Party panders to all those who cannot deny themselves their sexual expressions, who worship their rights more than life itself (abortion), or who excuse and exempt themselves from self-discipline, self-denial, or selfish personal conduct, resulting in emotional or physical harm to others who disagree.

Conflict is inevitable when diversity and equality overshadow integrity. Each of us must decide where our loyalties lie and what our standards will or will not accommodate. Forget "social truth" flowing from political correctness; rather, listen to the words of the well-known Christian hymn, *Rise Up O Men God*, "Rise up oh men of God! Have done with lesser things, give heart and mind and soul and strength to serve the King of kings!"

"I still haven't found what I'm looking for" are haunting words from the world-famous rock band, Bon Jovi. Whether this is profound, heartfelt angst to express a personal void in their real life or simply made-up words to complete the song's story narrative, everyone identifies with their power, knowing when something is missing in their lives.

Deep in your soul, in the fabric of your very being, you realize you will never be at peace or secure in a joyous manner until you find and grasp what you are looking for. Imagine living a lifetime, searching for who you really are and what you were meant to become, and not finding it. A life of searching in vain with unfulfilled potential would characteristically describe those who gravitate toward politically correct moral autonomy because they have no true direction, foundation, or purpose.

The Rolling Stones' hit "Satisfaction" has the refrain, "I can't get no satisfaction," repetitively expressing frustration with certain conditions or circumstances that cannot seem to be overcome. While they may not resonate as deeply as an unfulfilled life expressed in the preceding paragraph, many will admit it resonates with them and negatively affects their physical and mental condition.

One more tune, and we will move on. "Running on Empty" by Jackson Brown nicely describes the condition in which many in the moral-autonomy crowd find themselves. The theme of the song is a search to find meaning, direction, or fulfillment. Phrases such as "I don't even know what I'm looking for; running behind, running blind, and looking to my friends; I see in their eyes, they're running on empty too" describe the multitudes today who vainly seek but don't find what they are looking for.

Situational ethics is an infamous ploy that humans embrace. The philosophy that right or wrong is fluid, according to the contextual circumstances at the time, and that individual judgment should be the determining factor has great appeal. It gives you a wide latitude of correct choices in a live-and-let-live society. The moral reasoning that it will bring about an expedited agreement or reconciliation begs the question: why would you want to reconcile or excuse a sin or evil as part of the solution to the problem or choice at hand? Context should not subvert truth.

To God, when you give someone else or yourself the right to accept a less-than-complete or less-than-accurate truth or a compromised principle, you are accepting a form of sin and giving your stamp of approval to commit it. Is that a right? Is it righteous? It may be the way many process pragmaticism as the answer to moral quandaries, but more important, is it acceptable to God? There is no safe way or right way to do something wrong or deceitful. The best of intentions, without the matching integrity required to implement it faithfully (according to scripture), are sinful.

In the same vein, who can say, with any degree of certainty, who is, okay? On what grounds do you base your decision that you or someone else is okay? What requirements must be met to declare anyone okay? If you do not personally know certain people, how can you say they are okay— because you like them, you agree with them, or they have something in common with you? Is anyone okay simply because you agree with them? If you apply that logic, then evil people who agree with each other are okay too. It all comes down to three points: (1) what authority or whose authority you choose to answer the question, (2) your motivation to choose that authority, and (3) where the power came from that your authority exercises to give or take away certain rights or freedoms that define what is okay.

Whenever any person, political party, or religious community declares they received a new revelation or different interpretation and then gives permission to others to modify past Christian orthodox theology and practice to fit current standards, run for the hills! Neither God nor the Holy Spirit deviates from scriptural revelation in either the letter or spirit it was originally intended and received. Scriptural discernment, as guided by the Spirit, forbids Christians from promoting or modifying historically accepted scripture to fit the current culture's morality and its corresponding doctrines for any reason, regardless of whether the pope, president, or any political leader gives you permission to do so. The truth never changes, nor does the scripture that supports that truth.

> All the words of my mouth are righteous; there is nothing twisted or crooked in them. (Proverbs 8:8)

> All scripture is breathed out by God and profitable for teaching, for reproof, for correction and for training in righteousness. (2 Timothy 3:16)

In Romans 13:1, Paul addresses the relationship of human authorities to God's governing standards, as he states, "Let every soul be subject unto the higher powers. For there is no authority except from God; and those that exist have been instituted by God."

All governments are held accountable to God, as he established them for his purposes. No government has the authority to tell their citizens they can decide for themselves which power to obey. The government that usurps God's authority puts itself in the unenviable position of facing God's wrath for their arrogance and duplicity in their disobedience.

In Matthew 5:19, Jesus clearly warns everyone, then and now:

> Therefore whoever relaxes one of the least of these commandments and teaches others to do the same will be called least in the kingdom of heaven.

In Luke 9:26, Jesus speaks to Christians and non-Christians regarding their rejection of him:

> For whoever is ashamed of me and my words, of him will the Son of Man be ashamed when he comes in his glory and the glory of the Father and of the holy angels.

"Judge not that you are not judged" is one of the most-often-used scripture verses to defend against someone criticizing a particular view or activity. It is the number-one fallback position to justify one's right to think and live according to one's beliefs, without outside interference or judgment. The question that we must ask, and answer is this: Is the use of that phrase a matter of a seductive, malevolent arrogance, fueled by self-righteous indignation; or is it a legitimate defense by a person of character or integrity? If you can validly determine the authoritative source of motivation and intent that supports the moral position, as well as the person's tone or demeanor in defending it, you can accurately discern if there is any truth or honor inherent in the view or activity.

There is, however, another side to the above: "Judge with a righteous judgment" introduces another element to consider. Does it accurately represent an explicit scripture verse? If not, why not? Can the interpretation or position taken be corroborated elsewhere in scripture verses? Does the Holy Spirit confirm its validation, and would God agree that it meets his scriptural criteria to be considered faithfully obedient? These tough questions must be answered by the one representing a certain moral viewpoint and by the challenger. Where the rubber hits the road is often where two sources of differing authority are introduced, which is the supreme authority on the specific moral issue? Different moral strokes for different folks have no scriptural basis and is never a valid defense. It might fly if you are "politically correct," but like all human-initiated philosophies and judgments, it is dead on arrival with God.

Let us go back to our historical Christian moral roots, coming together as country to fight our Goliath, Great Britain, up to the years of our Civil War. Many of our political leaders were Christians who believed that God was the foundation for any future national success and was necessarily a key to national survival throughout our history.

> It is the duty of all nations to acknowledge the Providence of Almighty God, to obey His will, to be grateful for His benefits, and to humbly implore His protection and favor. (George Washington, October 3, 1789, proclaiming a National Day of Prayer and Thanksgiving)

> God who gave us life gave us liberty. And can the liberties of a nation be thought secure when we have removed their only firm basis, a Conviction in the minds of the people that these liberties are a gift of God? They Are not to be violated but with His wrath? Indeed, I tremble for my

country when I reflect that God is just; that His justice cannot sleep forever. (Thomas Jefferson, 1781)

If we abide by the principles taught in the Bible, our country will go on prospering and to prosper; but if we and our posterity neglect its instructions and authority, no man can tell how sudden a catastrophe may overwhelm us and bury all our glory in profound obscurity. (Daniel Webster, 1821)

It is fit and becoming in all people, at all times, to acknowledge and revere the Supreme Government of God; to bow in humble submission to His chastisement; to confess and deplore their sins and transgressions in the full conviction that the fear of the Lord is the beginning of wisdom; and to pray, with all fervency and contrition, for the pardon of them past offenses and for a blessing upon their present and prospective action. (Abraham Lincoln, declaring a National Day of Prayer and Fasting following the Battle of Bull Run)

Our Constitution was made only for a moral and religious people. It is wholly inadequate to the government of any other. (John Adams)

For my part, I sincerely esteem the Constitution, a system which without the finger of God, never could have been suggested and agreed upon by such a diversity of interests. (Alexander Hamilton)

The only foundation for a republic is to be laid in Religion. Without this there can be no virtue, and without virtue there can be no Liberty, and liberty is the object and life of all republican governments. (Benjamin Rush)

Another warning from Jesus about acknowledging and honoring him before others is found in Matthew 10:32:

> So everyone who acknowledges me before men, I also will acknowledge before my Father who is in heaven, but whoever denies me before men, I also will deny before my Father who is in heaven.

It does not get any more definitive or explicit than that!

Truth or consequences is a universal application of God's natural laws, powered by his Word and will, administered by the Spirit. Those divine laws work independently, outside the ability of any human attempt to thwart them. They are set in stone. Proverbs 1:24–27, 29–33 warns us of the folly of ignoring God's penalty for insolence:

> Because I have called and you refused to listen, have stretched out my hand and no one has heeded, because you have ignored my counsel and would have none of my reproof, I also will laugh at your calamity; I will mock when terror strikes you, when terror strikes you like a storm and your calamity comes like a whirlwind, when distress and anguish come upon you. Because they hated knowledge and did not choose the fear of the Lord, would have none of my counsel and despised all my reproof, therefore they shall eat the fruit of their way, and have their fill of their own devices. But whoever listens to me will dwell secure and will be at ease, without dread of disaster.

God's justice is obligatory; his mercy is not. It may not have crossed your mind that God *hates*! He does not allow his love, holiness, or mercy to minimize his other attributes, which require judgment against all who flagrantly or deceitfully break his commandments, Word, or will. God's wrath, in many circles, is played down, as if it was only applicable in history. But consider his tone in Proverbs 6:16–19 as equally applicable to us today:

There are six things the Lord hates, seven are an abomination to Him; haughty eyes, a lying tongue, and hands that shed innocent blood, a heart that devises wicked plans, feet that make haste to run to evil, a false witness who breathes out lies and one who sows discord among brothers.

Psalm 7:11 also underscores God's demeanor every day of our lives as it reveals, "God is a righteous judge, and a God who feels indignation every day." After reading these verses, you might want to take a closer look at self-introspection and subjective self-interpretation.

Do you know which two sins scripture declares raises God's wrath and brings about judgment? Suppression or intentional distortion of his truth and man's ingratitude toward him.

For the wrath of God is revealed from heaven against all ungodliness and unrighteousness of men, who by their unrighteousness <u>suppress</u> the truth. For what can be known about God is plain to them because God has shown it to them. For His invisible attributes, namely His eternal power and divine nature have been clearly perceived ever since the creation of the world in the things that have been made. So, they are without excuse. For although they knew God, *they did not honor Him as God or give thanks to Him*, but they became futile in their thinking and their foolish hearts were darkened. Romans 1:18–21, (italics added)

True justice weeds out the undeserving by not rewarding them for immoral behavior. If you want to arrive at true justice or equity, Proverbs 3:5–6 lays out the proper due diligence:

Trust in the Lord with all your heart and do not lean on your own *understanding*, in all your ways acknowledge Him and He will make straight your paths.

Regardless of our current political and moral morass, Christians find solace and hope in these words from Isaiah 46:5–11:

> To whom will you liken me and make me equal, and compare me, that we may be alike? Those who lavish gold from the purse, and weigh out silver in the scales, hire a goldsmith and he make it into a god; then they fall and worship! They lift it to their shoulders, they carry it, they set it in place, and it stands there; it cannot move from its place. If one cries to it, it does not answer or save him from his trouble. Remember this and stand firm, recall it to mind, you transgressors, remember the former things of old; for I am God and there is no other; I am God and there is none like me, declaring the end from the beginning and from ancient times things not yet done, saying, my counsel shall stand, and I will accomplish all my purpose, calling a bird of prey from the east, the man of counsel from a far country. I have spoken and I will bring it to pass; I have purposed, and I will do it.

Jonathan Edwards put it this way: "the will is the mind, choosing."[2] Intended or unintended, consequences reveal the nature of the choice. On a national level, every choice is compounded. Where there is peace and harmony or where Christians are faithfully transforming others, the Spirit of God is present and building up. Where there is conflict, human evil is present and tearing down. Divine authority or natural law, ordained by God, metes out consequences according to his choice, his will. Absent the Spirit of God, there is no good, regardless of how humans define or defend their actions or good intentions. As William Barclay states, "Love without obedience (Christian) is an impossibility."[3]

Hebrews 4:12 speaks to the effect of the divine word and truth of God on human choices:

> For the Word of God is living and active, sharper than any two-edged sword, piercing to the division of soul and of

spirit, of joints and of marrow and discerning the thoughts and intentions of the heart.

Paul speaks an assertive warning through the impetus of the Holy Spirit as he writes:

> Take care brothers, lest there be in any of you an evil, unbelieving heart, leading you to fall away from the living God. But exhort one another every day, as long as it is called "today," that none of you may be hardened by the deceitfulness of sin. (Hebrews 3:12–13)

Is there an explicit scripture that gives you the explicit manner that explains how believing in Jesus comes about? It is answered in John 16:12–15, as Jesus explains the workings of the Spirit:

> I still have many things to say to you, but you cannot bear them now. When the Spirit of truth comes, he will guide you into all the truth, for he will not speak on his own authority, but whatever he hears he will speak, and he will declare to you the things that are to come. He will glorify me, for he will take what is mine and declare it to you. All that the Father has is mine; therefore, I said that he will take what is mine and declare it to you.

Standing firm is the individual Christian's and church's mandate. It is how we each put that into play that will affect what the results will be. Those who are Spirit-oriented will get it right, while those on the margin, influenced by social pressure, will exacerbate the problems. First Corinthians 16:13 guides us through that struggle: "Be watchful, stand firm in the faith, act like men, be strong. Let all that you do be done in love." Engage others with an attitude of humble gratitude, not a superior attitude. The words chosen and the tone in which they are delivered will reveal the true extent of your understanding and applications of your personal faithfulness to the letter and spirit of God's laws. Frauds will be exposed by their words and attitude.

Paul describes and defines what is scriptural and Christian-validated, regarding what is correct and what is love, assigning each to the work of the Spirit:

> But the fruit of the Spirit is love, joy, peace, patience, kindness, goodness, faithfulness, gentleness, self-control; against such things there is no law. (Galatians 5:22–23)

Paul assigns what is not correct or true to the works of the flesh (human pride):

> *Now the works of the flesh are evident*: sexual immorality, impurity, sensuality, idolatry, sorcery, enmity, strife, jealousy, fits of anger, rivalries, dissensions, divisions, envy, drunkenness, orgies, and things like these. I warn you, as I warned you before, that those who do such things will not inherit the kingdom of God. Galatians 5:19–21, (italics added)

Psalm 8:3–4 is an example of King David's putting man in his proper place and noting his insignificance and inability to control much of anything:

> When I look at your heavens, the work of your fingers, the moon, and the stars, which *you* have set in place, what is man that you are mindful of him and the son of man that you care for him?

As God speaks to Jeremiah concerning Israel's infidelity, we read words of anger and judgment, which are eternally arrows in God's quiver, as we consider the ramifications of national and individual morality run amok:

> I have paid attention and listened, but they have not spoken rightly; no man relents of his evil, saying what have I done? Everyone turns to his own course, like a horse plunging headlong into battle. How can you say, we are wise, and the law of the Lord is with us? Were

they ashamed when they committed abomination? No, they were not ashamed; they did not know how to blush. Therefore, they shall fall among the fallen; when I punish them, they shall be overthrown, says the Lord. (Jeremiah 8:6, 12)

On the other hand, the Spirit celebrates when a Christian celebrates scripture. The autonomist celebrates when skeptics and progressives denigrate scriptural authority over their lives. Self-righteous indignation, in many ways, can be malevolence disguised. Arrogance is a harsh but appropriate word for those who engage in actions that contradict and deny Holy Scripture as God's inviolate word. If pride is the essence of sin, autonomy its core, and defiance its heart, arrogance would seem to be an appropriate description for those who attempt to make scriptural evil legal. But consistently, morally correct autonomists, where possible, attempt to go as far as possible to falsely proclaim that their "corrected" changes and choices are gospel compatible. You have heard the maxim, "garbage in; garbage out," but can you image hearing God sigh, "We need bigger trucks"? Choice may be a human right, but defying God is never a desirable choice.

Proverbs 28:5, 9 are instructive warnings for those who live according to their own inclinations, standards of justice, and laws:

Evil men do not understand justice, but those who seek the Lord understand it completely. If one turns away his ear from hearing the law, (God's) even his prayer is an abomination.

Solomon, one of the wisest men who ever lived, makes the point that everyone's life experience hinges on the understanding that God is sovereign. His justice and mercy are indisputably in his hands and are exercised according to his will and purposes. Every man who ever has lived has received God's justice, and by God's mercy alone, some received grace. Each of us is responsible for our actions and reactions to that sovereignty:

> I perceived that whatever God does endures forever;
> nothing can be added to it, nor anything taken from
> it. God has done it, so that people fear before him.
> (Ecclesiastes 3:14)

In other words, God is part of every single action or human involvement, and they last because he alone has the power to see everything he starts brought to its fruition. Each human generational undertaking is built up or torn town, according to the standards and practices to which they subscribe.

Paul acknowledges that he too recognizes that man is inherently sinful, as he writes through the inspiration of the Spirit, "None is righteous, no, not one; no one understands; no one seeks God, all have turned aside; together they have become worthless; no one does good, not even one" (Romans 3:11–12). Without God, godlessness becomes moral normal. In our day, "whatever works for you is right for you" seems to be the current moral favorite. "I'm okay; you're okay" sets the moral bar at the lowest common denominator because it indifferently accepts opposite or contradictory values, without objectively, scripturally qualifying the debits or credits associated with a particular lifestyle or practice.

CHAPTER 6

Christianity, the Only Objective Faith

In American society today, we are bombarded by claims of class warfare and economic unfairness. Political expedience and autonomy subjectively suggest that taxing the wealthy to pay for bigger entitlement and spending programs is only fair; that it is the right thing to do to address the imbalances between the upper and middle classes. That same issue roiled the American culture 125 years ago. Rev. William J.H Boetcker, a conservative thinker who spoke out about industrial relations at the turn of the twentieth commented on ways not to resolve the economic and social divisions, *but* today's political and economic wise men did not get the message. Someone, someday, would do well to consider what is still sound advice:

> You cannot bring about prosperity by discouraging thrift. You cannot strengthen the weak by weakening the strong. You cannot help the wage earner by pulling down the wage payer. *You cannot further the brotherhood of man by encouraging class hatred.* You cannot help the poor by destroying the rich. *You cannot keep out of trouble by spending more than you earn.* You cannot build character and courage by taking away man's initiative and independence. You cannot help men permanently by doing for them what they could and should do for themselves.[1] (italics added)

What we are seeing today in our towns and cities are elements of "progressive" institutionalized vanity. These are everyday people and authorities who exhibit humanistic arrogance, ascribing to themselves God-like attributes. Matthew Henry put it this way: "There is not a greater enemy to the power of religion and the fear of God in the heart, than conceitedness of our own wisdom."[2]

Have you ever thought what would happen to human civilization if there were no laws or codes of conduct or if the existing ones were not enforced? The answer to that is easy; there would be chaos and violence everywhere. The strong would exploit the weak; the evil would terrorize the good. There would be no recourse, only capitulation.

In similar fashion, what happens today when historically accepted Judeo-Christian moral laws are widely circumvented or haphazardly enforced? Pockets of chaos, rebellion, deceit, and violence coalesce around and take advantage of the least restrictive enforcement mechanisms (lax civil morality, progressive liberalism).

Hebrews 11:6 addresses the key principle that is required to please God:

> And without faith, it is impossible to please him, for whoever would draw near to God must believe that he exists and that he rewards those who seek him.

The conclusion one can draw from that one verse is that no matter your principles, your passion, your knowledge, or your religion, without faith in Christ, you cannot please God. Further, to be a child of God, you must have the faith that comes from the Holy Spirit.

Paul provides a detailed framework and description of Spirit and flesh, truth or consequences sorted out and placed in their rightful condition:

> But I say, walk by the Spirit and you will not gratify the desires of the flesh. *For the desires of the flesh are against the Spirit and the desires of the Spirit are against the flesh,* for these are opposed to each other, to keep you from doing the things you want to do. But if you are led by the Spirit, you are not under the law. Now the works of the flesh are evident; sexual immorality, impurity, sensuality, idolatry,

sorcery, enmity, strife, jealousy, fits of anger, rivalries, dissensions, divisions, envy, drunkenness, orgies, and things like these. I warn you, as I warned you before, that those who do such things will not inherit the kingdom of God. But the fruit of the Spirit is love, joy, peace, patience, kindness, goodness, faithfulness, gentleness, self-control; against such things there is no law. Galatians 5:16–24 (italics added)

And those who belong to Christ Jesus have crucified the flesh with its passions and desires.

When bad decisions and irresponsible behavior, resulting in known negative consequences, are repeated over and over, do those engaging in that behavior deserve equal respect and validation with those who made wise decisions and ethical choices? If everyone operates under their own subjective standards, and the politically correct validate opposite moral standards as equally viable, should you expect greater integrity, honor, and responsibility or less? The lowest common denominator of morality and integrity—in most cases involving large numbers of people—becomes the baseline normal for the government to use as its justification to modify laws, raise taxes, or validate new rights previously withheld.

Jesus, speaking to the Pharisees, said:

Whoever is not with me is against me and whoever does not gather with me, scatters. I tell you on the day of judgment people will give account for every careless word they speak, for by your words you will be justified, or you will be condemned. (Matthew 12:30, 36)

Christ's justice balances compassion with deserved consequences.

"Misery loves company" is a well-known axiom that suggests individuals who experience tough times or tricky situations prefer to commiserate with others who experience the same conditions or circumstances. The politically correct are, from many Christian perspectives, birds of a feather, sticking together, using arrogance, self-righteous indignation, and personal biases to force society to submit to their version of right and wrong.

By submitting truths by degrees (not the whole truth and nothing but the truth) and fixating on identity rights by decrees, not by scriptural instructions, they are painting a false picture.

Rebellion and defiance have been with us from the beginning. Scripture, from start to finish, emphasizes both the human earthly consequences and eternal damnation that results. Listen to the words of God in Proverbs 8:13: "The fear of the Lord is hatred of evil. Pride and arrogance and the way of evil and perverted speech, I hate."

In Amos 5:15, we read the same condemnation of evil as God speaks these words:

> Hate evil, and love good, establish justice in the gate; it may be that the Lord, the God of hosts, will be gracious to the remnant of Joseph.

Evil within a church is to be managed in the manner described in 1 Corinthians 5:13:

> God judges those outside [the church]. Purge the evil person from among you [within the church].

Second Timothy 3:12, 16 brings us full circle from evil to godly:

> Indeed, all who desire to live a Godly life in Christ Jesus will be persecuted, while evil people and impostors will go on from bad to worse, deceiving and being deceived. All Scripture is breathed out by God and profitable for teaching, for reproof, for correction and for training in righteousness that the man of God may be complete, equipped for every good work.

Finally, from 3 John 11: "Beloved, do not imitate evil but imitate good. Whoever does good is from God; whoever does evil has not seen God."

Politically correct adjustable morality is no less than God's truth obstructed, slandered, and manipulated to represent an inconvenient human truth— individuals, governments, and aligned organizations manipulate human standards, good works, and reasoning as both the means and ends for their "correct" version of human successes, goodness, and socially acceptable behavior, frequently in opposition to historic Christian practices. The very act of leaving God out of any human transaction or relationship and substituting human standards and reasoning is blatant rebellion and suppression of truth. You can take this to the bank—unquestioned political loyalty leads to unbalanced authority, which evolves into deception, suppression, and immorality.

Scripture guides us explicitly and implicitly regarding the validity or fallacy of our words, beliefs, and actions. A good example is Philippians 4:8-9:

> Whatever is true, whatever is honorable, whatever is just, whatever is pure, whatever is lovely, whatever is commendable, if there is any excellence, if there is anything worthy of praise, think about these things. What you have learned, received, and heard and seen in me—practice these things and the God of peace will be with you.

Paul was pointing out that before you speak, act, or profess a belief, cross-reference each of the eight conditions listed in the scripture verse when taking an ethical position or a judgment of good and evil or when evaluating the pluses and minuses of your subject or actions with God's example. Is what you propose coordinated with the divine requisite "trust and obey"? Further, God blesses or gives you and others his peace when you follow Jesus's lead and bring honor and glory to him in the process.

It is the Spirit, not our political or social spirit, from which all blessings and correct behavior flows. Faithful Christians who are obedient to the leading of the Spirit can discern that an obedient fellowship must separate false teachers to deny them spheres of influence within their congregations. Paul conveys that Christians and non-Christians are judged by the same standards, and God shows no partiality:

> There will be tribulation and distress for every human being who does evil, the Jew first and the Greek, but glory and honor and peace for everyone who does good,

the Jew first and the Greek. For God shows no partiality.
(Romans 2:9–11)

Here is a key component of all Christian evidential truth, which is supported and sanctioned only by scripture: whatever violates scripture violates truth, and whatever validates scripture is truth. All truth comes from God. There is no acceptable alternative, such as an I'm-okay/you're-okay truth for faithful Christians. We are warned to be wary of false prophets and pandering:

> Preach the Word be ready in season and out of season, reprove, rebuke, and exhort with complete patience and teaching, but having itching ears *they will accumulate for themselves teachers to suit their own purposes and will turn away from listening to the truth and wander off into myths.* 2 Timothy 4:2–4, (italics added)

If you want to arrive at true justice or equity, Proverbs 3:5–6 lays out the proper due diligence:

> Trust in the Lord with all your heart and do not lean on your own understanding, in all your ways acknowledge Him and He will make straight your paths.

What one thing affects everything in your life, your dreams, your relationships and associations, and your success or failure in achieving them? What word comes to mind? That key word is *trust*. The degree to which you are trustworthy and your ability to find and keep trustworthy people, associations, and groups within your inner circle will determine the quality of your life and your ability to find success and peace. The problem for each of us is universal—who do you trust, and who can you trust? Get it wrong, and life becomes one problem after another. Get it right, and life is far more rewarding. Are you at peace with God and your neighbor, or do you love your neighbor and accept his or her sin?

"Correct" standards tend to accommodate and lean toward their own understanding of what the Bible would readily call corrupt. Do you look to and trust the Holy Spirit or follow and trust the human spirit?

Any trust in someone without their respect for and recognition of divine truth is worthless. Empowering state-driven diversity and equality at the expense of equity and divine justice is a recipe for chaos. When individuals are solely dependent on other men and women, who are solely dependent on human institutions and values to determine what is fair and what is just, you are inheriting and incorporating human error into the equation. Not one president, Supreme Court judge, religious leader, or self-styled cultural icon or political ideologist is completely in control of anything during his or her life. Any day, they could get something wrong, misjudge, have an accident, become seriously ill, lose a loved one, or die themselves. Like everyone else, they are inflicted and conflicted with doubt, worry, truth, justice, equity, and failure.

They are all subject to illness, depression, anger, frustration, self-doubt, and lust in one form or another. If you get one thing from this chapter, let it be this: humans are hopeless and incapable of living an obedient, abundant life without the Spirit of God within and without. When you do not know how much you do not know, concerning any given topic or situation, and you act like you do so others will follow your lead, you are an instigator, not a leader. If you are not humble enough to acknowledge your shortcomings or to admit you are not sure, and you proceed, regardless of your lack of certainty, you become a dangerous person, irrespective of your position, authority, or credited wisdom.

It may be true that scriptural instructions are not always explicit. The implied message of instruction is sometimes abused, as it becomes a timely opportunity to further one's personal interpretation. But the remedy for any instruction that is not clear to you is to look at the letter, spirit of all instruction, and seek other related or similar passages that may be applied to the one with which you are dealing. The *Westminster Confession*, along with reference Bibles and concordances, is an excellent resource. Since the Holy Spirit was the inspiration for all of scripture and not the attributed author, what was written through the author by the Holy Spirit will be consistent and concise enough to all who genuinely want to find the intended meaning or answer.

We would do well to remember that we can measure something by seeing the visible effect, but some effects are unseen until God makes them known. Those who have prepared themselves to scripturally discern and read events and signs that proceed from both the visible and invisible will be in a better position to accurately discern what is transpiring.

Hebrews 11: 6 addresses the key principle that is required to please God:

> And without faith, it is impossible to please him, for whoever would draw near to God must believe that he exists and that he rewards those who seek him.

The conclusion you can draw from that one verse is that no matter your principles, your passion, your knowledge, or your religion, without faith in Christ, you cannot please God. Further, to be a child of God, you must have the faith that comes from the Holy Spirit.

Do we want to know the truth, or do we hear what we want to hear and disregard what we do not? In John 18:37, Jesus clarifies—to Pilate and all the worlds—his mission of bearing witness to the truth and how we can determine who is of the truth:

> Then Pilate said to him, "So you are a king?" Jesus answered, "you say that I am a king. For this purpose, I have come into the world-to bear witness to the truth. Everyone who is of the truth listens to my voice."

Remember the Serenity Prayer of Reinhold Niebuhr, a twentieth-century theologian in Germany? If we would take it to heart and embrace it daily, the world would be a much better place. Here are his powerful and prescient words:

> God grant me the serenity to accept things I cannot change, courage to change the things I can, and the wisdom to know the difference.

Jesus, speaking to the Pharisees, said,

> Whoever is not with me is against me and whoever does not gather with me, scatters. I tell you on the day of judgment people will give account for every careless word

they speak, for by your words you will be justified, or you will be condemned. (Matthew 12:30, 36)

Christ's justice balances compassion with deserved consequences.

In Dr. Michael Youssef's book *Hope for This Present Crisis*, the noted pastor, writer, and scholar from Egypt points out the alarming immoral and deceitful trends in our culture that need to be assertively addressed through these following steps:

1. Remember the truth: stand firm for biblical morality on a foundation of "irrefutable evidence."
2. Restore the soul: seek the approval of God over others.
3. Revitalize the family: pray fervently for our children and raise them to know and love God's Word
4. Reestablish the classroom: care for public school teachers, know what our children are being taught, and consider Christian schools or homeschooling, where necessary.
5. Respect our freedoms: know our rights, defend the rights of others, and pray for boldness.
6. Reform our society: seek moral and spiritual purity for ourselves while praying for our nation and sharing the gospel with all people.
7. Revive the church: always demonstrate the forgiving love of Jesus as we "put on the whole armor of God" (Ephesians 6:11) and seek opportunities to share our spiritual gifts.[3]

Those who espouse moral autonomy attempt to separate themselves from historically accepted moral and ethical guidelines containing certain restrictions and parameters ordained by God. They consider themselves a law unto themselves, independent from and outside of the jurisdiction of those requirements. Proverbs 21:2 reminds us of our propensity to stray: "Every way of a man is right in his own eyes, but the Lord weighs the heart."

A good example of gross misrepresentation of the highest priorities and secondary priorities of the "corrects" is how they vastly overemphasize the place of rights and freedoms and practically dismiss the command of Jesus, speaking to his disciples:

> And Jesus came and said to them, "All authority in heaven and on earth has been given to me. Go therefore and *make disciples* of all nations, *baptizing* them in the name of the Father and of the Son and of the Holy Spirit, *teaching them to observe all that I have commanded you.* And behold, I am with you always, to the end of the age." (Matthew 28:18–20, italics added)

If you cannot admit you are a sinner or cannot confess your sins, you will not be forgiven. In 1 John 1:8–10, clarity is amplified:

> If we say we have no sin, we deceive ourselves and the truth is not in us. If we confess our sins, he is faithful to cleanse us of all unrighteousness. If we say we have not sinned, we make him a liar and his word is not in us.

There is no integrity when one neither stands for what is scripturally right nor protests what is scripturally wrong. Saint Augustine made a salient observation when he stated that evil is what results "when the will abandons what is above itself and turns to what is lower – not because that is evil to which it turns but because turning itself is wicked."[4] Neutrality, used to avoid a necessary conflict between competing moral positions, is an excuse, a sign of lukewarm commitment and indifference when scriptural discernment is required.

Integrity requires uncompromised standards, truths, and honor by adhering to sound doctrines and practices that demand discipline, commitment, demanding work, and the sacrificial lifestyles that are necessary to rise above today's good-enough mentality. Compromise in any ethical or morality issue eliminates one from belonging to that elite status. Reaching an acceptable agreement that does not adhere to the highest standards and conduct demonstrated and demanded by scriptural requirements nullifies one's claim of being a person of integrity. Christian integrity is Spirit-driven and powered. All other claims of human integrity that use a human standard of measurement do not meet scripture's definition of Christian honor or integrity, which is gospel-faithful and God-purposed.

Those who question God's ability to manage all the comings and goings and affairs of every human would do well to read the above sentences several times. God does everything his way, according to his Word and his timing. One modern-day theologian J. I. Packer spoke of God's providence in all things as "the unceasing activity of the Creator whereby, in overflowing bounty and goodwill, he upholds His creatures in ordered existence, guides and governs all events, circumstances and free acts of angels and men and directs everything to its appointed goal, for His own glory."[5]

The Triune God of the universe is always present, works independently, and is completely resistant to any human efforts to thwart his created natural order of all things. The politically correct operate as if their order of things acts independently, outside the authority of God's prescribed order of natural laws. This conflict of interests pits a titan (God) against a philosophy (politically correct) that considers itself superior to all others and beyond the constraints of heretofore historically respected ethical laws. That appeal is so tempting that millions see it as an attractive, pragmatic replacement that allows them to create and exercise "rights" as they go; protocol in which everybody becomes their own independent agent, with the power to self-determine what is moral or right.

We like to believe that subsequent human efforts alone can undo the crisis, and order can be restored. Alexander Carson reminds each of us that there is a right way and a wrong way to govern and be governed:

> As God can protect his people under the greatest despotism, so the utmost civil liberty is no safety to them without the immediate protection of his Almighty arm. I fear that Christians in this country have to great a confidence in political institutions, rather than the government of God.[6]

American values should not be predicated on American morality or political correctness but on Christian fidelity. Values are always local, just as we say all politics are local. Values and human morality are all subjective; Christian fidelity is godly objective. In 1821, President John Quincy Adams made this salient observation: "The highest glory of the

American Revolution was this: it connected one indissoluble bond of principles of civil government with the principles of Christianity."[7]

The ever-present conundrum is reaching the proper balance. The problems are who or what has the final say or authority to declare their validity, and who decides that they are equitable and equally applied in an objective manner? With varying types of governments, national foundation documents, institutions, and majority rule, we try to reach a fair and just system that protects certain rights and freedoms but also denies or restricts certain acts or lifestyles that are considered morally harmful, from both an individual and corporate perspective.

Pretentiousness is everywhere—in our homes, businesses, institutions, and national moral makeup. The word clearly is divisive because many will deny it applies to them or their identity group. Dictionaries have numerous definitions, such as "a claim to something, such as a right or privilege, a right asserted without foundation, demanding or claiming a position of distinction or merit especially when unjustified." Wherever you come down on this assertion that we all are guilty of pretension, be wary of individuals and groups who assert their claim as valid or correct, simply because they say so or are in the majority, which they believe, by default, makes it right. All politically correct moral autonomy flows from various degrees of pretentiousness, whenever subjective criteria are used as the basis of the fact being represented.

Cognitive dissonance is another term that applies to those who go out of their way to defend their political or moral truth, which is essential to justify or validate their position or dogma. A definition might be something like, "a condition of conflict resulting from inconsistency between one's beliefs and one's actions."

Just as there are physical laws or natural laws, there are God's ethical laws. Each of those are set in stone as absolutes to guide our moral compass. When those lines are crossed or God's laws are subverted, a built-in trigger mechanism kicks in and sets in motion God's laws of cause and effect—or, as we like to say, truth or consequences. What most despots and the politically correct do not seem to understand is that whether you believe it or reject it, you cannot undo or prevent the penalty or discipline that will be imposed when you cross God. It may be immediate or delayed but in God's time, it will be brought to bear.

Human nature cannot rise above itself; it takes God's influence and grace. Only deceived men and women with a separate agenda and an arrogant I-know-better attitude would dare tell others to follow their lead and to reinterpret what is the unchanging Word of God for the changing word of man. If you know scripture, you know it is sacred as it is. If you do not know scripture, it never was nor will be for you, unless you honor it as God's very voice. This is speaking to you in 2 Timothy 3:16–17:

> All scripture is breathed out by God and profitable for teaching, for reproof, for correction and for training in righteousness, that the man of God may be complete, equipped for every good work.

Proverbs 8:8 further declares, "All the words of my mouth are righteous; there is nothing crooked or twisted in them." The truth never changes, nor does the scripture that supports it.

Which is more odious—the evil that is played out by a bad person who knows he is evil and makes no effort to hide it, or evil that is hidden by a "good" person with the right credentials and pedigree, who leads others into the evil under the guise of self-righteousness and moral autonomy? Which is the more effective way of getting people to come over to your side? Satan struck gold when he enticed the politically correct to convince themselves and others that moral autonomy did not deny God, per se; rather, it elevated humans and empowered them to decide for themselves what is true and what is an illusion?

In Leviticus 19:15, God is giving instructions to Moses to help the people of Israel live faithfully: "You shall do no injustice in court. You shall not be partial to the poor or defer to the great, but in righteousness shall you judge your neighbor." Every judgment must equitably take into consideration the merit of the opposing positions in each circumstance in an impartial and unbiased manner. No person of integrity or government dedicated to justice and honor will forcefully impose their subjective will on another, one who tries to be faithful to the Lord, simply because they can by fiat law.

Because they have taken it upon themselves to act independently and outside God's sole instruction, they are, in effect, fighting against his divine plans and purposes. Christians within this coalition have been duped and are sinning mightily against their namesake. Listen to Paul's warning:

> I appeal to you, brothers to watch out for those who cause divisions and create obstacles contrary to the doctrine they you have been taught; avoid them. For such persons do not serve our Lord Christ, but their own appetites and by smooth talk and flattery they deceive the hearts of the naïve. (Romans 16:17–18)

The politically correct forces of compromise and equality are waging a battle of wills with the Christian mentality that it is better to weed out impurities and unfaithfulness that infects the body, even if it means confrontation and division. Dr. Carl Trueman, a former professor of church history at Westminster Theological Seminary in Philadelphia, wrote:

> A movement that cannot or will not draw boundaries, or that allows modern cultural fear of exclusion to set its theological agenda, is doomed to lose its doctrinal identity. Once it does, it will drift from whatever moorings it may have had in historic Christianity.[8]

Each Christian community must conclude that by separating and removing false teachers from the congregation, it denies them a sphere of influence to corrupt Christ's word and will. *When* that becomes reality is a matter of spiritual discernment. What is certain is that by gradually allowing and accepting the increase of incompatible teaching within a church or congregation, the conflict becomes bigger and spreads wider.

Truth or consequences is a universal application of God's natural law, powered by his Word and will. Those laws work independently, outside the ability of any human attempt to thwart them. They are set in stone. Proverbs 1:24–27, 29–33 warns us of the folly of ignoring God's penalty for insolence:

> Because I have called and you refused to listen, have stretched out my hand and no one has heeded, because

you have ignored my counsel and would have none of my reproof, I also will laugh at your calamity; I will mock when terror strikes you, when terror strikes you like a storm and your calamity comes like a whirlwind, when distress and anguish come upon you. Because they hated knowledge and did not choose the fear of the Lord, would have none of my counsel and despised all my reproof, therefore they shall eat the fruit of their way, and have their fill of their own devices. But whoever listens to me will dwell secure and will be at ease, without dread of disaster.

John Calvin, the inspired Reformation leader, amplified the above when he wrote,

It is the summit of all evils when the sinner is so void of shame that he is pleased with his own vices and will not bear them to be reproved and also cherishes them in others by his consent and approbation.[9]

Jeremiah, a prophet, and priest in the Old Testament around 600 BC, lived during a time of great turmoil for the nation of Israel. He spoke a message from God that no one wanted to hear. God's anger against the people of Israel for their flagrant violations and disobedience is disclosed in the following words; thus says the Lord:

Cursed is the man who trusts in man and makes flesh his strength, whose heart turns away from the Lord. Blessed is the man who trusts in the Lord, whose trust is the Lord. (Jeremiah 17:5, 7)

Compromising in good faith and pragmatic rationalization are two of the most frequent ways we begin the process of self-destruction. It may be true that they bring a temporary peace or cessation of harsh rhetoric, but it is certainly true they do not solve the issue or ever achieve the highest truth or greatest good. Whatever you settle for, without resolving the heart of the issue, determines the degree and nature of your next conflict. The closer you are to the truest resolution of the ethical issue, the smaller your future problems. The farther away you are from a true resolution of the moral or social issue, the greater your future conflict. You be the judge of whether we have more conflict or less conflict today in our national, political, or religious arguments than in years past.

A growing perception among many citizens is that there is a deficient checks-and-balances system within the liberal, politically correct fiefdom that inherently undermines their sincere, compassionate attempts at redress. *Washington Post* columnist E. J. Dionne referred to the Affordable Care Act website crash that occurred several years ago:

> There is a lesson here that liberals apparently need to learn over and over; good intentions without proper administration can undermine even the most noble of goals.[10]

Our system of jurisprudence is framed by our Judeo-Christian heritage, passed down over many generations. The original laws that established our jurisprudence were taken from the Old and New Testaments and incorporated into our Declaration of Independence, Constitution, and Bill of Rights. From there, they have been codified and amended, depending on the integrity of those who decided adaptations were necessary to address contemporary problems and standards of conduct. Relationships between private citizens and corporate and institutional entities determine what is right or correct for all its citizens. Where the rubber hits the road is when individuals and interest groups are the tail wagging the dog.

The morality behind adaptations and reform can take the form of a tyrant, a majority rule perspective, or godly equal equity that ensures the minority's positions are weighed and measured equally with the majorities. Only godly equity prevents the majority from dictating a party-based morality that uses its superior numbers to forge laws and relationships that suits its subjective means to an end. While the minority can hold accountable the misdeeds of the majority, both the majority and minority tend to be hypocritical in the process of working things out by not using godly equity as the core standard for equal justice.

Individuals never discover a moral truth undisclosed in scripture or outside the Spirit's revelation. What is a given today is fabricating a claimed "new understanding" of scripture that fits contemporary morality.

"There is no human objectivity," according to Robin DiAngelo, in a *Washington Post* article printed on November 9, 2015. As a former Seattle-based professor of multicultural education consulting on racial justice, she states, "Human beings can only make sense of the world through the lens they were socialized to make sense of it through."[11]

Can we then logically conclude if individuals are unable to be objective—because they are innately unable to rise above their socialization—all human sources of group authority are also tainted by the group's inability to be objective? While this one authority's conclusion does not make the case closed, it does suggest that we all have innate biases that coalesce around opportunities to exploit and promote any biases or personal-identity leanings that favor our points of view.

CHAPTER 7

❦

Sin Hidden in Good Intentions

This book attempts to address the great indifference and deceit by many so-called Christians, whose theology and practice is predicated on which way the political wind is blowing on any current religious or social issue. Not much has changed in two thousand years. Jesus warned his followers in Matthew 7:15, "Beware of false prophets (teachers) who come to you in sheep's clothing but inwardly are ravenous wolves." In a similar vein, Jesus takes aim at the same false teachers, whose works, charity, and announced "good intentions" are timed and promoted to take effect when they will be seen and heard by the largest possible audience that favors their position is in attendance.

In Matthew 6:1, he warns, "Take heed that you do not do your charitable deeds before men to be seen by them. Otherwise, you have no reward from your Father in heaven."

In Mark 7:5–9, Jesus, in a biting, stinging manner, addresses the "politically correct" of his day, the Pharisees, when he says to them:

> Well did Isaiah prophesy of you hypocrites, as it is written, *this people honors me with their lips but their heart is far from me; in vain do they worship me, teaching as doctrines the precepts of men. You leave the commandment of God and hold fast to the tradition of men.* (Italics added)

As evidence of such a claim, Sean Trende, a political analyst, wrote this astounding political arrogance regarding the 2012 political campaign for the president:

> Consider that over the course of the past few years, Democrats and liberals have booed the inclusion of God in their platform at the 2012 convention.[1]

Anything originating from man cannot improve on anything already settled by God. Anything originating from God is inherently already the one and only acceptable position or truth. When two versions of the same truth or position collide, only one can be closest to the highest truth or principle, and it too could be off center. Close enough or good enough is less true, less good, and less right. Simply supporting alternative, good-enough or close-enough interpretations to keep the peace or maintain harmony is sinful.

Politically correct morality, ideology, psychology, or any related institutionally approved conduct comes from the minds of humans alone. It is not based on sound scriptural interpretation, nor does it submit to humbling itself under scriptural authority. It is an authority controlling itself, distinctly of human origination, and designed for human consumption, and it sees itself outside of the demands, commands, and requirements of Holy Scripture. It refutes and rejects passages and verses of the Old and New Testaments that limit personal autonomy and independent, self-governing lifestyles.

The Westminster Confession of Faith is in stark contrast to the moral autonomy so fondly embraced by the "correct." It clarifies and stipulates how we are to approach and interpret Holy Scripture. In chapter 1, it addresses how we are to faithfully discern both the reading and understanding of scriptural insights and wisdom:

> The infallible rule of interpretation of Scripture, is the Scripture itself; and therefore, when there is a question about the true and full sense of any scripture (which is not manifold, but one), it may be searched and known by other places that speak more clearly. The Supreme Judge,

> by which all controversies of religion are to be determined,
> and all decrees of councils, opinions of ancient writers,
> doctrines of men and private spirits, are to be examined,
> and in whose sentence, we are to rest, can be no other but
> the Holy Spirit speaking in Scripture.[2]

Can you fix someone or something that is broken or divided by accentuating victimology, unmerited equality, contrived rights, indiscriminate tolerance, or moral relativity? Does continually adding more of the same components or psychology into the mix that caused the initial fracture seem like a logical way to get different results? Does moral relativity, which reflects an individual's subjective life experience, increase or decrease the likelihood that emphasizing greater social and moral diversity will bring about a superior, ethically united society?

When you resort to using contradictory scriptural positions to make your case, you debase scripture; you seduce yourself and lead others to accept truth by degrees—humanity's accepted version—resulting in compounding your sin and theirs. God inspired every word in scripture. He did not spell out exact details on every possible sticking point, but he did give us exactly what he wanted us to know and accept and delineated the importance of separating the wheat from the chaff.

The gulf between the politically correct mindset and orthodox Christian doctrine and practice is *insurmountable.* The former is pulled up and down and all around to satisfy the many human-rights groups and various political blocks' needs and demands. It rises and falls from issue to issue, politician to politician, and changes its philosophy, as required, to gain approval from the masses. It often leads from behind, depending on which way the wind is blowing. It vociferously stands for everyone's rights but is silent in demanding everyone's accountability and responsibility.

Where do ministers, priests, bishops, and everyone else read into scripture that Christians are free to settle for either/or? Why do they personally endorse, promote, and validate opposite scriptural positions, claiming they come from deep prayer or Spirit revelation? Whose gospel are they proclaiming as they seek to find harmony in gray areas? Could it be, in their deception, that their moral values are skewed to a reoriented social gospel of rights and freedoms, powered and promoted by and for the people, rather than a salvation/truth gospel powered by Christ in conjunction with the Holy Spirit?

Human rebellion against God's authority is pointed out in Psalm 2:2–3:

> The kings of the earth set themselves and the rulers take counsel together, against the Lord and against his Anointed (Christians) saying, "Let us burst their bonds apart and cast away their cords from us.

A good case can be made that civil and political conditions today very much mirror the above refrain. If that is the case, then even the prayers of the rebellious are considered wicked, as written in Proverbs 28:9, "If one turns away from hearing the law, even his prayer is an abomination."

"Oh, what a tangled web we weave, when at first we practice to deceive" pretty much encapsulates the thrust of any type of moral autonomy. Appealing to our baser nature may help gain initial traction, but, inevitably, all lies, and deceits have consequences that will reveal their true nature—malevolence. Smiling faces and impassioned rhetoric can convey good or evil. Thomas Aquinas reminded us to be wary and to dig deeper when he said, "Man regards the deed; God sees the intention."

There is no escape from God's eyes or justice. Nebuchadnezzar, king of Babylon—arguably the mightiest nation on earth at that time—found out the hard way that no person or nation is beyond God's reach. After God humbled him in Daniel 4, God restored him to his right mind; here are the words of a defiant pagan who learned his lesson:

> All the inhabitants of the earth are accounted as nothing, and he (God) does according to his will among the host of heaven and among the inhabitants of the earth; and none can stay his hand. (Daniel 4:35)

Human intentions are grounded in human motivations. The major problem within that relationship, when the intention is not Spirit-motivated, is that it becomes self-centered and self-serving, even when the motivation is to positively impact others. Charles H. Spurgeon, the great nineteenth-century English theologian, put it this way in his book *Holy Spirit*:

> I want you to keep this truth in your mind, never forget it; whatever does not glorify Christ is not of the Holy Spirit and what is of the Holy Spirit invariably glorifies our Lord Jesus Christ.[3]

Adding another piece to the conundrum, Jesus emphasized the importance of putting things in the right order and then making being faithful to those eternal truths your highest priority, when he said, "For where your treasure is, there your heart will be also" (Matthew 6:21). We can walk the walk and talk the talk all we want about a specific social or ethical issue; we can pray unceasingly about the issue, but love without obedience is not love at all, and faith without the Spirit's guidance and scriptural corroboration is worthless.

What have they wrought? A politically correct, religiously corrupt utopia, where right and wrong, truth and fact, are blurred enough that individuals or churches no longer need to solely look to scripture for inspired revelation but simply turn to the politically correct leaders and pastors in politics, culture, and Christianity to be told what is acceptable. They are taking us back to the time of judges in Israel, thousands of years ago. The Old Testament book of Judges reads, "In those days there was no king in Israel; everyone did what was right in his eyes" (Judges 21:8).

Justice is God's equity that objectively rewards the good and objectively punishes the bad. Equity determines what is just and what is not equal. Assigning equality to unequal relationships or attributes is neither justice nor true equality. You cannot assign equality to an identity group or special-interest group that seeks it unless its merit and integrity can be definitively demonstrated as having the same ethical qualities inherent in both entities. It can be nothing else than applying God's explicit instructions in scripture, demanding to discern his will and purpose, and putting into place both the letter and spirit of that instruction. Any political or institutional attempt to exchange divine equity—one which requires objective, scriptural truth and fact standards—for human equality, based on subjective agendas or human morality, is no better than exchanging the truth for a lie.

The essence of politically correct moral autonomy is man's ascendant self-importance and moral self-determination. The essence of politically correct authority is moral self-validation. Together, they represent a malevolent spirit, dedicated to separating individuals from God and from other men and women. Every moral autonomy self-determination means someone has lost something precious—a truth, a trust, a relationship, or even life itself.

All humans battle their human nature, as all are born of flesh, which, in and of itself, is a death sentence, both physically and spiritually. In John 3:5–6, Jesus responds to Nicodemus as he says,

> Truly I say to you, unless one is born of water and the Spirit, he cannot enter the kingdom of God. That which is born of the flesh is flesh and that which is born of the Spirit is Spirit.

Because all are cursed with the sinful influences and evil inclinations passed down from the beginning, all are subject to a daily battle of good or evil, truth or consequences. No one can find fulfillment or complete peace, in and of their own volition. You cannot earn it or acquire it, no matter what you accomplish or how you live and relate to others.

In the very beginning of human creation, there were no issues, but that did not last long. Adam and Eve passed on to every generation the desire to be judge and jury, each deciding to judge what was right and wrong for them, and each deciding to be their own jury, using their own standards to acquit themselves of any wrongdoing. It is called *excuses*. Thousands of years later, contemporary Adams and Eves have taken the judge-and-jury psychology to new levels of complicity. They bend the rules and change the moral standards to accommodate human standards, claiming them to be kinder and gentler than God's outdated Old Testament version. But the icing on their cake is that they have convinced themselves and others that the church too needs to be reformed by outside influences and transformed to meet the modern-day philosophies. Claiming God's blessing falsely, they integrate their new rights as part of a more user-friendly church of universal appeal—something to accommodate everyone's taste.

Social and economic progress are dependent, in large degree, on each successive generation's passing on the necessary ethical or moral values and standards to the next. When one generation fails to do so, the next suffers greater degrees of economic or social breakdowns. We are in a downward cycle, arguably because baby boomers failed to emphasize the merits of personal sacrifice, patience, responsible sexual behaviors, and equal individual and corporate accountability for everyone, regardless of their social or economic status. When ethical behavior is not learned or valued, it inevitably causes social digression from personal honor and integrity into personal laxness and self-absorption. We have met the enemy but failed to recognize and address its root causes—human rebellion and ingratitude towards our Creator. Absent the Spirit, sin abounds.

Our inclination is to see, hear, and believe what we want, according to our human nature rather than through the wisdom of scripture and inspiration of the Spirit. In the process of rejecting that guidance, the indifferent, the ignorant, and the arrogant decide which Christian moral positions they want invalidated so they can avoid any past stigma being associated with their lifestyles. Then, they must work together to make those positions more palatable and allow themselves and others the luxury of benefitting from the increasing numbers associated with their cause. Put another way, they took God's sweet lemonade, made it bitter, and declared it better. The acidic aftertaste was easier to swallow because the camaraderie associated with working together to pull it off lessened any feeling of guilt, as vast numbers of politically correct agents indulged too, lessening the chance of being singled out.

In the past, the proper attitude concerning differences of opinion was, "I disapprove of what you say but will defend your right to say it." Today, the typical politically correct response would be, "I disapprove of what you say; it offends me; therefore, stop saying it."

In God's process of cleaning up our mess, he empowers those who know his truth to bear the slings and arrows that inevitably follow every attempt to justify the watered-down version of common morality. The best way to defend scripture and Christ's gospel is to trust and obey his Word and will as inspired by the Spirit. We do not need to browbeat or coerce others to turn them to God. We do have to live as God instructs, to speak and demonstrate the truth, and then step back and allow the Spirit to quicken the hearts of the elect. The Spirit will enter the hearts of the unrepentant, not because of our efforts but because God's grace elected or selected each to receive it. From the day we are born until the day we die, God will be judge and jury, while each of us must decide whether we want to be the defendant on trial or the faithful follower who is forgiven.

Human law is only as equitable and honorable as the legal system and the people who legislate it, explain it, justify it, and apply it, which means every step of the way is fraught with potential error. Human justice is dependent on the validity and veracity of the laws and the ability of the enforcing authority to always punish the wrongdoer and reward the honorable. Since that is humanly impossible, justice ebbs and flows, even under the best circumstances, so that what passes as justice is a matter of compromise, trial and error, political will, legal manipulation, and current social standards; unfortunately, it also dependent on who you are and where you live.

Human rights are only as validly applicable as the integrity, honor, selflessness, and self-control of those seeking them. They should be socially acceptable when the ethical motivation and intentions of those who put them into motion are corroborated by scripture. As that is seldom taken into consideration, from either a legal or ethical perspective, there is a high probability that the "right" under consideration will conflict with scripture yet be judged as equitable due to the lack of integrity and honor of those seeking and using them in a selfish, you-owe-me, or I-deserve-it psychology.

Human faith is only as good as the source of truth and proof used to substantiate, convey, support, or verity it. All human-claimed truth is conditional on the communicated testimony of humans to other humans. Often, it is initiated by a dramatic event, an unverifiable association with deity, a combination of inspiration/dreams or a transmitted doctrine, or belief limited by the nature and source of the authority transmitting it. In the end, faith is only as good as the source authority that inspires it. Christianity alone is fully divinely inspired, empowered, and transformed by the life, death, and Resurrection of Jesus Christ. It alone enjoys God's goodwill and blessing, now and throughout eternity.

Equity ethics is superior, in all cases and in all times, when determining the validity or any moral ideology. Ethics are God's intended way of measuring right and wrong, good, and evil. Equality is the politically correct moral autonomy's measuring stick because equity would reveal its hypocrisy. Merit-based equity is justice applied. Morality is top-heavy, with subjective accommodation of the many squeaky wheels who demand equality or equal respect, even when there is little merit or integrity to back up their claims.

In short, moral standards are human mechanisms and disguise incorporating both fact and fiction in their moral makeup. No moral standard or human-designed belief system can hold water in God's court of appeals. Every human-designed and -orchestrated moral system that claims to be just, or fair is flawed, to the degree that it considers itself superior to scriptural admonitions.

Your choice of standards carries with it a mixture of known or expected results. While the politically correct want you to believe choice, with different moral outcomes, can be equally valid and equally acceptable, common sense tells us that moral opposites cannot be either. A negative trait cannot exhibit positive traits, nor can it claim that a different outcome is equal to any other outcome. That which represents itself as equal in degree and value must adhere to logic and reasoning to be valid; any difference in any outcome precludes any possibility of being equal with what it is being compared to. If it is not a duck, nothing else is equal to a duck. It may look like a duck, and it might walk like a duck, but if it cannot quack like a duck, it is not a duck. The obvious point is that nothing can be made into or become what it is not, not by law, tradition, or majority vote. The corollary with that is that it can only be what it is; it cannot become what it is not. To beat a dead horse, any change or alteration in any degree makes it different; therefore, it cannot be equal.

It is illogical and absurd to think that opposite ethical positions, in which one violates scripture, can both be validated by scripture. Here is a key component of all Christian truth, which is supported and sanctioned only by scripture: *whatever violates scripture, violates truth, and whatever validates scripture is truth.* For those who blur the differences between right and wrong, doesn't that bother you? A prochoice stance identifies you as one who does not care enough to know the difference and one who cares too much about what others think of them. When you serve two authorities with opposing standards, you are unfaithful to both. Instead of standing faithfully with one, you hide unfaithfully behind two. Your only saving cover is that you have a large crowd, in which you can all hide behind each other.

Christian apologetics acknowledge our guilt and dependency on God, while the "correct" folks promote gay pride and abortion on demand. The politicians look to civil laws, Supreme Court decisions, the Constitution, rights groups, and majority vote to justify their positions. Spirit-directed Christians reject the superior authority of civil laws, Supreme Court decisions, the Constitution, rights groups, and majority rule, as well as politically manipulated themes and tenets, whenever they deny, subvert, subordinate, or rescind Spirit-instituted truth that is corroborated by Spirit-inspired, inerrant scripture.

Christian truth has stood alone on its own merits and the test of time for over two thousand years; politically correct truth is always local and temporary. It is not equally true or equally valid. Politically correct truth has been aligned with liberal theology for a few decades and gets much of its influence and authority from that association. But the name "liberal theology" defines a modified, misleading apologetic, steeped in compromise and exception. Genuine Christian theology is neither liberal nor conservative, as we are prone to label ourselves. No, it is God's theology, centered entirely on his Word and his will, as is revealed in scripture, and validly discerned by Spirit inspiration.

Listen to what the Spirit communicated to Timothy:

> All scripture is given by inspiration of God and is profitable for doctrine, for reproof, for correction and for instruction in righteousness. Preach the Word. Be ready in season and out of season. Convince, rebuke, exhort with all long suffering and teaching. (2 Timothy 3:16; 4:2)

In 2 Peter 1:20–21, the Spirit spoke these words:

> Knowing this first, that no prophesy of scripture is of any private interpretation (origin) for prophecy never came by the will of man, but holy men of God spoke as they were moved by the Holy Spirit.

The entire Bible is the work of the Spirit and is, in fact, the Spirit's book. That means that the Spirit not only inspired the written words but was himself as a present witness to its truthfulness. In so many words, the authority flowing from God's Word in scripture is confirmed by God himself!

What that proclaims is that God's Word never teaches error. It is the very Word of God proclaimed and revealed by the Spirit, making it the supreme authority over all people. God is the author, scripture his ultimate writing, and the Spirit, proclaiming Jesus, is the ultimate messenger. The ultimate message and truth that holds everyone and every institution accountable is "trust and obey."

Where the rubber hits the road today—and over the past century—is Protestant liberalism conflicting with the letter and spirit of Reformed Christianity. According to liberal theology, humans are basically good. It advocates the belief that the universal Fatherhood of God and universal brotherhood of humanity is acceptable and is to be incorporated as truth to all, whereas scripture declares humans as universally evil. Only God's chosen are considered His children.

This false doctrine and practice of liberal theology gives humans moral autonomy and greater choice. It also implies that it gives the benefit of the doubt to "good" people, when push comes to shove, regarding ethical or spiritual intentions. Further, it plants the seed that your charitable deeds or compassion cancel out your errors and misinterpretation of scripture. Compounding their slanted version, God overlooks or quickly forgives what we consider to be "small sins."

Truth is not a matter determined by human belief; it is not a matter of being politically correct or being inclusive. It is not a matter of majority rule or minority view. It is a matter of Christian facts, individually and corporately discerned under the influence and guidance of the Holy Spirit. Truth is the essence of God, which only those under the tutelage of the Spirit will recognize and validly proclaim. When any nation's or person's proclivity to frame truth around their understanding—their experience— acts upon it in such a way as to promote equal protection for unequal, unsubstantiated biblical truth, it portends grave consequences for all its citizens.

That above summation succinctly hits the nail on the head, as it reveals that a person's or group's actions—executed on their command and orchestrated so they result in problems and unintended negative consequences—cannot be trusted to resolve the problem or issue using the same people, processes, or judgments that created the problem. The "correct" group have had twenty-five years of using their legal and moral manipulations to get the country back on track but have progressively made the divide wider than when they started. You should not trust any political party whose arrogance exceeds its ethical acuity.

New scripturally discerning citizens who use higher ethical standards and more objective and equally equitable Christian policies and procedures for arriving at God's intended purposes are required—not the same personal-agenda culprits getting together again to figure out how and why they screwed up in the first place. Would you hire the same contractor to fix the mess he created?

The problem of trying to figure out what works, socially or morally, when undertaken by a political party is a huge gamble. If mistakes are made, people die, or problems get bigger, not smaller. It is a fool's errand to ask identity groups or special-interest organizations what is fair and equitable, as they will take advantage of any political largesse to help them get what they want, not what is fair and equitable to all parties involved in the issue or debate.

Reinhold Niebuhr, a theologian, and writer of the twentieth century, blasts theological liberalism as proclaiming and worshipping "a God without wrath who brought men without sin into a kingdom without judgment through the ministrations of a Christ without a cross."[4]

Christians who favor the progressive moral changes and push to legislate and legalize the revamped secular ethics that now endorse the equality of those recent changes are to be scrutinized as to where their true loyalty and obedience lie. Dr. John MacArthur, a contemporary theologian and author, put that warning up front and center when he said,

> We have been called into battle against every unbiblical, anti-god, and anti-Christ ideology. The world is filled with false ideological fortresses void of truth that cannot

produce true righteousness or peace with God, and sinners are imprisoned within them.[5]

We must hold Christians and non-Christians accountable for both their actions and their sources of reference that authorize changes in scriptural interpretations and applications heretofore prohibited. Explicit scripture should never be undermined by non-scriptural implicit interpretations. Scripture in question must be held up against other scripture that corroborates its unity. It is evil to take an implicit scriptural verse or read between the lines of an explicit verse and incorporate it into an explicit core that points in one direction and then changes that direction.

Morality is a tough nut to crack. It can be good or evil, righteous, or self-righteous, depending on who or what is defining it. Human definitions will include a combination of both and declare it to be moral normal. If you break down the attributes of any human morality, the flaws within it will be adopted according to the degree of self-righteous indignation or arrogance. A compelling case can be made that the non-Christian attributes of politically correct moral autonomy put it in the evil or self-righteous category because it is not Spirit-inspired or scripturally accurate. A godly assessment of any claimed moral autonomy is a destructive permissiveness that masquerades as moral enlightenment and is promoted by deceived beings who function as if they are outside the jurisdiction of scriptural authority and divine providence.

Systemic Christian revisionism by the politically correct perpetuates scriptural violations, while at the same time providing a false sense of security that allows people to get away with any potential negative consequences that might ensue. Moral autonomy, political or otherwise, is a satanic ideology that slanders Christians, denies culpability, and exonerates sinful acts.

Every ungodly moral authority thinks of itself as a self-sufficient, self-exonerating independent agent, devoid of any need to exercise godlike wisdom and measured grace over lost souls and desperate people. It is a progressive evil that infects all who neglect God. Sin's door is always open to all who knock. It results in making scriptural evil morally and legally nonbinding to all who swallow its poison. It redefines and acquits sin, making it "in"!

Let us take a quick look at the forces driving politically correct moral autonomy. The state has crafted and regulated, by political fiat, a system of checks and balances that authorizes a license to kill the unborn; it allows judges and juries to acquit politically correct authorities, as well as targeting systemic attacks against Christian theology and practice. Intimidation and crafted legislation are designed to break the will and spirit of individuals and Christian groups by forcing them to do or accept what scripture prohibits in the name of social progress.

Jesus's admonition in Mark 12:17 "Render to Caesar the things that are Caesar's and to God the things that are God's"—has been manipulated by the state to read, "Render to the state that which it claims is the state's and the things of God we determine are now ours." Indiscriminate tolerance and expanding rights are used by political agendas to tempt citizens to abandon heretofore accepted and enforced standards and principles of Christian teaching and practice. Normalizing prohibited behavior has become a full-time enterprise for progressive thinkers.

On the opposing side, Christians anointed by the Spirit are designated as God's messengers and witnesses. They are keepers of the faith and blessed with God's peace that passes all understanding. They are authorized to go boldly into a world that sees itself as independent, self-contained, and outside the standards and boundaries of Christian apologetics.

The challenge for all Christians is to rely on the Spirit and the words of scripture to faithfully live and die, according to the purposes and will of God. The moral and spiritual conditions of the world are in God's hands. All events and conditions at any given time in history are ordained or allowed, according to God's known and unknown purposes. As the words in the hymn say,

> This is my Father's world,
> Why should my heart be sad?
> The Lord is king, let the heavens ring,
> God reigns, let the earth be glad!
>
> This is my Father's world,
> Oh, let me never forget

That though the wrong seems oft so strong,
God is the ruler yet.

Genuine Christians know that luck, chance, coincidence, and fate are all made-up excuses, plausible explanations, or an inability to explain the timing of something unexpected. Everything happens, predictable or unpredictable, for a reason; it is the working of God's providence. He created all things, seen and unseen, for his divine reasons and purposes. His plan for humans and all that transpires has a purpose that he alone knows. Daniel 2:21 reminds us of God's power and purposes and how they come together: God "removes kings and sets them up."

God raises up the good and bad leaders of our nation and all nations. He determines who rules and for how long, as Isaiah 40:22–24 reminds us:

> It is he who sits above the circle of the earth and its inhabitants are like grasshoppers; who stretches out the heavens like a curtain and spreads them like a tent to dwell in; who brings princes to nothing and makes the rulers of the earth as emptiness. Scarcely are they planted, scarcely sown, scarcely has their stem taken root in the earth, when he blows on them, and they wither, and the tempest carries them off, like stubble.

God's providence and sovereignty bring about or ordain, in some sense, both the big events and insignificant things that may be good or evil, as both are incorporated to complete his sovereign purposes, which are, in many instances, not cipherable to humans. Putting words in God's mouth to justify a political or moral position is dangerously destructive. God holds accountable all who take his name in vain and who deceptively lead astray the millions who have lost their way.

He is in complete control of all things; nothing is out of his control. Whatever happens, even though we do not know why, it is all for arriving at his ultimate, eternal good and glory. Many of our whys will never be answered or understood, but as the hymn above states, God is the ruler yet. We are not in control of anything—how long we will live, when we will die, the future, and what we refer to as accidents or heartbreaks are all in

God's hands. Christians take comfort from this promise: "And we know that for those who love God, all things work together for good for those who love the Lord, for those who are called, according to His purpose" (Romans 8:28).

Deeply divergent views or faiths primarily come from one's source of inspiration and motivation. For faithful Christians, each of those are derived from the authority of scripture, coupled with our maturity regarding Spirit discernment. "Because He Lives" is a favorite hymn for many Christians. The refrain is a cause for tears for those who recognize how blessed they are:

> Because he lives, I can face tomorrow
> Because he lives, all fear is gone
> Because I know he holds the future
> And life is worth the living just because he lives

What separates genuine Christians from casual ones is their attitude of gratitude for what God has done and will do for those he has called through his grace. We know that God does not owe us anything. He does not need us to accomplish what he wants done. We are relieved to know we cannot earn our way to salvation by how we live; it is only through his grace that it is made known to us. We are not better, yet by his grace, he calls us through the Spirit and his grace to follow his lead as we are given discernment through prayer, scripture, and our call to action on his behalf.

A governing morality, where truth is abused and people are used, becomes confused. Yet we have a system where checks and balances have been restricted to allow greater leeway for chicanery. It has been gutted to reduce inconvenient truths. It is a system where the leading cause of death and destruction is not from criminals or diseases but from laws designed to encourage and protect abortion. Life, liberty, and the pursuit of happiness, as intended by our founding fathers, has been hijacked by political fiat, not protected by it.

Domestic tranquility will never happen if domestic fidelity is not required. We are in serious trouble because about everything thing we do to be fair or to seem just is designed to provide equality, rather than the more pressing issue of insisting on equal equity. While God's equity is "truth or consequences," politically correct moral autonomy is focused on granting equal respect and honor to unequal effort and integrity of thought, word, and deed. We might even say that many of us, consciously or unconsciously, present to others a God who mirrors our priorities. We hear what we want to hear; we read between the lines of scriptures and add or subtract according to our priorities. We see what we want to see or believe what our "identity" position determines is in its best interest, and we disregard what makes us uncomfortable or hits too close to home.

We may be agents who assist in compassionately caring for others' well-being and security, but God alone ordains the outcome in any event or circumstance, according to his plan and will. He determines what transpires in any given life. As God speaks to Moses in Exodus 33:19, he powerfully brings to bear his authority on every human: "I will be gracious to whom I will be gracious and will show mercy on whom I will show mercy."

Isaiah 14:24 continues the same path: "The Lord of hosts has sworn, as I have thought, so it shall be, and as I have purposed, so shall it stand."

In Isaiah 55:11, God states,

> So shall My word be that goes out from My mouth, it shall not return to me empty, but it shall accomplish what I purpose, and it shall succeed in the thing for which I sent it.

The truth you accept, rightly or wrongly, will reflect in the faith or truth you project. A false accepted faith or truth cannot be overcome by any degree of passion for it. Know the truth, lest your faith undermines it. Faith is truth dependent. Truth is not faith-dependent; it stands alone on its merit and validity.

The Word (Jesus) was and is the empowering instrument of God's creation.

> In the beginning was the Word, and the Word was with God and the Word was God. He was in the beginning with God. All things were made through him and without him was not anything made that was made. In him was

life, and the life was the light of men. The light shines
in the darkness and the darkness have not overcome it.
(John 1:1–5)

That truth and all other truth is indivisible and unassailable. Spoken or written, truth is timeless, the same—yesterday, today, and tomorrow. No power on earth or authority under heaven can breach its walls or prevent its ultimate triumph. The Word of God reveals it, the will of God sustains it, and the Spirit of God seals it in our hearts. The power inherent in God's truth is that exceptions or conditions have absolutely no grounds to stand on. However one argues in defense of a false truth, no matter one's faith, it will not stand the test of time.

Self-will often directs the mind to find a source or reference authority with just enough credibility to allow us to rationalize and give approval to overrule the source of all truth—God. In a corollary comparison, the source of our wisdom determines its impacts on our relationships:

The wisdom from above is first pure, then peaceable,
gentle, open to reason, full of mercy and good fruits,
impartial and sincere. And a harvest of righteousness is
sown in peace by those who make peace. (James 3:17–18)

For faithful Christians, all conversations, relationships, and debates must obediently convey both a message of hope and a requirement for self-discipline. Equal emphasis will ensure that what you preach and what you practice will reflect Christ's love, not your self-directed expectation. What separates the godly from the ungodly are the barriers we erect that separate us—we become so blind that we cannot recognize the truth when it is before us! Our field of view has too many options that cloud our judgment and the needed conviction to act precisely.

God's truth, not man's truth, is the sum of all things that gloriously represents and points to the grace of God, as proclaimed in Holy Scripture. Individually or collectively, it alone conveys legitimacy and validates only that which God declares meets *his* definition. All truth begins and ends according to his word and proclamation. It is universal in nature, uniform in its applications, and united in its purpose. It applies equally to all people;

it was made known through covenant and perfectly illustrated through the life of his Son, Jesus. Only God has the authority to judge what is true and who faithfully represents his truth.

Truth is unbiased, but man's representation and application often are not. The source of your truth will drive your truth. Every source outside of scripture is biased, influenced by its author, not the divine author. Every human has a built-in bias that is influenced by gender, nationality, race, sexual disposition, political persuasion, religious affiliation, and social standing.

Paul reminds us of what happens when a nation or church allows individuals a license to interpret scripture according to their understanding:

> For this reason God gave them up to dishonorable passions. For their women exchanged natural relations for those that are contrary to nature and the men likewise gave up natural relations with women and were consumed with passion for one another; men committing shameless acts with men and receiving in themselves the due penalty for their error. Though they know God's righteous decree that those who practice such things deserve to die, they not only do them but give approval to those who practice them. (Romans 1:26, 32)

On a more positive note, getting back to basic Christian doctrine and practice, John Wycliffe wrote, "Holy Scripture is the highest authority for every believer, the standard of faith and the foundation for reform in religious, political and social life."[6]

In contrast, the Reformed or authentic Christian compares social progress through classic orthodox standards of ethical conduct and Spirit guidance, based strictly on scriptural laws; godly principles, as demonstrated by Christ; and lifestyles whose relationships are divinely sanctified. An objective Christian understanding of where American society is in relationship to scriptural requirements would show, across the board, that moral standards today are socially deficient and misleading regarding their definition of good and evil and what is and is not acceptable to God.

Again, we can point to C. S. Lewis to weigh in on faulty moral reasoning, taken from his book *God in the Dock*: "Every preference for a small good to a great, or a partial good to a total good, involves the loss of the small or partial good for which the sacrifice was made."[7] No matter what your good intentions might be for social equality via political or legal contrivances, if, in the process of achieving the good intention, you forfeit a greater good—required individual obedience to scripture. Whenever the secondary emphasis (social acceptance, tolerance, or political correctness) becomes more important than the higher, primary importance (righteousness or ultimate truth), neither can be fully achieved. It is only in putting first things first that secondary goals may be reached.

Let us insert God into the equation at this point. God is far less interested in equality, tolerance, or inclusion than he is in obedience and truth. Sadly, in far too many instances, Christians will marry questionable civil rights with politically correct personal belief systems and incorporate the two into a new updated version of an old, settled truth. For instance— and I do not say this lightly or condescendingly—I am hard-pressed to understand how moral opposites or scriptural prohibitions can be equally right or equally true. The commandment, "Thou shall not kill," is by far superior to any woman's right or man's right to choose death for the unwanted unborn child. Surely, life or death choices should not be equally right or equally true or that one is no better or worse than the other, yet abortion today is the number-one killer in the United States and world.

Isaiah spoke to the same problem three thousand years ago to those who manipulated language and morality to make it something it was not when he spoke these words:

> Woe to those who call evil good, and good evil, who put
> darkness for light and light for darkness, who put bitter
> for sweet and sweet for bitter. (Isaiah 5: 20)

God has many attributes, all perfectly balanced, all perfectly righteous, and all perfectly exercised. Humans too have many attributes, all imperfect in their makeup, their motivations, and their manifestations. The best that people have to offer carries with it those imperfections, tainted with strands of evil. Our highest goodness, put into effect by our sincerest motivation, is tainted by our sinful nature. Yet we choose to equate our understanding and actions as acceptable to God as his are. Any deference to another faith in matters of faith mocks our reverence for Christ. Superior Christian truth always trumps any degree of competing religious or secular truth.

It is overwhelming to think that millions who call themselves Christians are in conflict regarding abortion are praying at cross-purposes for God to affirm their sin as good or right. Two thousand years after Christ, society decided it was acceptable in their sight and that it was a human right because everyone seems to think God accepts false faith or truth if it is passionately believed.

Jesus warns against looking the other way or accepting the unacceptable when confronted with evil:

> Temptations to sin are sure to come but woe to the one through whom they come. It would be better for him if a millstone were hung around his neck, and he was cast into the sea than that he should cause one of these little ones to sin. Pay attention to yourselves! If your brother sins, rebuke him, and if he repents, forgive him. (Luke 17:1–3)

David asks, "If the foundations are destroyed, what can the righteous do?" (Psalm 11:3). A few verses later, we read:

> Save, O Lord, for the godly one is gone; for the faithful have vanished from among the children of man. Everyone utters lies to his neighbor; with flattering lips and a double heart they speak. (Psalm 12:1–2)

> The fool says in his heart, "There is no God." They are corrupt, they do abominable deeds, there is none who does good. The Lord looks down from heaven on the children of man to see if there are any who understand, who seek after God. They have all turned aside; together they have become corrupt; there is none who does good, not even one. (Psalm 14:1–3)

After a long discourse, David hits the nail on the head in as he says, "Unless the Lord builds the house, those who build it labor in vain" (Psalm 127:1).

Spirit-initiated faith trumps human effort every time. Combine it with Spirit-initiated power, and you become a divine messenger, with God himself by your side. Ask yourself when the last time was that you heard political leaders or social activists say that they labor for the glory of God, or they seek discernment from the Spirit as they read scripture for guidance to corroborate its fidelity. How often do you use scripture as your first source of authority? If you do not, why not? Is there ever a time of personal doubt or uncertainty where it could not apply?

Alan Redpath, a renowned pastor in England and the United States during the mid-twentieth century, wrote these insightful, charged words in his commentary on the book of Nehemiah: "There is no winning without warfare; there is no opportunity without opposition and there is no victory without vigilance." Whenever and wherever a man or woman of God says, "Let us arise and build," Satan says, "Let us arise and oppose."[8]

The lesson here is that God cannot effectively bring about a blessing or use you until your eyes have been opened and your heart prepared by the Spirit and made to see things as they really are—not through man's eye but through God's Spirit.

Christians must choose between accepting and promoting American political and cultural standards that encourage compromise to achieve peace and equality or Christ's standards and commandments, which demand self-sacrifice, self-discipline, humility, and obedience to his absolute standards.

> Do not think I have come to abolish the Law or the Prophets: I have not come to abolish them but to fulfill them. For truly I say to you, until heaven and earth pass away, not an iota, not a dot, will pass from the Law until all is accomplished. Therefore, whoever relaxes one of the least of these commandments and teaches others to do the same will be called least in the kingdom of heaven but whoever does them and teaches them will be called great in the kingdom of heaven. (Matthew 5:17–19)

Gospel compatibility with natural truth, corroborated by scriptural truth, has been upheld under the power and authority of the Holy Spirit for two thousand years. The church heretofore followed that inspired truth through divine inspiration, which separated the wheat from the chaff. Great care and discernment through prayer and sacrificial obedience applied and underwrote the church's instructive authority. Apostasy continually raised its ugly head but was overcome, repeatedly, as the Spirit intervened to refute it.

CHAPTER 8

Divine Inspiration or Cultural Intimidation?

The nations in the Old Testament, including Israel, were held accountable for their willfulness and sinfulness. Warnings dismissed by individuals and nations resulted in a loss of God's patience, and judgment ensued.

Christians, God's agents, and servants on earth, are called to witness to Christ's authority by faithfully discerning and demonstrating Christian theology and practice to all nonbelievers. That is what each of us is called to do in both a loving and assertive manner, as divinely instructed in corroboration with Holy Scripture. The response of others to gospel truth is out of our hands. We are called to act and witness on Christ's behalf; the rest is up to the divine intervention of the Spirit to convict and convert.

Reformed Christianity emphasizes the importance of the inspiration and inerrancy of Scripture. The Chicago Statement on Biblical Inerrancy provides insight and clarity as to how that doctrine instructs us:

> We believe that God, who is Himself truth and speaks truth only, has inspired Holy Scripture in order thereby to reveal Himself to lost mankind through Christ as Creator and Lord, Redeemer, and Judge. Holy Scripture is God's witness to Himself.

> We believe the Holy Scripture, being God's own Word, written by men and superintended by His Spirit, is of infallible divine authority in all matters upon which it touches; it is to be believed as God's instruction, in all that it affirms: obeyed as God's command, in all that it requires: embraced as God's in all that it promises.

> We believe that the Holy Spirit, Scripture's divine author, both authenticates it to us by His inward witness and opens our minds to understanding its meaning.

> We believe that Scripture, being wholly and verbally God-given, is without error or fault in all its teaching, no less in what it states about God's acts in creation, about the events of world history and about its own literary origins under God, then in its witness to God's saving grace in individual lives.

> We believe the authority of Scripture is inescapably impaired if this total Divine inerrancy is in any way limited, disregarded, or made relative to a view of truth contrary to the Bible's own; and as such lapses bring serious loss to both the individual and the church.

The next item connected with the above affirmation is the proper interpretation of scripture. How do we understand what is required to rightly interpret and apply scripture? Again, we look to the Chicago Statement on Biblical Inerrancy:

> We believe that the meaning expressed in each biblical text is single, definite, and fixed, though capable of multiple applications.

> We affirm the necessity of interpreting the Bible according to it literal, or normal sense. The literal sense is the grammatical-historical sense, that is, the meaning that the writer expressed. Interpretation according to the literal

sense will account of all figures of speech and literary forms found in the test.

We believe that the Bible's own interpretation of itself is always correct, never deviating from, but elucidating the single meaning of the inspired text. The single meaning of a prophet's words includes but is not restricted to the understanding of those words by the prophet and necessarily involves the intention of God evidenced in the fulfillment of those words.

We believe that since God is the author of all truth, all truths, biblical and extrabiblical are consistent and coherent, and that the Bible speaks truth when it touches on matters pertaining to nature, history, or anything else. We further affirm that in some cases, extrabiblical data have value for clarifying what Scripture teaches and for prompting correction of faulty interpretations. [1]

Friedrich Nietzsche insisted that the "will to power" is the basic drive in our human nature. We Christians know that our baser nature always tempts us to grab as much of it as is humanly possible, to control as much as possible. C. S. Lewis reminds us "a proud man is always looking down on things and people; and of course, as long as you are looking down, you cannot see what is above you."[2] That should bring us back to reality and remind us of the vital requirement for appropriate humility in all our acts and relationships. Reverend Rick Warren helps bring us back to how we should act and see ourselves: "Humility is not thinking less of yourself but thinking of yourself less."[3]

The defiant will of man and the lawlessness of his actions are the cause and effect of our eternal struggle for control of our passions and deceptions. We are who we are, and we do what we do because we prefer our way to God's way. The Westminster Confession of Faith, taken from the 1646 Reformed Confession, subordinate to the initial revelation of the Holy Spirit's divine instruction concerning Holy Scripture, provides additional clarification and guidance to all who seek greater insight and spiritual discernment concerning the meaning and intention of that divine instruction. The Church of England, Scotland, Presbyterian churches, and other Reformed Christian communities embrace the words and wisdom of those inspired reformers who skillfully articulated in this Confession of Faith, God's Word and will, based on the power and wisdom of the Holy Scripture via the Spirit's guidance. Read the following excerpts from chapters 1, 2, 3, 11, 16, and 23 to better understand what faithful Reformed Christians believe and represent:

> 1. The authority of the Holy Scripture, for which it ought to be believed and obeyed, dependent not upon the testimony of any man or church, but wholly upon God (who is truth himself), the Author thereof; and therefore, it is to be received, because it is the Word of God.

> All things in Scripture are not alike plain in themselves, nor alike clear unto all; yet those things which are necessary to be known, believed and observed, for Salvation, are so clearly propounded and opened in some place of Scripture or other, that not only the learned, but the unlearned, in a due use of the ordinary means, may attain unto a sufficient understanding of them.

> The infallible rule of interpretation of Scripture, is the Scripture itself; and therefore, when there is a question about the true and full sense of any Scripture (which is not manifold, but one), it may be searched and known by other places that speak more closely.

> 2. God hath all life, glory, goodness, blessedness in and of Himself; and is alone in and unto Himself all sufficient, not standing in need of any creatures which He hath made, nor deriving any glory from them, but only manifesting His own glory in, by, unto and upon them; He is the alone foundation of all being, of whom, through whom and to whom are all things; and hath most

sovereign dominion over them, to do by them, for them, or upon them whatsoever Himself pleased.

3. God from all eternity did by the most wise and holy counsel of His own will, freely and unchangeably ordain whatsoever comes to pass; yet so as thereby neither is God the author of sin; nor is violence offered to the will of the creatures nor is the liberty or contingency of second causes taken away, but rather established.

11. God doth continue to forgive the sins of those that are justified; and although they can never fall from the state of justification, yet they may by their sins fall under God's Fatherly displeasure, and not have the light of His countenance restored unto them, until they humble themselves, confess their sins, beg pardon, and renew their faith and repentance.

16. Good works are only such as God hath commanded in His holy Word, and not such as, without the warrant thereof, are devised by men out of blind zeal or upon any pretense of good intention.

Their ability to do good works is not at all of themselves, but wholly from the Spirit of Christ.

23. And as Jesus Christ hath appointed a regular government and discipline in his Church, no law of any commonwealth should interfere with, let, or hinder the due exercise thereof, among the voluntary members of any denomination of Christians, according to their own profession and belief. It is the duty of civil magistrates to protect the person and good name of all their people.[4]

A necessary reminder might be prudent at this early stage of developing points of reference and order of authority: scripture alone is the first and highest order of divine revelation. It alone has the power and presence of the Holy Spirit's words to bring people to receive Christ and to bring them to subsequent salvation. All writings by men of any stature are inferior and are not to be received as equal revelation or instruction, no matter the apparent wisdom or scriptural insights. It is the Word of God alone, conveyed by the Spirit alone, that both convicts and saves every sinner who confesses Jesus as Lord!

Using the two above sources of authority concerning scriptural accuracy and instruction and adding the Ligonier Ministries Statement of Faith, let us review a Reformed stand on two key issues—abortion and homosexuality—currently escalating the divide between and among Christians and non-Christians.

The Sanctity of Life

Since 1973, there have been approximately sixty million abortions in the United States alone. This is an evil on an almost unfathomable scale. Because this is one of the great crimes of the century, Ligonier Ministries has emphasized the need to declare what God's Word has to say about this crime to those who willfully support it.

> We believe that human beings are creatures made in the image of God. They are, therefore, worthy of protection under the law from the first moment of their existence. There is no dispute that the fetus is a genetically distinct individual human being from the moment of conception and from the earliest stages of embryonic development. Since the fetus is a human being, and since the unjust killing of an innocent human being is murder, then abortion is murder.[5]

All abortions are complex, replete with good reasons, real concerns, and hardships. It is a life-changing decision with valid, humanly legitimate arguments for and against. What is lost on today's men and women is the value that *God* puts on life in the womb. However you choose to value or devalue that life or even what you call that life, it comes from God's plan for procreation and is seen by God as a life to be preserved and revered.

Listen to what God, not Moses, said, and determine for yourself how egregious it is to directly or indirectly take the life of the unborn:

> When men strive together and hit a pregnant woman so that her children come out, but there is no harm, the one who hit her shall surely be fined, as the woman's husband shall impose on him, and he shall pay as the judge determines. But if there is harm, then you shall pay life for life, eye for eye, tooth for tooth, hand for hand, foot for foot, burn for burn, wound for wound, stripe for stripe. (Exodus 21:22–25)

You can argue or debate every exception or good reason that legitimizes the killing of an innocent unborn life and tell yourself it is for the best; that it is the lesser of two problems, both of which have consequences that harm you, your future, or your current situation. God himself, in the above passage, declared that men who accidently or intentionally killed an unborn child were put to death as a warning to all that all life, even unborn, is sacred.

The Sanctity of the Family

> Our culture is witnessing an attack on the family like it has never seen, and because of this, it is necessary that the church reemphasize the biblical teaching on marriage and the family. Ligonier has long attempted to come alongside the church to assist in this task.

> We believe that God gave man the institution of marriage in the garden and that this institution has been under attack by the evil one ever since. we reject the idea that the redefinition of marriage by judges, legislatures, executives, philosophers, or anyone else changes the reality of what God created. Since God defined marriage to be between one man and one woman, there is no such thing, therefore, as a homosexual marriage.[6]

Christians sometimes fall into the trap of accepting deceit that can only be "sanctified" by corrupting or substituting a specific scriptural instruction by overlaying on it a general theme that encompasses undefined boundaries. Always, they do so because of two compelling human forces, outside of Spirit acceptance and Spirit instructions. One force is a desire to include and compensate those who currently fall outside of the good graces of orthodox, historic interpretation. The other force is the secular pressure of falling in line with like-minded politically correct thinkers who prefer to keep the peace by compromising truth, rather than holding fast to the scriptural truth that will separate the wheat from the chaff.

Submission to the Spirit is a prerequisite for harmony and inner peace.

> What causes quarrels and what causes fights among you? Is it not this, that your passions are at war within you? Submit yourselves therefore to God. Resist the devil and he will flee from you. Humble yourselves before the Lord and He will exalt you. (James 4:1, 7, 10)

Christians with a backbone do not tolerate or reconcile with abortion, homosexuality, or any misleading doctrines, either inside Christianity or outside in the secular world. The civil laws in every country are built on a combination of force, compromise, and local moral standards. Not one of those countries' moral or legal standards, when held up to scripture in its entirety and under total introspection, would pass muster in God's court. Following human standards precludes you from obeying God's standards. Mixing the two is attempting the impossible of being faithful to each. By simply putting the word "human" in front of standards or using "politically correct" instead of Christian correct, you instantaneously disqualify yourself from being faithful to God.

What is stunning, though, is the extent to which everyday people have been converted to accepting and then promoting the deceit themselves as new truth. But stunning is in the eye of the beholder. We all hate to admit that it is far more prevalent than in previous times. Comparisons are difficult to accurately portray because of time and culture variables. Let us not compare our times with previous times but strictly rely on the historic, unchanging words and wisdom of scripture. Isaiah warned, "Woe to those who call evil good and good evil, who put darkness for light and light for darkness" (Isaiah 5:20).

The differences between politically correct, self-righteous, moral indignation and scriptural righteousness are the differences between what is human and what is divine. The word *self* modifies *righteous*, making human what was divine. The liberal, politically correct emphasis on the self is contradictory to what God demands from each of us—fidelity first to him, second to others, and then to ourselves. Their attempts to correlate liberal, humanistic characteristics with divine virtues cannot mask their deceitful intentions of making what is subjective morality a mainstream truth.

For anything to qualify as being righteous, correct, or of a divine nature requires that the conditions of mercy, purity, objective justice, and divine purpose be included and corroborated by scripture. Further, the motivation must be initiated by the work of the Holy Spirit. Everything else initiated by human means, by human standards, and cannot rise above its human nature; it is eternally engaged in a battle it cannot win. It is the Spirit alone that changes the human heart into a soul with an attitude of gratitude. Humanity is trapped, boxed in, with no ability to change itself, outside divine intervention.

There is no hope for any person or government to correct that which cannot be corrected "man's heart." Scripture says "suppression of the truth" is universal; man distorts and rejects God's truth and worships the creature's truth. If you want to "correct" society, the means to that end require God's changing our individual and collective hearts, not government policy, social directives, or legal mandates. William Barclay got it right when he said, "The Christian hope is not in the human spirit, in human goodness or human achievement, it is in the power of God."[7] What most politically correct and liberal thinkers fail to understand is that self-reliance and self-determination inevitably mean self-defeat. Barclay nailed the summation of Christian understanding and faith when he stated, "A written code can change the law; only the Spirit can change human nature!"[8]

Our current chaos and divisions, without exception, reveal broken people, broken laws, and the presence of evil. No number of new rights, regulatory laws, money, or education can fix evil. But if you were to ask politically correct, progressive authorities, most would say "more of all the above" is the answer. Oh, and for good measure, they will add that more tolerance and more self-governing authority, outside the interference of conservative Christian influence, will solve our racial, moral, and relationship issues.

Quick questions here: Have you ever seen harmony, goodwill, and peace replace animosity, hatred, and conflict, when one political side, continually and arrogantly, undeservedly gains at the other's expense? You have not and will not because that runs counter to God's natural law of cause and effect. Can partial truth, composed of compromise and subjective self-enhancement, compete on its own merits with godly truth, the whole truth, and nothing but the truth? It cannot because any right, any entity, or any person whose basis of support or authority accepts ethical compromises automatically introduces a fatal flaw—deception that can only be maintained if the truth is not revealed. That means, in some cases, that millions must be coconspirators to prevent the truth of God from being exposed and accepted. Again, without exception, using force of law or the threat of personal harm by the politically correct coconspirators eventually will be overcome by the more honor-bound, uncompromised-truth adherents. God sides only with the whole truth; the ethically compromised settle for whatever satisfies their immediate gratification or expected future entitlements.

Ask yourself if anyone or anything can opt out of the sovereign operating laws and standards, eternally set in motion by God the Father, Son, and Holy Spirit, because they do not like them or do not think they are fair or even exist. Are you willing to bet your future and others' futures by thinking that you are in control and that natural or divine laws have little or no bearing on you or anything else? Do invisible forces interact with the visible, and are they able to counteract your intentions? Who would know?

> I form light and create darkness, I make well-being and create calamity, I am the Lord, who does all these things. (Isaiah 45:7)

Colossians 1:16–17 emphatically reminds us:

> For by him all things were created, in heaven and earth, *visible and invisible,* whether thrones or dominions or rulers or authorities-all things were created through him and for him. (Italics added)

Hebrews 1:3 declares,

> He (Jesus) is the radiance of the glory of God and the exact imprint of his nature, and He upholds the universe by the word of his power."

Acts 17:28 describes where a Christian's power and life come from: "In him we live and move and have our being." The essence of Christianity is God's grace and our responding gratitude. He ordains all that comes to pass, and we are privileged to recognize and understand that truth.

Jesus reminds all of us that those who believe and trust in their own goodness, wisdom, or authority or who proclaim that their ways and means of doing things are equally as good and acceptable as anyone's, are living and teaching a lie.

> *He who speaks on his own authority seeks his own glory*; but he who seeks the glory of him (God) who sent him is true, and in him there. (John 7:18, italics added)

Paul, speaking to the Corinthians, said, "For Godly grief produces a repentance that leads to salvation, without regret, whereas worldly grief produces death" (2 Corinthians 7:8–10).

Every person and every nation, eventually, must deal with a crisis that precipitates a tipping point. It is a time when a culmination of events—wars, social crisis, monetary crisis, health crisis, family crisis, or spiritual crisis—requires decisive choices and actions that expose the nature of our characters and reveal where we stand with God. Frequently, those who claim they are of God—but in truth do not stand with God or fully commit and submit to him—are considered good people by their contemporaries and even are seen as charismatic leaders by many. But

God sees all things in the light and darkness; nothing is hidden or missed. Each of us wears a mask, rebels against God, and deceives to save face or fool others. Christians are guilty too as they lose their salt and light due to compromises, scriptural ignorance, and indifference.

Even if everybody played by the "correct" rules and standards, which would not enable us to rise above our human shortcomings. To paraphrase William Barclay, the brotherhood of man is never going to happen outside the Fatherhood of God.

To turn our individual and national shortcomings around, we each need to do several things:

1. Expect and demand greater individual and corporate honor and integrity, as defined and demonstrated in scripture
2. Hold accountable all who are responsible for their misdirection and deception
3. Depend less on human goodwill and more on God's divine guidance and justice
4. Individually and corporately repent and pray for Christian unity and God's grace to see us through troubled waters

God does not judge us by how much good we do and then subtract the evil to see if we have debits or credits. According to God's scriptural standards, individual and corporate debits are so great that no one has done enough or is good enough for him to give them a pass. You are forever in debt, unless God forgives it out of his grace, sends the Spirit to open your eyes and heart to your sins, and provides the means, Jesus, to overcome your sin debt.

God does not judge us so much on whether we win or lose an argument as on how we have prepared ourselves and comported ourselves as we give evidence to our faith and scriptural discernment regarding our testimony with another.

The problem with the "correct" group is that they consider themselves a cut above those who disagree; thus, they deserve additional rights and dispensations, as they purport to know how things should be. To add insult to injury, not only do they think they have a right to take charge but that they also have the right to redistribute money by robbing from the rich and those who disagree with them and giving to those who agree with them. In effect, they render to Caesar what is Caesar's via our pocketbooks as they forever rob Peter to pay Paul.

The essence of politically correct moral autonomy is an individual's ascendant self-importance and moral self-determination. The essence of politically correct authority is moral self-validation. For the politically correct moral autonomist, the emphasis is defiantly centered on human capabilities and the government's progressive authority and right to determine what is acceptable. Their motto might be, "Rights rule; choice reigns." None is so blind as he who exudes an arrogant attitude of ingratitude. Politically correct moral autonomy, by its very definition, eschews any degree of scriptural due diligence. If those who promote and embrace its clarion call made even a small effort, they would not falsely equate political or civil morality with gospel fidelity. Christian theological differences in motivation and intention that conflict with philosophical differences of liberal government management and goals negate any claims of moral-autonomy equality with past historically interpreted and accepted scriptural mandates and standards.

Our founding fathers established a framework that consists of a three-tiered system of government, designed to provide checks and balances in our legislative, executive, and judicial institutions. The *intention* was obviously to ensure that no one branch would dominate the other two. When that does happen, who or what is to blame—the framework designed to prevent that, or the political party that takes advantage of its power to change rules or enforce its will on the other party?

For most, the answer is straightforward—the ruling political party has the power to set policy and determine what it believes is "correct." The line of thinking is that power ebbs and flows between the two political parties, and it is expected that the winner in an election will dictate—or more delicately put, determine—what is acceptable or "correct," according to its agenda, regardless of scriptural instruction.

To answer the question of whether the framework or party is at fault, the framework is objective (it does not change; the structure/conditions are set), and the ruling political party is subjective (it vacillates or changes), according to its political muscle, vis-à-vis the other party. The previous paragraph has two key words that help us determine a political party's motivation in governing—its ability to *dictate* or *determine* what is correct or right. Proportion or degree can be a matter of semantics and no doubt open to vigorous debates too.

In Philippians 3:17–19, Paul spelled out a distinction that defines the nature of those who serve human nature:

> Brothers, join in imitating me, and keep your eyes on those who walk according to the example you have in us. For many, of whom I have told you and now tell you even with tears, walk as enemies of the cross of Christ. Their end is destruction, their God is their belly, and they glory in their shame; with minds are set on earthly things.

Ethical deviations reveal different moral values or standards and end in different results; they corrupt. If the historically accepted truth is modified to suit the current moral pendulum, as all politically correct modifications must do, the pendulum may temporarily swing to honor the lie. Every lie, however, that is overlooked, understated, or hidden by human will or human justice will become known when God corrects it. Those who rallied around it will, at God's chosen time, answer for their deceit. Those who knew better but did not speak and those who led others to believe the lie will endure greater consequences, for theirs is an even greater sin. Remember Jesus's words in Luke 1-2:

> Temptations to sin are sure to come but woe to the one through whom they come. It would be better for him if a millstone were around his neck, and he was cast into the sea than that he should cause one of these little ones to sin.

There is an eerie parallel today in the United States with the moral situation in Israel, found in the book of Judges, during its transitional stage over three thousand years ago. The loosely held-together tribes were governed by a series of judges rather than a king, and we are legally bound by a Supreme Court of judges. The parallel is not with the form of governing but with the terrible conditions that resulted from not trusting and obeying God and, instead, following their own instincts, inclinations, and assimilations from surrounding influences. The infamous last verse in Judges could be written today: "In those days there was no king in Israel. Everyone did what was right in his own eyes" (Judges 21:25). In our day, it does not matter who is in Congress or who is president. God seems irrelevant or subservient to what they decree.

In our time, to paraphrase that last verse, everyone does what they are told is the right thing to do because the government and civil society say it is politically correct. Tens of millions have chosen the government and rights groups as their effective moral compass. As a result, just like in that dark time for early Israel, we are experiencing moral relativism, confusion, degradation, and assimilation of false gods into our theology and practice. Idol worship today is not so many idols made by human hands, but idols made by human minds—the idols of wealth, authority, sex, fame, unlimited freedoms, and pleasures. The resulting outcome for citizens in Israel was constant turmoil and subjugation as God gave them over to their evil practices. Always, then, and now, God warns us that his judgment and punishment are an ever-present possibility for our disobedience.

What happens when the spiritually ignorant pose as moral authorities? They teach the commandments of men as doctrines. They signal to all who will listen that human authority and institutions are more in tune with today's enlightened thinking than ancient writings and theology given to us by the Spirit of God himself.

What we have today is a socially false starting point that combines the best of human nature (which is still evil) with the liberal ideology and theology that leads us to falsely accept and believe we are better than we really are. Using feelings rather than principles, coupled with the belief that what is new or modern is superior to previous Christian practices and principles, our moral standards fail to take into consideration that God's version of goodness and honorable relationships requires far more self-control, proper balance of our physical and spiritual bodies, and first things first in our priorities, if we are to lead a God-designed, purposeful life, as taught in scripture.

What is the point of debating or arguing a moral issue or social problem? Isn't it to prove a point and arrive at a logical answer or conclusion, based on proven facts, logical reasoning, sound theology, and the known consequences of an action? Shouldn't it be to seek and find the highest integrity and the ultimate truth that overwhelms and supersedes all other arguments or conclusions? Isn't that the point? Ask that to an identity group or progressive moral agenda, and you will be ridiculed or attacked for including sound theology and proven facts.

Today, it is more dangerous to be conceived in America than it was in any pagan or hedonistic society in history. Do you find it hypocritical to focus on the rights of the mother to kill her unborn son or daughter and protect her and to deny the victims, the weakest and voiceless, the same rights and protections? The killing of certain animals or abusing them frequently results in prison sentences and fines, but it is safe to kill an inconvenient, unborn child! Equality, inclusion, and tolerance are all the rage but saving the life of an unborn human is a nonstarter.

The worse thing a Christian can do is to try to reach an agreement or find common ground that does not require the sinner to give up the sin. Reconciliation to keep the peace, at the expense of equitable justice for both parties, is sin. Whatever became of "love the sinner and hate the sin"? Isaiah 5:20 reminds us of God's wrath for those who choose sin:

> Woe to those who call evil good and good, evil; who put darkness for light and light for darkness; who put bitter for sweet and sweet for bitter.

John Bunyan, who wrote *The Pilgrim's Progress*, reminded us of the importance of integrity and honor when he said, "If my life is fruitless, it doesn't matter who praises me, and if my life is fruitful, it doesn't matter who criticizes me."[9] What a difference it would make if more Christians took that to heart and tried less to please others who are scornful or indifferent to the things of God.

In all ethical debates or moral arguments, you cannot allow assumptions, predilections, or public opinion to influence the outcome at which you hope to arrive. What are major conditions that must be met to arrive at an unbiased, unvarnished truth?

First, remove all authorities and institutions (these change over time, depending on the makeup of their political leanings), as well as eliminating all authorities and institutions made up of elected officials who represent special interests or a particular popular sentiment. Neither majority rule nor minority tyranny changes relevant facts or historically validated truths. Again, all truths and facts must stand alone on their own merits. If they cannot, how valid or true can they be? Truth stands because its source and its known author, God, does not need outside assistance or coercion in any manner to buttress its case.

Do you know what many liberals, progressives, and the "politically correct" are working on, night and day, to change? Greater acceptance and dependence on man, his systems, and his standards, to replace Christian principles and standards. Many of those within the ranks of the above are nominal Christians or Christians in name only. While many may take offense at such a harsh declaration, the truth is they are substituting good works, sincere beliefs, and the need for approval in their fashioning of compromised, false new standards for social and moral behaviors. Evil can deceive and disguise as it gives the appearance of approximating true Christian practices and lifestyles.

In 2 Corinthians 11:13–15, Paul warns of false teachers urging deceptive practices:

> For such men are false apostles, deceitful workmen, disguising themselves as apostles of Christ. And no wonder, for even Satan himself disguises himself as an angel of light. So it is no surprise if his servants, also, disguise themselves as servants of righteousness.

The question is, how can you distinguish between false practices and genuine truth? Well, first you need to be scriptural sound and Spirit-inspired. No one who is not of the Spirit is scripturally sound. You may know what the scripture says, but your human nature reads into it what seems right to you. Because each one of us has a distinct perspective on what is acceptable and unacceptable, ten people can read the same scripture and interpret it ten ways. Only the Spirit-guided will discern both the letter and spirit of what they are reading. Everyone else will add or subtract, based on what motivates them and what their intentions are.

All moral rights exercised outside of scriptural integrity are evolving wrongs. It does not matter if they are legally validated, majority supported, or believed by "good people." Political correctness is anti-scriptural.

Supporters do not refer to scripture or Christian tradition or practices as their source of truth or highest authority. Why? Because they are not, in most cases, in agreement with politically correct motivations and intentions.

When playing a piano, when you hit a different key, the sound is different. Holding the same note for different lengths of time changes the sound too, as does the intensity of the playing the note. However you look at it, the sound is not the same; it is not equal unless it is the same note played with the same measure and intensity. The different notes may sound good or even better but that is a subjective judgment, not objective validation. People may say that different moral values or variations that are not found within the original construct are equal, even if they are opposing. The only way that one moral value compared with another that contains different elements can be claimed to be equal is when false subjective logic attempts to remake something it is not into something they want it to be. That is what political correctness attempts to do.

Ethical deviations reveal different moral values or standards and end in different results; they corrupt. If the historically accepted truth is modified to suit the current moral pendulum, as all politically correct modifications must do, the pendulum may temporarily swing to *honor the lie*. Every lie overlooked, understated, or hidden by human will or human justice, however, will become known when God corrects it. Those who rallied around it will, at God's chosen time, answer for their deceit. Those who knew better and did not speak and those who lead others to believe the lie will endure greater consequences, for theirs is an even greater sin.

Contrasting objective truth (God's), subjective logic is viewing objective logic as conditional to an opinion or widely held belief; it is not necessarily valid, even though it *is* valid by almost any other objective measure. The Webster's II New College Dictionary definition of *subjectivism* is "the quality of being subjective; the doctrine that all knowledge is restricted to the conscious self and its sensory states, the theory that individual conscience is the only valid standard of moral judgment."

What person with integrity and honor would stoop to say that nothing is fixed or settled in and of itself; that everything is open to personal interpretation; that every previous understanding is relative to a person's experiences or senses, and one person's consciousness is as good as anyone else's in matters of right or wrong? If that were true, then nothing would be true unless you say it is.

The path of least resistance is, unfortunately, the road most traveled. It is paved with rights, entitlements, tolerance, and self-righteous indignation. But the straw that broke the camel's back is their attitude of ingratitude and the arrogance with which they disdain the divine. Today's culture insists on getting something for nothing. They feel they are owed something just because they exist. They look to themselves and their political party as superior entities that control their destiny by giving each identity group free rein to set their own standards and rules, with little or no boundaries or accountability. Today, it is a right to kill your unborn child but wrong to criticize those who do or who encourage others to enshrine the practice of abortion as a legal and moral prerogative.

It is constructed using identity politics as a moral base and implemented by progressive ideology to attract all those whose temperament is to get what they want, however they can, in the soonest viable way, with the least pushback from outside forces that would deny them their indulgences. One of their most popular programs offers a get-out-of-jail-free pass to all who get caught up in a frenzy of expressing themselves or who are chastised by faithful Christians for suppressing God's truth. That pass gives each person who identifies with moral autonomy free rein to box God into a corner or completely disown him in whatever manner they choose. Their world is devoid of thanking God for what they have; most insist they deserve more and are doing everything in their power to seize more freedoms.

The God-inspired and known ethical truths, as taught in scripture, are being trampled by politically correct moral autonomists and their arrogance. Effectively, they say that we are not bound by past principles and truths taught by faithful followers of Christ, and no one religion or organization is superior to another. That is, we each can decide for ourselves, using whatever sources of authority we choose, to do what is right for us, regardless of hurting others or denying them their due in the process or refuting Christian theology and practice as irrelevant today.

Human history has shown, over the millennia, that when the letter and spirit of God's laws and authority are not obeyed, the truth is abused, nations become confused, and people are used. Many of our political and social issues are rooted in our misplaced belief that tolerance, inclusion, and equal respect for unequal truth is the "correct" way to achieve greater peace and personal fulfillment. They are all fundamentally misguided.

In contrast to the above, Spirit inspiration, the source of all truth and power, enables and empowers the faithful Christian to discern and define scripture's content and meaning, to separate human influences from its rightful interpretation, and to proclaim that truth as the Spirit leads. Every other understanding, no matter the source of authority, is simply ungodly. Trust and obedience are the attributes of the humble, faithful practitioner. "I'm OK; you're OK" is a good example of how far we have become detached from scriptural instruction.

Romans 12:2 is a good starting point of reference and instruction:

> Do not be conformed to this world but be transformed by the renewal of your mind, that by testing you may discern what is the will of God, what is good and acceptable and perfect.

The sanctioning of state, corporate, and institutional practices that create legal opportunities to get around either the letter or spirit of God's ethical standards and that politically repudiate and replace God's Word and will with human substitutions, as well as their following premeditated defiance in enacting laws and rights heretofore considered sinful to legitimize them as civil rights, is a good example of the "lawlessness" Paul warned us about in 2 Thessalonians 2:3–12:

> Let no one deceive you in any way. For that day will not come unless the rebellion comes first, and the man of lawlessness is revealed, the son of destruction, who opposes and exalts himself against every so-called god or object of worship, so that he takes his seat in the temple of God, proclaiming himself to be God. Do you not remember that when I was still with you, I told you these things? And you know what is restraining him now so that he may be revealed in time. For the mystery of lawlessness is already at work. Only he who now restrains it will do so until he is out of the way. And then the lawless one will

be revealed, whom the Lord Jesus will kill with the breath of his mouth and bring to nothing the appearance of his coming. The coming of the lawless one is the activity of Satan will all power and false signs and wonders, and with all wicked deception for those who are perishing because they refused to love the truth and so be saved. Therefore, God sends them a strong delusion, so that they may believe what is false in order that all may be condemned who did not believe the truth but had pleasure in unrighteousness.

You can accept or reject the scripture above. Either way, you need to support your viewpoint by choosing an authority to support your reasoning. You must ask and answer what you are looking for, what you are living for, and what you stand for or are against. Then you must figure out who or what you will follow or trust to help you get where you are going and enable you do what you want to do, in the name of the authority you chose.

This being a skeptical, legalistic, and individualist generation, the chances are great that the multitudes will look for sources that give them permission to indulge and engage in whatever floats their boats. Unfortunately, they are spitting into the wind, and the blowback will knock them off their feet.

In these times of uncertainty, we want certainty. In all relationships where there is disrespect and hostility, we want wise counsel. In times of desperation, we seek security and a light at the end of the tunnel. Where do you find certainty, wise counsel, and hope? Who can you trust and count on in every situation? Who or what authority can bring answers to the table for the political parties and identity groups that will be objectively equitable for all involved?

There is no question, in some aspects of our lives, that progress has resulted in physical and mental improvements. We are more educated. We have benefitted from new scientific discoveries. For some populations, life itself is easier and less demanding. But nothing of a more permanent nature for people from all levels of society seems to be in our immediate future. Temporary truces or political compromises are routinely seen as the only way to get from A to B in a responsible way.

All our major problems, such as ethnic or identity equality, economic parity, or religious differences are always present and percolating resentment that is fomenting civil rebellion. Permanent, long-lasting results regarding an equitable resolution for every major moral and social issue always seem to slip through our fingers. The process of achieving equal justice and equity based on merit and integrity is thwarted by powerful forces and spirits in high places that seek to use various individuals and organizations to maintain their grip on power and a greater ability to control their desired destiny.

Romans 8:28 brings comfort and security to faithful Christians in times of stress and chaos:

> And we know that for those who love God all things work together for good, for those who are called according to his purpose.

No one likes stress or discord but knowing that you are experiencing something that God has brought about brings Christian's peace and comfort in the time of a personal or national heartache. Everyone, Christian or not, should be reminded that the trustworthiness of the message depends on the trustworthiness of the messenger, sent by the authority commanding both the message and messenger. Are all messages and messengers in any human organization or institution always truth-bearers from an objective source? Or is their message and messenger part of a subjective source of authority with subjective ways and means, used to achieve their end goal?

Today, we are pulled in different social directions because the underlying liberal secularist and materialist philosophers tell us they can deliver something for everyone, without asking much of anyone. In their progressive, liberal dogma, the mantra is "vote for me, and I will set you free."

Speaking of shame, nobody does a better job of blaming someone or something for all that is wrong with Americans today than the politically correct. Have you ever heard them admit they have been wrong or made a mistake and apologize for it? Do they chastise and discipline their guilty party members, or do they sweep under the rug those actions and decrees, causing harm to others? We all must do better and not throw the first stone, but we need to call a spade a spade. Jesus provides the way that we are to call out evil or sinful behavior:

> The one who speaks on his own authority seeks his own glory but the one who seeks the glory of him who sent him is true and in him there is no falsehood. Do not judge by appearances but judge with right judgment. (John 7:18, 24)

The authority to make a righteous judgment only comes to the person who is under the tutelage of the Holy Spirit in Christians. *When the Word of God is rejected, sin, without guilt or shame, is accepted.* Across-the-board arrogance in our boardrooms and political parties replaces submission and humility in the form of intellectual and moral superiority by an elite group of people who see themselves as the holders and transmitters of information and knowledge, to which lesser groups or opponents are not privy or have not fully grasped.

Without ethical due diligence, coupled with corroborated scriptural discernment from the Spirit's guidance, the moral values and scriptural interpretation one teaches to others often leads to promoting a false social gospel that cherry-picks and distorts both the letter and intent Christ intended. By throwing in half-truths and teaching self-reliance, temptations and distractions are introduced into the mix, and our human baser nature sees an opportunity to rationalize greed, envy, and lust as moral normal. Malevolent forces or spirits of the world constantly slander and deceive each of us, to distract and tempt us to take things into our hands. By elevating our emotions, they are egging us on to rely on ourselves, our judgments, and our rights that we hold so near and dear to our subjective hearts. Twisting the truth is their forte.

False teaching that leads to false values creates false security. In the process of arriving at a point where false security is embraced and sanctioned in politically correct morality, the Ten Commandments are nonbinding platitudes that may be opted out of because politically correct moral autonomy allows for both self-justification and self-exoneration. In other words, you are given free rein to indulge in whatever seems right to you.

Deception rules where satanic forces are given a free ride. Moral autonomy and moral self-determination are both masterful deceptions. Twisting the truth about God and man's relationships is one of the greatest threats to every individual who is not sure of either, or who is searching for something to resolve the emptiness or hopelessness he or she is experiencing. The ideology that more freedom is always better than more reliance on God is a real crowd-pleaser. Promoting everyone's right to determine their own rules and standards and using the familiar deceitful slogan "I'm okay; you're okay" has done far more harm than good because of the ungodly freedom it gives to all who worship rights and self-determination.

Because moral autonomy does not distinguish between various forms of godlessness, evil is seen as more of an irritant than a major concern. If you are a supporter of politically correct forms of morality, you are probably not overly concerned about what Christian's regard as sin. But if you are a Christian, you are told to love the sinner and hate the sin. There is a fine line delineating the two. Getting it right is of the highest priority. Sometimes, to show the superiority of faithful Christian teaching and practice regarding politically correct moral positions on social issues, you may be prone to alienate the sinner by speaking in a tone of condemnation, rather than listening to them and discovering why they act as they do. Every Christian must learn this if they are to have any chance of defending the Word and will of God as he intended it to be represented.

CHAPTER 9

Who or What Do You Trust?

"In man we trust; in God, not as much"—this is the new, improved slogan or mantra that succinctly and explicitly depicts the politically correct moral viewpoint. It has reversed the rule of godly governing by substituting its moral ideology as the new guiding light, whose authority supersedes God's. We now bow and pray to the idols we have made.

Politically correct moral choice or autonomy is either an oxymoron or a free ride to do and say what pleases you. Today, the latter is the prevailing view that Christians must address. This book takes the view that it is an evil ideology with far-reaching consequences for both non-Christians and Christians. We are so far off track from what God expects and demands that killing an unwanted, unborn innocent life is a primary plank in progressive liberal theology. However, you must give the "correct" people credit for their chutzpah, as they are able to make rotten eggs smell like cooking bacon.

The prayer of Saint Francis of Assisi, who lived in twelfth-century Italy, is a good starting point to compare the nature of Christian theology and practice with politically correct ideology and practice:

> Lord, make me an instrument of your peace,
> Where there is hatred, let me sow love,
> Where there is injury, pardon
> Where there is doubt, faith.

Where there is despair, hope.
Where there is darkness, light.
Where there is sadness, joy.

O Divine Master, grant that I may not so much
Seek to be consoled as to console.
To be understood as to understand.
To be loved as to love.

For it is in giving that we receive.
It is in pardoning that we are pardoned.
And it is in dying that we are born to eternal life.

Ask moral autonomists who are politically correct how they feel that the faith and grace Saint Francis exhibited in the above prayer would play out in their ideology or practices? How would they pray for forgiveness, understanding, and discernment from God? Or in lieu of God, what standard or ideology do they commit themselves to? Can they recite an equivalent commitment to their higher power? See what their response is. Does their faith reside in their wisdom and their system's ability to bring about equity for all people? Will they bow in reverence to God's holiness and perfection, or will they bow and pray to the gods they have made?

Most individuals want to believe that God loves everybody equally. Is that true, or is there a caveat that states that the context determines whether his love is conditional on our obedience and his sovereign choice? Finally, scripture will corroborate that God is love, but the context needs to be discerned. He separates the believer from the unbeliever finally. In conclusion, God's love incorporates myriad factors that determine the kind and degree of that love and how it is manifested by God on earth and in heaven. Lest we forget, wrath is just as much an attribute of God's as is love and mercy!

Examine the attitude and behavior in the above paragraph, let us look again at a previously used scripture verse: "Claiming to be wise, they became fools" (Romans 1:22).

The follow-up verse describes what happens when that occurs:

> Therefore God gave them up in the lusts of their hearts to impurity, to the dishonoring of their bodies among themselves, because they exchanged the truth about God for a lie and worshipped and served the creature rather than the Creator. (Romans 1:24)

That is an explicit, pointed indictment against all who look to their own interests and standards as the measurement of something's value or validity. There may be free will, but God clearly lets it be known there is no free ride!

There is an old commercial about car repairs that played out decades ago. The line was something like, you can pay me now, or you can pay me later, but you will eventually have to pay me. The car repairman was telling the man who brought in the car that preventive maintenance was less costly than waiting until the car broke down and then paying for repairs. Applying that logic to today's excessive impulses for immediate gratification, there are great spiritual costs for our procrastination or denial that something is amiss; the foolish plow ahead anyway, thinking they can get away with what they know is wrong or will break down.

God has given everyone free will. On the other hand, no one is given moral autonomy to redefine or self-determine what is or is not acceptable or righteous in God's eyes. When you lead others to believe there are no moral repercussions, negative consequences, or social stigma when you assign a different value or label to an act, you become an accomplice or coconspirator in the deception you are validating.

Is evil in the eye of the beholder, like beauty? Many would say yes. Christians worth their salt would emphatically say no. Likewise, the revised "correct" thought that is postulated by moral autonomists is so subjective that it could be a positive or negative, depending on who is defining it. The emphasis that should be substituted for "correct" should be, "Is it God's truth, his Word?" The Bible often uses the phrase, "thus says the Lord," when it wants to magnify or emphasize that the words come from God, and the position being posited is validated by God himself. It reminds today's hearers that only what God says, or institutes is eternal and forever true. What God says is the highest truth, the supreme "correct," and the zenith of all peace and wisdom. Everything spewing from the mouths of men and women in contradiction or rejection of God's Word and will is subject to a wrath that ends in discipline or destruction to those who embrace or approve the defiance or perversion.

Tolerance of false teaching and perverted actions is sin, regardless of whether it is legally correct. Granting anyone permission to indulge themselves as they see fit is an egregious sin that will at some point, be brought to God's judgment.

No one wants to hear harsh biblical pronouncements are true or that they apply to contemporary men and women. You understand why the politically correct have cobbled together an ideology and protocol of media and institutional programs and pundits that daily proclaim their superiority over all who challenge or resist their claims of social enlightenment or moral advancement. They self-righteously broadcast that they have the answers or wherewithal that usurps or negates God's authority, and they claim the ability to more successfully resolve problems and social issues through greater indiscriminate tolerance and progressive something-for-everyone ideology. If their proof is in the word and will of political protocol being bandied about as "correct," but the ensuing real consequence is widespread turmoil, which clearly depicts moral and social chaos, correct is the wrong word; *corrupt* might be closer to the truth!

No debate or argument should be sidetracked by insisting that everyone has an equal right to be heard and that their subjective, self-serving values should be equally respected with scriptural admonitions. Rather, it should concentrate on the reason for the debate or argument in the first place. The end goal should be to arrive at the one highest truth and the one definitive scriptural answer that settles the debate. Each time you settle for a compromised ethical solution that saves face or makes both sides look good for political purposes, you exacerbate the problem and delay its correction. Why? Because both sides become more entrenched and prefer to protect any gains or illusions of progress, rather than risk being discovered as a fraud.

The book of Proverbs, which is attributed to King Solomon—considered one of the wisest men in history—is a good starting place to winnow out the wheat from the chaff concerning how to tell the difference between God's truth and wisdom and everyone else's subjective, humanly biased version.

Proverbs 1:23 reminds us of the importance of humility and trusting the Lord:

> If you turn at my reproof, behold I will pour out my spirit to you; I will make my words known to you."

> Better is a poor person who walks in his integrity than one who is crooked in speech and is a fool. (Proverbs 19:1)

> A false witness will not go unpunished, and he who breathers out lies will not escape. (Proverbs 19:5)

> The fear of the Lord is instruction in wisdom, and humility comes before honor. (Proverbs 15: 33)

> The fear of the Lord is the beginning of wisdom and the knowledge of the Holy One is insight. (Proverbs 9:10)

Everyone must evaluate the intent, content, and motivation of politically correct moral autonomy against God's required ethical standards and restrictions, as they apply equally to all humans, whether they accept or reject them. A good starting reference point would be Micah 6:8, as it explicitly expresses God's intent:

> He has told you, O man, what is good; and what does the Lord require of you but to do justice, and to love kindness and to walk humbly with your God?

William Law, a Christian living and writing in the early eighteenth century, puts it like this: "If you have not chosen the kingdom of God first, it will in the end make no difference what you have chosen instead."[1]

C. S. Lewis asserted, plainly, the discerning insight of the above as he wrote,

> We shall have missed the end for which we are formed and rejected the only thing that satisfies. Does it matter to a man dying in the desert by which choice of route, missed the only well?[2]

We are systemically dealing with conflicting values today, with the advantage of added historical insight and hindsight, as compared with yesteryear. Yet we do not appear to have advanced ethically in dealing with and resolving problems such as life or death (abortion), sexual purity and restrictions (homosexuality), racial and gender equality, economic disparity, church, and state relationships, and individual and interest-group demanded changes.

Honor, integrity, and truth, each in and of themselves, have stand-alone godly merit. All honor, integrity, and truth flow from God's revelation and grace. No one and no institution can add or subtract to what is required and expected by God. Claiming to be wise or superior to others is either an act of arrogance or an attempt to hide the flaws and errors inherent in one's theology or political ideology.

Humility is a sign of strength and confidence, flowing from a faith that first trusts and obeys God. It is in God that Christian humility finds its strength. Politically correct arrogance is dependent on human collusion and private and corporate moral disinformation. First, arrogance is a sign of weakness, insecurity, or lack of confidence. If you must boast of who you are or what you stand for, it means something is lacking when others assess your character or integrity. If what you represent cannot stand on its own merit, others will determine you are a hypocrite or fraud falsely posing as one with elevated wisdom.

God's order of things and the human order of things are eternally at odds. There is God's divine plan and laws to implement his order and humans' mortal plan and laws to implement their order. Neither the order nor plan of humans falls under God's good graces. Political correctness is underpinned with a combination of religious, civil, legal, and political dichotomies, selectively picked to cover all their moral bases, without being hamstrung by anyone. God's plan has unfolded flawlessly over billions of years, whereas man's plans have collided with God's from the start. In refusing to honor and obey God's natural order and divine laws, man honors and obeys his alternative order by manipulating his moral laws.

Using self-righteous indignation as an excuse for invoking moral self-determination, the politically correct have unleashed all manner of decay and corruption on a scale never achieved by tyrants and demagogues of the past. Yet their arrogance grows daily as they throttle all venues of resistance. The evils sanctioned by the politically correct exploit human weaknesses, regarding their understanding of free will, and turn the weakness into destructive acts of self-degradation. The arrogance of the moral autonomists knows no bounds. They aggressively seek to use their victims as fodder for their controlling authority to authorize even greater evil and to demand more rights that will counter damages previously accrued.

Good and evil are not in the eye of the beholder; they are defined and defended by God. It is never a matter of "I am right, and you're wrong," or vice versa. It is always a matter of written and inspired truth, as directed in Holy Scripture. Only God's truth is always objective and eternal; every other embraced truth or truth embraced by humanity is subjective and destructive. When competing with God and obedient Christians, the "correct" group will win some battles and at times, designated by God, gain temporary legal or moral superiority, but like clockwork, nothing and no one can turn back what God is moving forward.

God does not want or need new methods of solving old problems. He is looking for new men and women who dismiss materialism, paganism, and indifference. He wants people to consecrate their lives by serving him faithfully, day in and day out. Commitment to him will unlock many doors that are currently closed because of the sins of being self-serving and self-independent from his Word and will. Willful disobedience prevents many a blessing that God is prepared to give to those who submit to his authority.

Looking back two thousand years, the early church was attacked and scattered by opposing political and social forces, just as it is today. In 2 Peter 1:20–21, we read this affirmation:

Know this first, that no prophecy of Scripture comes from someone's own interpretation. For no prophecy was ever produced by the will of man, but men spoke from God as they were carried along by the Holy Spirit.

In 2 Peter 3:17, Peter conveyed a follow-up warning:

You, therefore, beloved, knowing this beforehand, take care that you are not carried away with the error of lawless people and lose your own stability.

Continuing along the same lines, but long before Peter spoke the above, Isaiah used an interesting illustration that parallels Peter's words. Isaiah was given a revelation or prophecy from the Holy Spirit, who spoke to him about corruption of the people and God, informing Isaiah that destruction was coming, but the faithful remnant would survive the storm:

Then I said, "How long, O Lord?" and he said: "Until the cities lie waste without inhabitant, and houses without people, and the land is a desolate waste, and the Lord removes people far away and the forsaken places are many in the midst of the land. And although a tenth remains in it, it will be burned again, like a terebinth or oak, whose stump remains when it is felled." The holy seed (Spirit) is its stump. (Isaiah 6:11–13)

The familiar axiom, "see no evil, hear no evil, speak no evil," was originally a kind of spoof about looking away from or excusing something wrong. No longer. Today, it is the compelled mantra of those in power or positions of authority who, by political fiat, attempt to deny its corruption and the destruction of existing moral protocol based on Christian theology and practice. It is an attempt to deflect public understanding of evil as heinous sin to where it is not so obvious but more a matter of personal preferences and nuanced perception. By embracing any form of evil (abortion, homosexuality, mass entitlements, moral autonomy) and claiming conservative Christians are misinterpreting scriptural content and intent or that past uneducated populations' views are invalid today, the political power structure unleashes pent-up and restrained evil to come out as normal moral human nature.

The various authorities are all pitted against God the Father, Son, and Holy Spirit. Faithful Christians who trust and obey the Word and will of God, as represented and empowered by the authority of the Holy Spirit, are the only bulwark against the spreading plague. Scripture is the Christian guiding light and source of authority and power, not dependence on physical or political domination. As a divided nation, we would do well to remember these words from Paul:

> For we do not wrestle against flesh and blood, but against the rulers, against the authorities, against the cosmic powers over this present darkness, against the spiritual forces of evil in the heavenly places. (Ephesians 6:12)

You have heard the phrase in sporting events, "The best defense is a good offense." That is true especially for faithful Christians. God does not want his followers playing defense or back away from those who see things differently and defiantly reject Christ. He wants our convictions to be such that others will see how deeply we are convinced of his love and power to change lives. Do not let satanic forces create doubt or to convince you that something, which you know to be scripturally true, is labeled as not true by progressives.

Moral autonomists know that coercion and intimidation are great tools to help them evade pointing out that scripture confirms the act or belief to be "evil!" To equitably answer the moral and social problems at hand—abortion, homosexuality, excess entitlements, equal acceptance of unequal truths, racial acrimony, and Christian persecution —objective truth, scripturally corroborated, not subjective preferences, should be the primary standard applied to each legal or moral issue.

Moral self-determination violates Christian apologetics, theology, and practice by distorting scriptural truth and Spirit interpretation divinely revealed and intended. Any so-called truth or "right" that circumvents or subverts the required sacrifices, disciplines, and self-denial demanded by God in any given social or moral issue ceases to be right in the moment it becomes a force unto itself, outside or independent of the scripturally required obedience and honor due God.

It is said that opposites attract. Politically corrects evil counterpart, or antithesis, then, might be the Christian doxology. The word *doxology* was specifically chosen to accentuate the radical lostness of all who worship politically correct dogma and practice. Doxology means "a liturgical prayer or hymn of praise to God." It concentrates and directs all of one's purposes and attributes to honor, glorify, and praise God through his Son, Jesus. It is a God-affirming and God-confirming allegiance that is sung as follows:

> Praise God from whom all blessings flow,
> Praise him all creatures here below,
> Praise him above, ye heavenly host,
> Praise Father, Son, and Holy Ghost.
> Amen.

How do the politically correct redirect people's perception or understanding of any ideology or theology and transfer their loyalty from one source or authority to another? They give them an alternative that provides more of what they want. You point out the new standard that removes the stigma from the existing theology/ideology that society finds too restrictive. The proponents of converting to the new standard will attempt to show you the superiority of their lifestyles as compared to the past standards. By adding something new and more attractive and taking away historical aspects that the people believe is holding them back, a state or institution can manipulate groups or populations into seeing things differently and follow their more enlightened lead.

Simply by changing the emphasis from scriptural rights and wrongs to individual personal preferences or individual sexual orientation or caving to group-identity demands, all of society is coerced to take sides. By redefining certain words or concepts or overemphasizing others, evil is made legal, and past prohibitions become today's correct behavior. Morality that depends on what various people determine is their correct standard or that they claim is detrimental to their pursuit of happiness soon becomes social anarchy, when they coerce others to fall in line or to keep their mouths shut.

The inherent problem in governing by the will of the people, for the people, and of the people, fixated on increasing freedoms and entitlements and reducing restrictions and moral boundaries, quickly becomes evident when various constituencies strive for the upper hand. By allowing various standards of self-determination in ethical situations, he said/she said, or I am right/you are wrong, predictably, becomes an emotional shouting match that prevents any chance of equitable resolution. In the worst-case scenario, both sides decide the ever-popular moral code of "I'm OK; you're OK" should be incorporated into the moral fabric of the times. It postulates that whatever works for you, do it, and do not worry about what others think or say; they too will look the other way.

If necessary, you explain why the new is more progressive or better able to meet the needs and aspirations of contemporary lifestyles and thinking. Is there a common thread that attempts to make the case that the old moral system or process of governing was flawed and that the new corrects those flaws?

John Dos Passos authored an essay in 1941, "The Use of the Past," to remind us of the relevance and importance of how the past can assist the present in recognizing and successfully dealing with the current set of conditions and problems that each generation faces:

Every generation rewrites the past. In easy times history is more or less of an ornamental art, but in times of danger we are driven to the written record by a pressing need to find answers to the riddles of today. We need to know what kind of firm ground other men, belonging to generations before us, have found to stand on. Despite changing conditions of life they were not hugely different from ourselves, their thoughts were the grandfathers of our thoughts, they

managed to meet situations as difficult as those we must face to meet them sometimes lightheartedly and, in some measure, to make their hopes prevail. We need to know how they did it. In times of change and danger when there is a quicksand of fear undermines reasoning, a sense of continuity with generations gone before can stretch like a lifeline across the scary present and get us past that idiot delusion of the exceptional, **Now,** that blocks good thinking. That is why, in times like ours when old institutions are caving in and are being replaced by new institutions not necessarily in accord with most men's preconceived hopes, political thought must look backwards as well as forwards.[3]

In the case of politically correct moral autonomy, the common thread is to redefine and reform Christianity and redefine evil and what is legal. Weaving that thread through the government, institutions, and everyday citizens is the understanding that each entity has the moral choice or right to reject God's authority by rejecting Christian theology and practice where it interferes with progressive thinking and liberal ideology. If you can persuade enough people to round off the sharp edges of certain Christian restrictions and prohibitions, the rest of the contested social issues will follow suit. The result is indiscriminate tolerance and consistent erosion of corporate moral integrity and personal honor.

Good and evil have been contending for our allegiance since the beginning of human history. If you were to ask others today which side is winning, you would get many different sentiments. That is because different people look to diverse sources or standards when they determine whether something is good or evil. How they respond will be influenced by where they currently find themselves, regarding their physical, financial, mental, and spiritual condition. We each see through distinct, personal lenses and are influenced by our physical environment, social standing, and spiritual health. If there is no central conforming standard of ethics, everything is up for grabs. Coercion and force inevitably take over and dominate the moral atmosphere in a nation.

It is the Holy Spirit and Christian Church that is holding back the malevolent forces of evil that arrogantly masquerade as forces of enlightened reasoning. No other religion or ideology has the Holy Spirit guiding and protecting the individual and corporate body associated with their religion.

Listen and diligently pray for inspired guidance in trying to understand and discern the dynamics and trust the words of what is called "the high priestly prayer" that Jesus prayed in John 17:1–26. Read the preceding lines in John 16:29–33 that explain the context from which Christ's words emanated. Here is his prayer:

> When Jesus had spoken these words, "he lifted up his eyes to heaven and said, "Father, the hour has come; glorify your Son that the Son may glorify you, since you have given him authority over all flesh, to give eternal life to all whom you have given him. *And this is eternal life, that they know you the only true God and Jesus Christ whom you have sent.* I glorified you on earth, having accomplished the work that you gave me to do. And now, Father, glorify me in your own presence with the glory that I had with you before the world existed.
>
> I have manifested your name to the people whom you gave me out of the word. Yours they were, and you gave them to me, and they have kept your word. Now they know everything that you have given me is from you. For I have given them the words that you gave me, and they have received them and have come to know in truth that I came from you; and they have believed that you sent me. I am praying for them. I am not praying for the world but for those whom you have given me, for they are yours. All mine are yours and yours are mine and I am glorified in them. And I am no longer in the world, but they are in the world, and I am coming to you. Holy Father keep them in your name which you have given me, that they may be one, even as we are one. While I was with them, I kept them in your name, which you have given me. I have guarded them and not one of them has been lost except the son of destruction, that the Scripture might be fulfilled. But now I am coming to you and these things I speak in the world, that they may have joy fulfilled in themselves. I have given them your word and the world has hated them because they are not of the world just as I am not of the world. I do not ask that you take them out of the world but that you keep them from the evil one.

They are not of the world just as I am not of the world. Sanctify them in the truth; your word is truth. As you sent me into the world, so I have sent them into the world. And for their sake, I consecrate myself, that they also may be sanctified in truth.

"I do not ask for these only but also for those who will believe in me through their word, that they may all be one, just as you Father, are in me, and I in you, that they also may be in us, so that the world may believe that you have sent me. The glory that you have given me I have given them, that they may be one even as we are one. I in them and you in me, that they may become perfectly one, so that the world may know that you sent me and loved them even as you loved me. Father, I desire that they also, whom you have given me, may be with me where I am, to see my glory that you have given me because you loved me before the foundation of the world. O righteous Father, even though the world does not know you, I know you, and these know that you have sent me. I made known to them your name and I will continue to make it known that the love with which you have loved me may be in them and I in them."

Truly it must be divinely inspired and revealed that what was said two thousand years ago by the Son of God in a prayer is still as powerfully as true and applicable today as it was then. No other faith or religion has the very words of hundreds of prophets, judges, kings, paupers and peasants hearing, receiving and accepting the word or God and his Son from thousands of years ago because none other has the Holy Spirit of God to inspire and protect the words and legacy that God himself spoke and recorded for his chosen followers to faithfully obey! *The Holy Spirit Nurtures Truth, Glorifies Christ, and Empowers Christians!* (Italics added)

The personality and power of the Spirit is described throughout the Old and New Testaments. The Spirit is real—a distinct being/person, not an indifferent, ephemeral force. It intercedes, adopts, unites, and empowers all who are of God by revealing universal truth that they alone receive and apply, as it is given to them by the grace of the heavenly Father. Without the Holy Spirit, Christ would not have risen; Christians would not be able preach Christ and be used by the Spirit to reach out to all whom God had chosen; and the final victory of Christ would not come to fruition. To many, the Spirit of God, the third person within the Trinity, is somewhat of a mystery and a lesser partner of the Trinity. But without the influence and power of the Spirit, the world would be hell on earth. Without the Spirit, the works of the Father and Son would be unknown, and salvation would be lost.

Numerous verses from the Old and New Testament are used to illustrate, define, and defend the authority, power, and wisdom that the Spirit shares as a member of our Triune God.

> The earth was without form and void, and darkness was over the face of the deep. And the Spirit of God was hovering over the face of the waters. (Genesis 1:2)

> And I will put my Spirit within you and cause you to walk in my statutes and be careful to obey my rules. (Ezekiel 36:27)

> The Spirit of the Lord was upon him [Othniel, Caleb's younger brother] and he judged Israel. (Judges 3:10)

Jesus promises to send the Holy Spirit to his disciples and followers:

> And I will ask the Father and he will give you another Helper, to be with you forever, even the Spirit of truth, whom the world cannot receive, because it neither sees him nor knows him. You know him, for he dwells with you and will be in you. (John 14:16–17)

> When the Spirit of truth comes, he will guide you into
> all the truth, for he will not speak on his own authority,
> but whatever he hears he will speak, and he will declare to
> you the things that are to come. He will glorify me for he
> will take what is mine and declare it to you. All that the
> Father has is mine; therefore, I said that he will take what
> is mine and declare it to you. (John 16:13–15)

Paul explains how the Spirit acts as an intercessory to overcome our
weakness and guide our prayer life and footsteps as we delve into additional
readings:

> Likewise the Spirit helps us in our weakness. For we do
> not know what to pray for as we ought, but the Spirit
> himself intercedes for us with groanings too deep for
> words. And he who searches hearts knows what is the
> mind of the Spirit, because the Spirit intercedes for the
> saints according to the will of God. And we know that for
> those who love God, all things work together for good; for
> those who are called according to his purpose. (Romans
> 8:26–28)

God sends the Spirit to those he adopts as sons and daughters to
enable them to cry to the Father as their source of power, faithful service,
and salvation, as Paul writes, "And because you are sons, God has sent the
Spirit of his Son into our hearts, crying, 'Abba! Father!'" (Galatians 4:6).

> The wind blows where it wishes and you hear its sound,
> but you do not know where it comes from or where it goes.
> So, it is with everyone who is born of the Spirit. (John 3:8)

> Now there are varieties of gifts but the same Spirit; and
> there are varieties of service, but the same Lord; and
> there are varieties of activities, but it is the same God
> who empowers them all in everyone. To each is given the
> manifestation of the Spirit for the common good. For to
> one is given through the Spirit the utterance of wisdom

and to another the utterance of knowledge according to the same Spirit, to another faith by the same Spirit, to another gifts of healing by the one Spirit, to another the working of miracles to another prophecy, to another the ability to distinguish between spirits, to another various kinds of tongues, to another the interpretation of tongues. All these are empowered by the same Spirit, who apportions to each one individually as he wills. (1 Corinthians 12:4–11)

Paul speaks to the early Corinthian church and encourages and confirms them:

And it is God who establishes us with you in Christ and has anointed us, and who also puts his seal on us and given us his Spirit in our hearts as a guarantee. (2 Corinthians 1:21–22)

The Spirit himself bears witness with our spirit that we are children of God and if children, then heirs -heirs of God and fellow heirs with Christ, provided we suffer with him in order that we may also be glorified with him. (Romans 8:16)

Jesus spoke out this warning against those who blasphemy the Spirit: Therefore I tell you; every sin and blasphemy will be forgiven people but the blasphemy against the Spirit will not be forgiven. And whoever speaks a word against the Son of Man will be forgiven but whoever speaks against the Holy Spirit will not be forgiven, either in this age or in the age to come. (Matthew 12:31)

Everyone needs the Spirit, but not everyone knows him or receives him. And for those who do not receive him and cause those of the Spirit to stumble, Jesus said, "It would have been better if they had not been born" (Matthew 18:6). But for those who do receive the Spirit, the good news is in John 14:26:

> But the Helper, the Holy Spirit, whom the Father will send in my name, he will teach you all things and bring to your remembrance all that I have said to you.

What does that encompass? Charles Spurgeon's book *The Holy Spirit* is a powerful, Spirit-inspired writing that instructs and clarifies the full and divine nature of the Spirit. He wrote:

> He instructs us as to our need and as to the promises of God that refer to that need. He shows us where our deficiencies are, what our sins are and what our needs are. He sheds light on our condition and makes us feel deeply our helplessness, sinfulness, and dire poverty. Then he casts the same light upon the promises of the Word and lays home to the heart that very text that was intended to meet the occasion- the precise promise that was framed with the foresight of our present distress. In that light He makes the promise shine all its truthfulness, certainty, sweetness, and suitability, so that we, poor trembling sons of men, dare to take that Word into our mouths that first came out of God's mouth and then come with it as an argument and plead it before the throne of the heavenly grace. Our power in prayer lies in the plea, "Lord do as you have said."[4]

All faithful Christians have the Spirit within them and are, in a sense, a letter or messenger from God. Corinthians 3:16–17 speaks to that:

> Do you not know that you are God's temple and that God's Spirit dwells in you? If anyone destroys God's temple, God will destroy him. For God's temple is holy and you are that temple.

Irreverence or rebellion against the Son or Spirit becomes an attack or rebellion against God. Christians are belittled and attacked in many places in our country today, but we can take comfort because although we may be persecuted, there is glory in it for us if we remain faithful, and there is destruction to those who neither revere God nor respect Christian theology and practice. Keep in mind that *everything done outside the Spirit's influence is unacceptable to God.*

Paul reminds us of the eternal war within our consciences as we battle various conflicts and tensions that seek resolution, as he implores us to take the higher road:

> But I say, walk by the Spirit and you will not gratify the desires of the flesh. For the desires of the flesh are against the Spirit and the desires of the Spirit are against the flesh, for these are opposed to each other, to keep you from doing the things you want to do. But if you are led by the Spirit, you are not under the law. Now the works of the flesh are evident: sexual immorality, impurity, sensuality, idolatry, sorcery, enmity, strife, jealousy, fits of anger, rivalries, dissensions, divisions, envy, drunkenness, orgies, and things like these. I warn you as I warned you before, that those who do such things will not inherit the kingdom of God. If we live by the Spirit, let us also keep in step with the Spirit. Let us not become conceited, provoking one another, envying one another. (Galatians 5:16–21, 25–26)

Do you know what some of the most terrifying words of scripture are? "God gave them up." Paul, in his scathing discourse against unrighteous people and behavior, reminds us of the cost of such impurity and dishonor:

> For although they knew God, they did not honor him as God or give thanks to him, but they became futile in their thinking and their foolish hearts were darkened. Claiming to be wise, they became fools and exchanged the glory of the immortal God for images resembling mortal man and birds and animals and creeping things.
> Therefore, *God gave them up* in the lusts of their hearts to impurity, to the dishonoring of their bodies among themselves because they exchanged the truth about God

for a lie and worshiped and served the creature rather than the Creator, who is blessed forever! Amen.

For this reason, *God gave them up* to dishonorable passions. For their women exchanged natural relations for those that are contrary to nature, and the men likewise gave up natural relations with women and were consumed with passion for one another, men committing shameless acts with men and receiving in themselves the due penalty for their error.

And since they did not see fit to acknowledge God, *God gave them up* to a debased mind to do what ought not to be done. They were filled with all manner of unrighteousness, evil, covetousness, malice. They are full of envy, murder, strife, deceit, maliciousness. They are gossips, slanderers, haters of God, insolent, haughty, boastful, inventors of evil, disobedient to parents, foolish, faithless, heartless, ruthless. Though they know God's righteous decree that those who practice such things deserve to die, they not only do them but give approval to those who practice them. Romans 1:21–32, (italics added)

If that does not make you think twice and cringe about some of the sins listed above and who you are and what you stand for, you are living in a make-believe world and believe that what is going on today is moral normal. As the title convicts us of our attitudes of ingratitude and defiance, it is worth repeating that individual or group moral self-determination inevitably leads to divine intervention and a lot of teeth gnashing.

As we each look at our lives and assess who we are and our moral condition, we determine differently whether our glass is half full or half empty. Even more revealing, many see us as in control of our own earthly and eternal destiny and that no one has the right to tell you to stop doing whatever floats your boat. Most understand that some people are ahead or behind of others in their worldly circumstances, simply by place of birth; some are moving forward by sheer grit and fortitude, and many others are treading water or falling behind in one or more areas for myriad reasons. A huge contributing factor to the malaise that humankind has experienced from the beginning is the so-called "progressive" ideology that individuals self-determine good and evil. Therefore, what God defined and instructed two thousand years ago in scripture is not applicable or morally enforceable because we have become enlightened and have moved past ancient cultures and standards.

You may or may not agree with what follows, but regardless of where you stand, you will be challenged, encouraged, or stimulated, one way or the other, to ascertain and examine where you are, what you stand for, and why you believe what you believe. The question we each must answer for ourselves is, *Can I defend the veracity of my facts and truth, using the Spirit in Holy Scripture as my source of authority?*

The separation of church and state is no longer binding in progressive liberal circles. They have gathered institutional forces to alter the balance of power between the two by using coercive legal, political, and institutional dictates that prevent Christian theology and practices from influencing the general public's moral and spiritual grounding.

Over the years, the tide has turned, as "thy will be done," found in the Lord's Prayer, is now "my will be done." Every part of our society is buying into political correctness and crowding out Christianity's demand for self-discipline, self-denial, and personal and corporate integrity. Personal and corporate dependence on scriptural obedience in all phases of our individual and corporate lives is smothered by malevolent ideology. Life or death is now an equally valid choice; sexual immorality is now the norm; "you owe me" and entitlement is embraced by millions; disrespect and civil disobedience is used as a weapon against those who do not agree with progressive politics; and God is boxed into a corner, where he is becoming increasingly gagged.

If we agree that beauty is in the eye of the beholder, does that mean evil is also in the eye of the beholder? We know beauty is subjective to the person defining it, using his or her criteria for making the case. It is a matter of personal perception. We give each other that right. The question is, do we (or does the state) give individuals the freedom or the autonomy to determine for themselves what is right or wrong? Does that hold true for good and evil? The answer is not blowing in the wind, nor is it human prerogative. It is written in the pages of Holy Scripture. Scripture is holy because it comes from God. Self-determination and moral autonomy are not holy because that comes from sinful hearts seeking to justify and exonerate their words and deeds. They have become an unholy authority unto themselves.

Suppose one of your core beliefs was based on a false premise? If so, you would be living out a counterproductive life, using those false pretenses. You would be in good company because many are convinced that they are good people who are doing the right things, according to most human definitions of morality. But here is where the rubber hits the road: man's standards are not God's standards. If you primarily compare yourself and your character with other people, you very well may be a better person or citizen. But your good, seen through God's eyes, looks bad, and your character or integrity fails to meet God's standards of personal accountability and obedience.

Another misconception is that God's providence is primarily involved in blessings or favor. Many believe God may or may not be a part of a blessing to an individual or country, but he will not intentionally bring calamities or disasters. Is it coincidental or plain bad luck that the worst fires ever in the western United States; the number and devastation of floods and hurricanes elsewhere; the worldwide pandemic; the millions who have lost their jobs; the most divisive political atmosphere in decades; and the rise in riots, suicides, and depression are all coming together at one time? Or is the hand of God in each?

The question must be asked and answered from a biblical perspective, using scripture as the core for discerning the degree to which God participates in allowing or creating terrible things to happen to all the people who believe they are good. A good starting point explicitly declares that God does, in one form or another, ordain calamities:

> I am the Lord, and there is no other; I form the light and
> create darkness, I make well-being and create calamity; I,
> am the Lord, who does all these things. (Isaiah 45:6–7)

Since God is in complete control of all events and circumstances and can stop them or intervene when disaster is imminent, and he does not, we can confidently deduce that he allows them or even ordains them for his purposes. Why he ordains or allows any calamity from a human perspective is hard to decipher. We cannot look at any disaster and be certain what went into his purpose and intention for it. It is important to remember that God uses physical or moral evil or rebellion, in whatever form we bring it about, to punish or discipline arrogant and defiant men and women who refuse to acknowledge him as sovereign over all human activities. That often comes with a high price.

We may question why terrible things happen and try to comprehend how we are to respond, but in the end, we know, regardless of our limited understanding, that God's purpose employs both good and evil for his and our ultimate good.

Contrast that with moral autonomy granted by the politically correct who try to convince you that individuals have within themselves—or can achieve within themselves—what they need to be good enough or righteous enough to attain God's favor and others' blessings. How many times does scripture explicitly demonstrate and deny the false belief that good words or charitable deeds by good people are sufficient to gain eternal life and personal earthly favor? Or how many do not believe that good Christians are just as likely to suffer dreadful things as everybody else? Think about how you would answer those challenges.

Everything attempted outside of God's justifying truth and grace is counterfeit. Outside an act of God—his intervention—no one can cure themselves or save themselves, no matter how good they are or how righteous they claim to be. You can care for others deeply, but you cannot cure them or yourself by following prescribed rules and regulations by any human person or institution. Vanity and self-righteous indignation exacerbate the false social gospel being posited by politically correct ideologists, as they postulate that they can fix whatever ails us.

The chances are good that few people reading this book are biblical scholars. Ask yourself how often you read the Bible or use Reformed commentaries or actively search through them to accurately discern and help you interpret a difficult passage or theme that is troubling you or others. We all can see and read what scripture is telling us on the surface, but we often interpret it using personal preferences or authorities that are not Spirit-inspired but socially progressive. Scripture is the only infallible rule for life and faith. Reformed commentaries are valuable in helping us understand and interpret correctly what the Bible says, not what we want it to say. Always first use other Bible verses to help you interpret difficult passages, and then take the extra step by using trusted commentaries or respected Christian authors to help you get it right and corroborate what you have interpreted.

When interpreting, you must understand a given passage within the context that it was written. Without the correct context, you, in a sense, isolate it or put it into a category that can be made to mean anything you want it to. We are all prone to interpret scripture by the contemporary times and places we live in and then falsely apply those understandings or leanings to interpret the passage to fit contemporary understandings.

The moral autonomists within politically correct circles have defiantly refused to bend the knee to God's authority. Their moral normal is now moral autonomy. They mock his cause-and-effect natural laws. Sanctimonious hypocrisy eventually comes back to bite you in some manner. For example, truth that is not defended becomes a lie in the making. Defended, a lie in the making eventually becomes the reversal of truth. Moral autonomy is a lie in the making, and by defended it, it becomes truth to millions of gullible lost souls. As a nation seriously at odds with divine authority, shades of Sodom and Gomorrah come to mind.

The above assertion requires you to take a stand for or against using personal tastes and attitudes as the defining filter to properly place or label something as positive or negative. If you consent with others to assigning that prerogative to individual morality, are you not saying that moral relativity is a matter of self-determining moral normal and, therefore, a matter of subjective personal interpretation? By granting that authority, are you implying we each are equally capable of separating fact from fiction and truth from lies? If so, by what authority are you giving that permission? A secularist worldview such as the above is incapable of accepting an objective reality.

New Testament theology is the Christian bridge that Jesus built to draw us closer to a more personal and accessible understanding of God as Father and Jesus as Son. Through the inspired revelation of the Holy Spirit, we are told that the only way anyone can be set free and live a joyful life is to follow Jesus and deny ourselves. Since moral autonomy, as promoted by politically correct progressives, is primarily about indulging and satisfying your needs, lusts, and preferences, you could make a compelling case that hell will freeze over before "correct" corrupted rights and freedoms will be acceptable to God. The fundamental need and requirement for every person is to be reconciled to God through repentance, trust, and obedience.

If God is out of your loop, that means you are out of his loop. If you do not care one way or the other, ask yourself what matters to you and why others find Christ's peace that passes all understanding so all-encompassing? How did you arrive at an understanding that rights, freedoms, tolerances, entitlements, and consent are all human orchestrated and, by varying degrees, acceptable to suit individual tastes and understandings of good and evil, if good and evil are all subject to millions of differing interpretations? Is one interpretation as good as any other? Are we each free to define and design our own understanding, which means we are free to be both judge and jury as we see fit? Are your rules and standards designed to incorporate the ideology of what seems right to you is acceptable and therefore should be adopted as morally valid? Morality is subjectively fluid, dependent on the nature and character of the individual or group. God's truth is objectively fixed, not subject to change due to subjective context or one's predilection.

Where did all of this he said/she said come from, regarding human moral persuasions? In the account of Adam and Eve, living in the garden that God prepared for them, the serpent, an incarnation of Satan, is conversing with Eve to convince her that they had more freedom than they thought.

> He (Satan) said to the woman, "Did God actually say, you shall not eat of any tree in the garden?" (Genesis 3:3)

Here is what God said in Genesis 2:16–17:

> And the Lord commanded the man saying, "You may surely eat of every tree of the garden, but the tree of the knowledge of good and evil you shall not eat, for in the day that you eat of it, you shall surely die."

Here, we have Satan's account and God's account. Satan goes to Eve, not Adam, with a deceptive nuance about what God had said earlier to Adam. Satan's intent is to tempt Eve by emphasizing God's prohibition of only one tree and not emphasizing but distorting God's provision that they can eat from all the other trees but not one specific tree. Satan successfully reduces God's command to a question, introducing and raising doubt about God's sincerity and motives, very much like moral autonomy, as proclaimed by the politically correct.

Should we question why God set aside one tree that was off limits? It would be hard to make a case that a tree or its fruit was evil. An inanimate object is not evil. But God called the tree "the tree of knowledge of good and evil." The fruit may have been poisonous or not. When they ate from it, they did not die immediately, nor was it the fruit caused their deaths many years later. So what are some explanations why God purposefully placed one tree that was off limits among many other trees that were bearing good fruit? No one can confidently know how the tree was different or what kind of tree it was. But God obviously had a purpose for placing that tree in the garden where they lived.

Could it be that the physical tree was not itself evil but was a symbol or manifestation of a divine separation that we should not attempt to breach through human pride, arrogance, or deceit? A qualified consideration might conclude that the tree was a symbol, a boundary of sorts or a standard bearer that required respect and obedience from the created human beings. We all are evaluated on a daily level. When we are told that something is off limits or inappropriate, we often test the will of the people or entity that warned us. We want to see for ourselves, or we question why we are denied the right to engage in something. In our minds, we challenge the authority denying us the right and ask does he or she really mean it, and to what degree will they enforce it?

Another thought—humans are funny in that they think they are clever or creative enough that they will not get caught, should they decide to break the law or prohibition against something. If they do get caught, they can blame others or their circumstances, claiming they did not know it was wrong or off limits. They then produce excuses and reasons why they should be exempt from discipline or punishment.

In conclusion, it was a combination of a malevolent spirit that was present in the garden and Adam and Eve thinking they could become godlike and thus free to decide for themselves, using human reasoning and deceit, what is good or evil, acceptable, or unacceptable, based on their standards, not God's.

CHAPTER 10

The Ten Commandments or Ten Suggestions

The Ten Commandments represent the core ethical and legal standards for Jews and Christians. When they become the "Ten Suggestions," as they have with politically correct proponents in the United States, the default is not to God but to human interpretation and application. What follows is an ethical and theological void that is filled with a presumptuous and arrogant defiance, enshrining heretofore sins as "corrected" rights. Sin is an assertion of moral autonomy, an independence from godly requirements that minimize any wrongdoing when changing the intended direction God demands and maximizing your right to make a change. It is a failure to trust God and a denial of his sovereignty.

When sin comes from within the church itself, it inevitably is bound up in secular demands to accommodate a wider net of diversity. Should diversity be driven by claims of feelings, of being hurt because of exclusion, or false claims of moral equality when using modified unequal scriptural criteria? Each claim must be looked at not so much as an inclusive or exclusive legal or moral issue but as a spiritual issue, properly grounded in scriptural merit and instruction.

Interpretation of scripture, first, requires using other scripture from either the Old or New Testament to properly corroborate that the intended letter and spirit are carried out faithfully. Understanding the written word, as guided by the Holy Spirit, is God's requirement. Everything else is subordinated and inferior.

Christians that choose to render to Caesar a blighted version of truth and render to God a blighted version of justice and integrity have much to answer for. Any country that revels in its respect for deceit and reverence for choice, in effect, labels itself as being at war with God. When the sacredness of the state and its authority usurps the sacredness of gospel truth, everyone loses!

But historically orthodox, Spirit-filled Christianity is different. It states that no one is good; no one is good enough to earn his or her way into heaven. Your good works cannot save you. You cannot believe or pray your way to salvation. The bottom line: you cannot justify your moral conduct or life in the eyes of God. Jesus touched on that in Luke 16: 15, when he said,

> You are those who justify yourselves before men, but God knows your hearts. For what is exulted among men is an abomination in the sight of God.

You cannot get much more explicit than that!

Scripture is quite clear on what God is for and against; what is acceptable and unacceptable behavior. It is consistent and never contradicts itself. The Spirit does not inspire one message to the liberal and another to the conservative. The Spirit does not concern itself with whether the message is liked or received well. It always points both adherents to the same written Word, helps to interpret it as God intended, and empowers those who strive mightily to seek it, understand it, and apply it to themselves and others. Where you stand on rights versus responsibilities will be revealed by what you first commit to and then submit to. There is no reward or gain in combining a little of each to please both. If you attempt to please the crowd, the majority, you will displease God, as God could not care less about your kowtowing to their standards. Finally, you can either please humans or God, but you cannot please by trying to do so. The quality of your life depends on your choice. Paul reminds us that "the wrath of God is revealed from heaven against all ungodliness and unrighteousness of men, who by their unrighteous suppress the truth. (Romans 1:18).

The acceleration of liberal theology juxtaposed with political correctness is picking up steam, to the point that something must give. In case you have not noticed, the divide between conservative Christians and Republicans with liberal Christians and Democrats is widening. The increasing separation of church and state, as well as the animosity between secular society and orthodox theology and Christian understanding of homosexuality and abortion is ever present and ever growing. Our political system is full of guilty people and politically complicit hypocrisy. There has been a constant barrage of various finger-pointing and giving the finger to Christian individuals and faithful churches. A simple but powerful reminder that should humble everyone is in order. There is not one legal, political, religious, or entertainment figure who is innocent. They are all guilty as sin of sin. The president is guilty; the Supreme Court judges are guilty; all political party leaders and their followers are guilty. We may consider them good or trustworthy because they agree with us on important matters. But using scriptural analysis, whatever good we attribute to them is tainted by our universally corrupted nature.

Disinformation would be closer to the truth than what is frequently presented by our political leaders as valuable information. Yet many continue to accept at face value whatever they present as factual and complete. What they promote—and hope you will subscribe to—is that all our conflicts and problems can be resolved by simply following their advice and lead. In so many words, "Trust us; we know what is best for you and the country." Anyone with common sense knows that peace, harmony, and progress require tough love, self-denial, self-sacrifice, self-control, and equal goodwill efforts by institutions and individuals. But even more important, truth, integrity, and honor must be demanded, embraced, and rewarded, and scriptural evil must be punished and held accountable across our political and social institutions.

But that will never happen! We will never come even remotely close. Why is that? Because there are always large numbers of misguided and selfish individuals and organizations who put their faith and trust in human institutions, human power, and human wisdom. What they do not understand or accept is that every human-originated endeavor has both built-in blinders and self-destructive tendencies. No matter how great your faith or trust in someone or some organization, you are doomed to eventual failure when God is not present in the decision-making and follow-through. Every foundation built on human ability or capability is an exercise in futility—harsh but scripturally factual.

Let us explore that line of thinking for a minute. Even if all the king's men and women worked together as best they could for their entire careers and lives, and everyone bought into the political correctness of their undertakings, failure is inevitable. No matter how hard a government or person tries to do the right thing in a politically correct atmosphere, if the basis of their actions is determined by human reasoning, goodwill, and human planning, God puts up roadblocks from start to finish. God ordains events to disrupt and undo any current or future human monuments to themselves. It is not that compassion, mercy, and goodwill are wrong in God's eyes; it is that the motivation, intent, and pride that is driving them are human originated by human standards that are intrinsically sinful!

> But the wisdom from above is first pure, then peaceable, gentle, open to reason, full of mercy and of good fruits, impartial and sincere. (James 3:17)

You cannot tout that you are doing God's work or claim it is the right thing to do when God has not been called upon to bless the work, and Scripture has not been consulted to winnow out the chaff, or when the Spirit is not leading the process, and the people doing the work have little or no understanding or relationship with God. The best of intentions can only go as far as the weakest links allow it. Eventually, human pride and human self-serving behavior finds a way to dishonor and bring down the most valiant human efforts.

For the past few decades, we have known of the half-truths and manipulated data used to make things seem better or look better than they really were. *Hope* and *change* were clever sound bites, but we cannot save ourselves by counting on everyone to do the right thing. Even if everybody played by the "correct" rules, which would not enable us to rise above our human shortcomings. To paraphrase William Barclay, a twentieth-century theologian, the brotherhood of man is never going to happen outside the auspices of the fatherhood of God. Humans cannot cure physical illness, mental maladies, or moral perversions. Humans care;

God alone cures. Humans, of their own volition, cannot overcome evil, despite their best efforts; God alone does. Education cannot resolve social strife; government programs and money cannot change people's hearts. God does that through the Spirit. Every human owes God. God's grace allows you to exist, and it is only God's grace that enables you—those he has chosen—to receive his blessing.

Our problem is that shame, guilt, remorse, and just compensation to victims of economic and political corruption are becoming a vanishing social requirement that will, as a result, undermine every attempt to arrive at a place of goodwill and equal respect. Cronyism is systemic; revolving corporate and political patronage are so common that it is expected that one will lobby for the other and then exchange positions, as both benefit at the expense of the public. Lobbying by business behemoths to selected political-party movers and shakers is rewarded with fat contracts and inside information.

You cannot force positive change by incorporating negative elements into the change. Opposite ethical views cannot be made equal by consensus or majority. Change, in and of itself, is neither good nor bad; it is dependent on the motivation and intention of those behind it and the means and ends that put it into effect.

Hostility and incrimination are everywhere. Each political party exploits the gaffes of the other, and many exploit every loophole for personal and political gain. Common sense and civility are less common than private and political outrage. Achieving common ground may be the goal, but in far too many instances, common ground means greater compromise and less truth and integrity. Common ground should not be the end goal or the means to achieve greater integrity, honor, and trust. Trusting that good people will come together, work together, and solve the problems they are addressing is an exercise in futility. Nothing of a permanent nature occurs if God is not the impetus and glue being embraced by those seeking greater peace and harmony.

Before we get too judgmental or self-righteous, each of us needs to remember that true Christians and honorable politicians, as well as every other religious and political perspective, are all answerable to God's standards and his directives. What is obvious is that few subscribe to that divine truth and fewer still believe any one standard is right for everyone.

Moral gridlock and identity diversity is front and center, a leading cause of social chaos. Individual integrity and personal honor no longer drive most relationships. Our ship is sinking!

Whether we hit bottom or struggle to keep our heads above water, greater conflict and pain are in the national forecast either way. Should the wind favor the current direction of political correctness, widespread conflict and division eventually will boil over into a national malaise that will not go away until God intervenes. At that point, whether it gets worse or better is known but to God. Should God determine that enough is enough sooner rather than later, immediate, and bitter pills will be forcibly ingested. Kingdoms will fall, while the faithful eventually will regain their rightful place.

At this point, you may be wondering why I—or anyone, for that matter—would project what God might do and what the consequences might be. Well, it is a sure thing, not a best guess. Scripture repeatedly tells us that every nation and culture, at some point, will stir God to action. It is not a matter of *if* but *when*. How he intervenes—and when—will be determined by our individual and corporate responses to his demands to cease and desist from our transgressions. We are all under his universal law—truth or consequences.

That being the case, making various moral standards acceptable or equal, being politically correct carries the imprimatur of being morally correct. What must be defined and extrapolated is what constitutes the politically correct version of who and what determines where moral autonomy begins, and where and what conditions determine where it ends? In other words, what constitutes "correct" standards that are necessary to claim moral autonomy, and from what source or sources of authority do they draw to arrive at those "correct" standards? Is the information published so that everyone knows the rules, or is it fluid and self-determined?

Therein lies a major concern. If there is no official, historic, printed documentation that clearly indicates what is acceptable, as there is in Christian doctrine and practice, and the only way to determine what is politically correct is from a political, civil, or legal authority's verbal declaration, how can anyone be sure they fall inside the parameters of being politically/morally correct? How can anyone conclude—correctly—what contribution comes from the political party platform, civil rights demand, constitutional requirements, or our Christian heritage? How do you put them together into a cohesive, on-target moral representation of accepted politically correct moral autonomy?

What happens when individuals and liberal political proponents take it upon themselves to encourage others to turn away from God's providence and rely on their own devices, their own resources, and their own wisdom? Exactly what they want—a new order, underpinned by relaxed relationships, self-serving political parties, and a God who has little relevance in their day-to-day affairs. God is not dead but subordinated to their agenda.

The special-interest protection laws that have created new civil and legal rights previously denied may have added to our sense of moral relativity freedoms, but they subtract honor and integrity from God's existing scriptural laws and plans. Whenever a human law becomes our preeminent focus and substitutes for an existing biblical law and expected code of conduct, it becomes a form of legalism. That word conveys a negative connotation, as legalism replaces the legitimate, intended version of a previously existing ethical law with a crafted, substitute human version that either adds or subtracts from its designed function. It becomes a form of idolatry, in that it takes on a different motivation and intention, outside of God's ordained written and spoken authority. In effect, moral relativity boycotts divine-instructed major and minor constructs in human nature's close-enough and good-enough constructs, which are the backbone of political correctness.

Today, legalism is the curse of the politically correct, raising its ugly head as the bane of much of our moral and ethical interpretations. It is a tool, used by Satan, to move us away from the truth. In 2 Corinthians 11:13–15, Paul instructed the early church to look out for those who were masquerading as Christians:

> For such men are false apostles, deceitful workman, disguising themselves as apostles of Christ. And no wonder, for even Satan disguises himself as an angel of light. So, it is no surprise his servants also disguise

themselves as servants of righteousness. Their end will correspond to their deeds.

If we allow individuals to select what works for them, what seems right to them, and what feels right to them from any corroborating source, we will get different results and opposing positions. Everyone has individual biases and different experiences, or they interpret the same experiences differently. It comes down to the sources they use, the authorities they choose, and their individual character, integrity, and moral and ethical makeup.

Jesus was quite explicit in his warnings to naysayers and rebellious entities regarding choosing whatever appeals to you: "He who is not with me is against me and he who does not gather with me, scatters" (Matthew 12:30). His clarion call is decisive and clear; opposition, indifference, and neutrality separate all those who do not commit and submit to his sovereignty.

It may be hard for them to believe, but their pride manifests itself by believing and doing the very things that prevent them from bringing the peace and harmony we all seek.

There seems to be a dangerous misconception in both Christian and secular thinking, which the politically correct believe and promote—the idea that God's love and compassion, in the end, will overrule his demand for purity and obedience in all things and lifestyles. Reinhold Niebuhr, a twentieth-century German theologian, depicts our destructive theological liberalism as proclaiming and worshipping "a God without wrath who brought men without sin into a kingdom without judgment through the ministrations of a Christ without a cross."[1]

Christians discern that all human ethical standards are God-imposed, all truth is God-created and defined, and no human has or will reach God's required perfection to be called "good." As far as God is concerned, good intentions, coming from false beliefs being proffered by good people, are dead on arrival! Mocking God's truth or consequences is the height of arrogance.

Who are the rulers, and what represents human authorities? Every government and all human institutions, at their absolute best, have been corrupted. Evil disguises itself, choosing the manner that will get the most bang for its buck. Sometimes it is obvious (abortion); sometimes it is subtle, but it infiltrates and infuses social, legal, and political institutions to give it credibility and make it appear benign. Always, it undercuts all attempts at lifting humanity to a higher spiritual level. In the rare instances, where church and state hold authorities or institutions accountable for abortion or homosexuality or any number of entitlements or sinful activities, the rulers and selected authorities collaborate with other like-minded evil spiritual forces to relabel or redefine the evil as part of an acceptable human moral nature, and they attempt to legislate it as a human right.

A civil law or moral law that is broken without consequence or repercussion is, in effect, a flagrant violation of the law. Evil can promote a partial good or tangential right in the process of building up a counterstrike that destroys what truly is good or right. God sometimes allows evil a short leash but is always in control of it. However, as in Hitler, Stalin, and Mao, when evil finds a willing partner (person or political party), it unleashes its fury to the degree that God allows it.

We are living in a time of unprecedented wealth and corruption. "Good people" everywhere are becoming political pawns, in that they buy and sell truth, people, and principles for the right price and label. Their agenda is human-centered, human-created, and human-promoted. They incorporate a mixture of right's psychology and moral ambivalence about truth, relationships, and principles of ethical behavior. Contrived legal validation of that ambivalence seduces many into accepting alternatives, rather than Christian teaching and practices. Political correctness is founded on the proposition that the majority of "good people" in the United States can be influenced or bought without their feeling they are doing anything wrong.

Paraphrasing Judges 21:23, in our time today, everyone does what they are told is the right thing to do because the political party or government says it is politically correct. This orchestrated process is determined to leave God out of targeted transactions or relationships by substituting ourselves or our organizations as the good guys. We are attempting to do the impossible, trying to meet the needs of others on our terms and conditions; in effect, we are trying to cure them with unclean hands and unfaithful, separate agendas. Concisely, the evil that is within each of us reveals its true nature when we attempt to picture ourselves as champions of goodness and rights for others. In the process, we focus on what we can do and what our group or party can do, rather than on what God has already done and will do, if we follow his lead, not ours.

What we each see and interpret is subjective because each of us is subject to different influences and conditioning factors that, by various degrees, shape how we reason or interpret what we see and feel. Men and women see the same thing and experience it differently. Different racial makeups see, experience the same thing, and react differently or process differently, and on and on. They are all subject to innate, normal human biases.

The final question is, what do we use that is always objective and always right? The only possible answer is, something or someone that is not human. God, through his Son, Jesus, as revealed by the Holy Spirit, is the only universally objective source of all truth. Everything else is subject to human bias and subjective interpretation.

No one likes to hear they are not good, but the Bible, in numerous places, affirms and confirms our inner disposition as evil. Romans 3:10–18 exemplifies that assertion:

> None is righteous, no, not one; no one understands; no one seeks for God. All have turned aside; together they have become worthless; no one does good, not even one. Their throat is an open grave; they use their tongues to deceive. The venom of asps is under their lips. Their mouth is full of curses and bitterness. Their feet are swift to shed blood; in their paths are ruin and misery and the way of peace they have not known. There is no fear of God before their eyes.

Remember, this is God speaking through his servant Paul. These are divine words breathed from God's human mouthpiece.

The only things that last forever, that are eternal, are of God and from God. The author of Ecclesiastes, King Solomon, considered one of the wisest men who ever lived, shared what God revealed to him in his writings. The long and short of it was that God was eternal and everlasting, and everything God planned, timed, and purposed has been completed in the past and will be in the future, according to God's will and purpose.

Man, on the other hand, is temporal. Solomon reminds us of what is happening today, has already happened in the past, and that which is to come—it too has already happened. What man attempts to add or subtract to what God has purposed comes and goes, and God, over time, puts everything man screws up back in the proper balance and order. When politically correct moral autonomy becomes an embraced ideology and philosophy that counters God's intended purpose, it too is temporary, as God brings back what man repurposed to deny and defy in every age.

"Pride and prejudice" is more than a book title. It is inherent in each of us, whether we deny it or not. Who is so arrogant or prejudiced as to tell others that we are correct, we are right, and our pride is so oblivious to God's being in control that we cannot help ourselves? One party's theology or ideology incorporates personal moral autonomy as being a "correct" value or right; further, we decide what is real and what is an illusion in the moral atmosphere in our contemporary culture. Many of us are familiar with the quote, "Pride goes before a fall." In several places, Proverbs reinforces the damage that false pride does in our relationships with others and God. Here are several reference quotes from Proverbs:

> When pride comes, then comes disgrace, but with the humble is wisdom. (Proverbs 11:2)

> Everyone who is arrogant is an abomination to the Lord, be assured, he will not go unpunished. (Proverbs 16: 5)

> Pride goes before destruction, and a haughty spirit before a fall. (Proverbs 16:18)

> Many are the plans in the mind of a man, but it is the purpose of the Lord that will stand. (Proverbs 19:21)

The key words in this writing are *politically correct* and *moral autonomy*. We must answer these questions: is "correct" subject to the people that define it, which is always subjective bias, or is it "correct" because it corroborates the only possible objective standard—God's? Every person and organization has a "correct" understanding or view of an issue that they have collectively agreed upon and endorsed publicly. Is it right because they say so, or is it right because it works for them? "Correct" from any human origin is subject to biased error.

Democratic and Republican views posited as being "correct" can be opposite. What, if anything, makes something of a political or moral nature right or correct? We live under the same laws and constitutional constructs, yet there are numerous different versions of "correct" that are derived from interpreting them.

One dictionary definition of autonomy is, "the quality or condition of being self-governing, self-contained, independent of the laws of another state or government, the right of self-government." Do you notice the word self appears several times, and independent asserts that it is not tied to a particular existing standard? Autonomy defines its own standard to judge or assess someone or something, based on one's selected authority. To be correct or to assume you have autonomy, do you go to various sources or only one, so as not to create the possibility of conflict or error in interpreting?

Vanity of vanities—what self-determination can conceive; it wants to believe. Those who espouse moral autonomy or moral self-determination are persuaded that if there is a God, you can bargain with him; even better, you can help him change his mind to suit your purposes. Or, if there is no God, you can become godlike, control your own destiny, and live how you want. Millions are buying into that illusion.

The moral character and ethical condition of humankind is all over the spectrum. The Bible says we are all evil in God's sight. Most individuals disagree with that assessment and claim that each of us is a "good person." The overwhelming consensus is that we do the right thing most of the time, so the balance tips to the positive side. Malcolm Muggeridge, a twentieth-century Christian journalist from England, aligned his assessment with scripture as he stated, "The depravity of man is at once the most empirically verifiable reality but at the same time the most intellectually resisted fact."[2] He was influenced by the carnage and atrocities he was familiar with in both World Wars. The twentieth century was the most violent and depraved regarding violent war deaths and ideological destruction in humankind's history. You cannot dispute facts.

A case can be made that "good" people are fabricating false doctrines to support the "I'm okay; you're okay" liberal theology. "Ultimately evil is done not so much by evil people but by good people who do not know themselves and who do not probe deeply."[3] spoken by Reinhold Niebuhr, a German theologian in the mid-twentieth century. That assessment reinforces scriptural themes and reminds us to search our own characters and souls. Are we objective or subjective when we assess our characters using scriptural demands and commands as our core reference points? Does self-righteous morality grease the way for us to assume godlike authority? Are progressive, ungodly authorities spreading a false social gospel by distorting the letter or spirit of scripture? Is moral relativity or pragmatic theology a contributor to our guilt-free hypocrisy regarding abortion, homosexuality, entitlements, etc.?

While there are many people with a clear-cut position, pro or con, on abortion and homosexuality, many more think they can have it both ways and still maintain their sense of integrity. Taking the stance that having an open mind and adopting a live-and-let-live pragmaticism will lead to less conflict, they know if they take a hard position that requires a strong scriptural defense, things could get messy, so the pro-choice supporters believe they have covered their bases adequately and deserve a welcome from both camps. What they deserve is condemnation for having no grounded faith and a weak moral backbone.

The Old Testament speaks to God's indictment when he said, "The heart is deceitful above all things, and desperately sick (wicked); who can understand it?" (Jeremiah 17:9).

Jesus speaks to his judgment of the state of man:

> What comes out of a person is what defiles him. For from within, out of the heart of man, come evil thoughts, sexual immorality, theft, murder, adultery, coveting, wickedness, deceit, sensuality, envy, slander, pride, foolishness. All these evil things come from within, and they defile a person. (Mark 7:20–23)

We sometimes tend to concentrate on our actions or deeds at the expense of our words. While we can have a sense about a person's character "by his fruits"—that is, the results or consequences of his actions—words too are tabulated on the day of judgment. Listen to what Jesus shares with us in Matthew 12:36:

> I tell you, on the day of judgment people will give account
> for every careless word they speak, for by your words you
> will be justified and by your words you will be condemned.

Is that scary or what?

Digging deeper into the above, wicked speech, within itself, has the power to deceive or worsen a volatile situation. Worthless, indifferent words also have the capability to widen any existent gap. What we are expected to do is to graciously address differences and build up the person or relationship, when appropriate, where it is most needed. We each must learn when to hold and when to fold and to properly discriminate, from a righteous scriptural foundation, in a tone that lowers the contentiousness of a heated discussion.

One concern that must be addressed, when examining and deducing what the scripture is conveying, is if the key principles being derived are verifiable or can be corroborated by other scripture, or if something is read into them by reading between the lines.

Our principles are prone to be skewed by the lenses we look through that distort what we see, but if it is not what we want to see, we find ways to erroneously defend them. One of the biggest mistakes we make is in deriving a key principle from a less-than-principled source. We can look at scripture through the assistance of the Holy Spirit in helping us discern correctly what we are reading or seeing, or we can read into the scripture what is not there because of our use of a faulty, biased lens that sees through humanistic eyes. The secular or human-oriented lens can look at scripture and read into it what it needs to see to validate its principle. The morally blind seem to be misleading the spiritually lost into believing they are in control, and all is well.

The major problem that the politically correct have with any understanding of what God requires is the view that he is too restrictive and, in certain places and times, unfair or unjust when he singles out certain people and practices for doing what comes naturally to humans.

In other words, what the politically correct see as moral normal or valid socially acceptable behavior, God labels as sin. To counteract or mollify those differences, like all other human ideology or philosophy, they define and defend their version of truth by reading between the scriptural lines or by reading into the explicit, implicit possibilities. Like the serpent that tempted Adam and Eve, they ask the question, "Did God really say that or mean that?"

Conservative Christians, on the other hand, because they see it as godly defiant, only deserve or qualify for full moral autonomy when their beliefs and practices comply with progressive ideology. The separation of church and state has been hijacked by a contrived moral autonomy that expands the state's control over the church, denying it the role God intended—to supervise and administer his standards and directives that will ensure human compliance with Christ's.

The problem with moral autonomy is in the details. Who defines what is acceptable, correct, or true, and what political or moral authority has the audacity to tell everyone that their standard is the only acceptable one? The only standard for Christians is the Word and will of God, as revealed in scripture. Moral autonomists insist they fall outside the influence of scripture and are not held to the same standards because those standards were meant for ancient times and people, not modern, educated autonomists. The battle lines are drawn; on one side, we have fundamental humanism, and on the other, foundational divine truth.

When the rule of civil law clashes with Christian directives, your response will indicate where your loyalty lies. The state cannot replace or babysit for God, trying to be neutral to be fair. "Government for the people, by the people and of the people" is a great slogan for those who spout out the rule-of-law ideology, but it is not high on God's list of accurate statements, unless those who are governed trust and obey his words and, in fact, are being governed by his people, for his people, and are a government of his people. Boxing God into a corner or out of our government's politically correct vocabulary is an exercise in futility.

Most of us have heard the phrase, "The devil is in the details." Have you ever considered that the word *devil* is identified by how it is spelled? The five-letter word has within it a four-letter word that self-describes its meaning. What does that have to do with anything? Moral self-determination, affirmed by politically correct moral autonomy advocates, identifies their progressive ideology as godless or God-subordinated political fiat. *Fiat* is defined as an arbitrary decree, authorization, or sanction. The bottom line: it is arbitrarily or subjectively conditional to a decreed, authorized, or sanctioned refutation of scripture, promulgated by political arrogance and hypocrisy that poses as rational enlightenment.

Choice is the biggest political weapon in the "correct" arsenal. You are authorized to choose to believe what seems right to you, and you have the corresponding right to do what seems right to you. Who is going to argue with that? Certainly not the politically correct. But on the other side of the equation, make the wrong choice, and there will be consequences! Christians too must choose to stand up for Jesus or choose to acquiesce to the attractive offer of moral autonomy. For Christians and non-Christians, hear these chilling words of Christ:

> For whoever is ashamed of me and my words in this adulterous and sinful generation, of him will the Son of Man also be ashamed when he comes in the glory of his Father with the holy angels. Mark 8:38

Should a person of good character and integrity read into a scripturally explicit statement or firm historic ethical distinction a hidden, implicit interpretation that nullifies its explicitness? Should we look for a rational, circumstantial alternative that rounds off sharp edges or that makes the restrictions less cut-and-dried and more palatable? Why or why not?

If scripture is explicit, but we reason or rationalize, from a contemporary perspective, that there is wiggle room to read between the lines or to interpret it from a more fluid perspective, various forms of legalism tend to skew either the letter of the law, the spirit of the law, or both.

One perspective is where we believe or convince ourselves and others that our honorable deeds and good will, done with good intentions, can justify us before God. Another is that past moral traditions worked for the past, but today's traditions allow men's and women's consciences to be their guides and lend themselves to accepting greater equality and tolerance as a fixture in the new moral order. The problem with legalism is the increased tendency today to constantly look for ways to get around the intended spirit of the law without appearing to break it. By adapting it to fit the political ideology being promoted, we are obeying the letter of the law, while, in our hearts, we secretly defy God.

Examining and assessing values, morals, and authority from various sources requires an objective starting point. The initial problem for many individuals is, who or what best represents that? Proverbs 1:7 points us to the highest possible objective truth source—God: "The fear (reverence) of the Lord is the beginning of knowledge; fools despise wisdom and instruction." What person has the arrogance to claim another source of authority is superior? No doubt, some will try to justify an alternative political truth as equally sufficient and equally correct. What do you think? Can any humans honestly think they are able, of their own cognition and volition, to express objective truth, as revealed and lived by Jesus himself? Is anyone capable, always and places, of discerning objective truth and demonstrating it correctly?

How can you and I put our faith and good works into play in the most effective manner? While there are many responses, C. S. Lewis puts it this way:

> I have received no assurance that anything we can do will eradicate suffering. I think the best results are obtained by people who work quietly away at limited objectives, such as the abolition of the slave trade, or prison reform, or factory acts, or tuberculosis, not by those who think they can achieve universal justice, health, or peace. I think the art of life consists in tackling each immediate evil as well as we can.[4]

Human wisdom or human reason has failed to permanently solve human problems for thousands of years. Our presidential election every four years reveals that we have the same problems and have created new areas of contention that the candidate boasts he or she will fix if elected. The problems of poverty, discrimination, disrespect, lawlessness, sexual depravity, envy, Godly rebellion, and ingratitude have been with us forever. No one or no group has the power to provide any long-term fix or to eradicate any sinful activity. Only God can objectively address and resolve every human problem.

Elections are a matter of which is the lesser evil or which party will bring about God's greater good according to His will and purpose? Which candidate and which political party will more astutely listen to the Spirit's voice and use their position of authority to put into play what God purposes? Without the involvement of the Spirit, God's word and will are sure to be broken and the election process will continue to drive individuals and institutions to look for answers in all the wrong places!

CHAPTER 11

Divine Dependence or Political Independence?

A compelling argument can be made that there are very few if any American moral values regarding a socially divisive issue which are scripturally negative in both the letter and spirit intended, that are nationally accepted and promoted. Even when they are specific and explicit, there are regional, state, or local values that ascribe to a variety of moral values, religious convictions, or acceptable positions. Every person has his or her priorities that are tailored to meet their most pressing needs. When politicians or moralists tell you to vote American values, they mean their values and priorities When politicians passionately say it is for the public good, and everyone should get on board, they promote what they determine is in their best interest, the party's best interest, or the best interest of the identity group they support, not necessarily yours. In many cases, they do not have a clue or sincerely care about your individual needs and wants, unless your position or party affiliation coincides with theirs. If you are a Christion trying to faithfully follow the scripture instruction intended that does not agree with their political agenda, too bad; you are wrong!

Moral autonomy granted by the politically correct, in varying degrees of acceptability, aligns individual free will with party ideology, dedicated to and validated by political fiat. The intent is twofold: to establish moral autonomy as a counterweight to godly authority and, to separate human functioning from divine influence. By molding social morality to "correct" standards that appeal to one's baser nature—what the politically correct determine to be moral normal—millions are given the green light to define and defend their various appetites or passions as simply acceptable, normal human behavior. The conundrum is this: when motivation and intention are primarily human centered and directed but fall outside historic Christian guidelines and acceptance, is it moral or right, considering God's standards? Will it hold up to Spirit-inspired scriptural scrutiny?

Pandering to permissive lifestyles grants identity groups godlike authority to violate scripture. It frequently evolves into an ungodly partnership of moral and political protocol. Sexual license grows exponentially when past sexual perversion and premarital sex, which were seen nationally as taboo, are now nationally moral normal, and the chaste are moral misfits. We live in a moral atmosphere where varying degrees of indiscriminate tolerance systemically presents itself as progressive, social enlightenment. If you were to promote a slogan that best represented the moral and political alliance that we are seeing in most of our elections, it would be something like, "Vote for me, and I'll set you free!" By validating scriptural violations, we are setting ourselves up as moral misfits.

The purpose going forward—the motivation and intent—is to disconnect or disassociate moral autonomy from more restrictive historic ethical standards in favor of contemporary accommodation and compromise of watered-down integrity, honor, and truth. Offering something for everyone, without corresponding limitations and restrictions posed by scriptural foundations, is a moral license to sin.

Scripture, from beginning to end, has a core thread running through it. Human pride, arrogance, and rebellion in every generation separates and destroys God's desired relationship with all humankind. Each man or woman who seeks their own way as they break away from God's authority seeks to disown or disavow God's authority and embrace idols of their choosing in attempts to satisfy their lusts or passions. Constructing new rights and entitlements allows them free rein to indulge at will.

Every human is guilty of sin and is guilty as sin, period. Anyone who denies that inherent human attribute is a liar. But all humans play down their guilt and present themselves as better than they really are. The lack of shame, guilt, remorse, and repentance compound sin, and the resultant evil finds a path to expand its hold.

Any so-called "truth" or "right" that circumvents or undercuts the required sacrifices, disciplines, or discernment demanded by God, in any given social or moral issue, ceases to be true or right the moment it becomes a force unto itself, outside of or independent of scripturally required obedience.

The politics of customizing morality through institutional indoctrination and follow-up legal validation is fabricated and designed to create the illusion that human values assigned by the politically correct agree with godly virtues. In other words, "corrected" human moral values, preached, and practiced as politically approved, are adopted as godlike virtues with which everyone can get on board. The bane of godly integrity, honor, and truth is human integrity, honor, and truth! In that they are dismissive of any deviation from orthodox scriptural interpretation and practice, the politically correct tweak the negative to look less disconcerting than it is, and they dismiss or diminish the relevance of the required positive Christian attributes as relics of the past historic orthodoxy that no longer applies to modern people.

Jesus's statement in Matthew 5:17–19 warns us of the importance of obeying God's law and fulfilling it:

> Do not think that I came to destroy the law or the Prophets. I did not come to destroy but to fulfill. For truly I say to you, until heaven and earth pass away, not an iota, not a dot, will pass from the Law until all is accomplished. Therefore whoever relaxes one of the least of these commandments and teaches others to do the same will be called least in the kingdom of heaven; but whoever does and teaches them, will be great in the kingdom of heaven.

Whenever you attempt to elevate the characteristics of any human ideology to godlike status, while also failing to acknowledge God in the process, it becomes fundamental idolatry. Excessive or obsessive adoration or worship of anything or anyone independent of God, which circumvents God or is humanistic by design, has within it the seeds of idolatry. Progressive humanism, through coordinated political intimidation or fundamental institutional change, is the result. It morphs into a catalyst that blames, shames, and disdains all who fail to bow down to its authority. As that becomes publicly and morally entrenched, just like in past ages, God will either give them over to their lusts or arrogance and let them receive their due reward or send someone or something to warn them of impending destruction. Either way, there will be a price to pay for every degree of insubordination.

Humanism is the elephant in the room that neither the politically correct nor Christians can evade. Its inherent pervasiveness is such that it is, front and center, an instinctive part of every conversation and activity, no matter how much we might try to control its influence. The dictionary definition of *humanism* is "a doctrine or attitude concerned chiefly with human beings and their values, capacities, and achievements. A cultural and intellectual movement of the Renaissance that emphasized secular concerns."

The conflict that is eternally present is how we respond to politically correct or socially correct strains of humanism. It is there, and no one with any degree of integrity can deny its existence and influence. What we each must confront is how deep it infiltrates our human experience and whether we choose to embrace it or subdue it. Since no one can fully control it, no one, of their own volition, has the power to hold back its sway.

To mitigate the hostility and mudslinging in any moral or political debate, the Serenity Prayer, attributed to the theologian Reinhold Niebuhr, would seem to fit a neutral but equally acceptable beginning point for all sides. Leave behind any arrogance or feeling of superiority over others, and incorporate the necessary wisdom required within the prayer as we consider its power to reflect a godly, equitable disposition in all disputes. An old Turkish proverb puts its stamp of approval on the importance of wisdom when it states, "Fear an ignorant man more than a lion." Ignorance and its frequently resultant arrogance often prevent the higher nature of human capability from exercising greater degrees of integrity, honor, and responsible behavior, when confronted with emotional social and moral issues.

Serenity Prayer

God grant me the serenity to accept the things I cannot change, the courage to change the things I can, and the wisdom to know the difference. Living one day at a time, enjoying one moment at a time, accepting hardship as a pathway to peace.

If you cannot win someone over to your point of view or political position by way of your lifestyle, personal conduct, or self-control, could it be seen by another as hypocrisy when you claim moral superiority without demonstrating it? If you must intimidate or force others by whatever means possible to accept your truth concerning any issue, there must be a flaw or self-serving interest that prevents another from seeing the superiority you claim is on your side. Time has a way of proving or disproving something's integrity, honor, or truth and whether it demonstrates any superiority or inferiority vis-à-vis a competing stance.

A neutral starting point for both sides to consider is the Beatitudes, as written in what is often referred to as the Sermon on Mount in the New Testament book of Matthew 5:2–12. Here, we see the ethics or highest morality of the kingdom of God, as compared to the varying moralities of any competing human kingdoms or institutions. Everyone should be reminded that humans, at their best, still come up short of God's standards. No one should be bent out of shape when scripture reminds us that our depravity can never rise above humanism's inherent bent to defy or deny God's holiness and justice.

> And he (Jesus) opened his mouth and taught them, saying:
> "Blessed are the poor in spirit, for theirs is the kingdom of heaven.
> "Blessed are those who mourn, for they shall be comforted.
> "Blessed are the meek, for they shall inherit the earth.
> "Blessed are those who hunger and thirst for righteousness, for they shall be satisfied.
> "Blessed are the merciful, for they shall receive mercy.
> "Blessed are the pure in heart, for they shall see God.
> "Blessed are the peacemakers, for they shall be called sons of God.
> "Blessed are those who are persecuted for righteousness's sake, for theirs is the kingdom of heaven.

"Blessed are you when others revile you, persecute you, and utter all kinds of evil against you falsely on my account. Rejoice and be glad, for your reward is great in heaven, for so they persecuted the prophets who were before you.

Obviously, many will disagree with the above assessment or will be outright angry in insisting that the scripture above reflects negatively on the politically correct. So let us look at the Beatitudes, line by line, at the motivation and intent of the words and line of thought Jesus used to explain what is required of each of us. Take a moment to compare how you and the politically correct or progressively enlightened might stack up against the stiff expectations incorporated into Jesus's teaching.

Poor in spirit describes those who recognize they are spiritually destitute, a moral poverty in which you humble yourself and admit your sinful nature

Those who mourn over their sin and other's evil, who recognize they have failed to give or acknowledge the proper glory or reverence due God will be rewarded

Meek as a view or attitude of humility and submission to God's will sets the proper relationship with God

Hunger and thirst for righteousness designates those who seek God's righteousness based on his standards, not human standards, or human righteousness.

Those who recognize the wonder of God's *mercy* toward them, its magnitude, are to treat others as God has treated them, knowing they cannot earn his mercy, nor do they deserve it.

The pure in heart can only attain that state of being by and through the intervention of the Holy Spirit that enables them to receive and see God through their faith.

Peacemakers, not peace lovers, is the correct emphasis. These are the children of God, who alone can bring together man under the Fatherhood of God.

Persecuted for righteousness's sake—God's infused righteousness; he grants to the followers of Christ who are intentionally discriminated against and targeted because of their faithfulness and obedience to him.

Speaking evil against you falsely—Christ rewards those faithful who endure slander and false accusations on his account.

The Canons of Dort forthcoming from the Synod of Dort, held in 1618–19 under the auspices of the Dutch Reformed Church, are used by Dr. Robert Godfrey as a background to give Christians insight, comfort and confidence on the sovereignty and saving grace God provides believers:

> The reality that some people are given faith by God in time, while others are not given faith, proceeds from God's eternal decree. "He knows His works from eternity" (Acts 15:18; Eph. 1:11). According to this decree, He graciously softens the hearts of the elect, however hard, and inclines them to believe. He also leaves the non-elect according to His just judgment in their wickedness and hardness of heart. This decree most powerfully shows us God's profound, merciful, yet also just distinction among people equally lost. This decree of election and reprobation is revealed in the Word of God. And although the perverse, impure, and unstable twist it to their own destruction, it gives inexpressible comfort to holy and pious souls.[1]

Each day, most of us are confronted with choices that impact our present or future. Those choices often affect others as well. When we make a choice at any time, at that moment it seems to be the best one; our mental and physical states of being agree it is correct for that circumstance. That is normal. But before we exercise the choice, do we consider the moral or ethical ramifications of how it impacts others or might put them at risk?

Faithful Christians believe that scripture is our highest authority, not the church. When the church is at odds with scripture, it flails, but scripture prevails. When the politically correct digress from scripture, it seems as if the squeakiest wheels prevail. Whether over time or suddenly, identity groups frequently force their agenda to the top of the political platform, pressuring the party to make it the new correctness or acceptable morality. Can that be equated to the tail wagging the dog?

If its party approved, and if it fits our social-issues agenda, it is morally acceptable. That sums up what some see as the new and progressive liberal agenda that is used to remove old restrictions and stigmas from our former ethical and political values. Notice the word *ethical* was used, not moral. Ethical in the purest sense is what should be or what is required, according to God's instructions in scripture. Ethical is established scriptural precedence or, better yet, fixed by God, not subject to human change. Moral is always subjective at any place or time as to what is currently acceptable by those defining it. From a biblical view, much of what is moral (acceptable) today is not ethical.

In the past, the proper attitude concerning differences of opinion was, "I disapprove of what you say but will defend your right to say it." Today, the typical politically correct response would be, "I disapprove of what you say. It offends me; therefore, stop saying it." The French writer Charles Péguy dealt with the same problem, as he noted, "It will never be known what acts of cowardice have been motivated by the fear of not looking sufficiently progressive."[2]

God raises up the good and bad leaders of our nation and all nations. He determines who rules and the timing of their rule, as Isaiah 40:22–24 reminds us:

> It is he who sits above the circle of the earth and its inhabitants are like grasshoppers; who stretches out the heavens like a curtain and spreads them like a tent to dwell in; who brings princes to nothing and makes the rulers of the earth as emptiness. Scarcely are they planted, scarcely sown, scarcely has their stem taken root in the earth, when he blows on them, and they wither, and the tempest carries them off like stubble.

There is not one social issue, one truth, that God considers unresolved or a problem. There is no list of problems that God must rethink or for which he must redo his truths that he set in motion and settled at creation.

To the Trinity, everything is clear, every truth is uncontestable, and every Spirit-inspired revelation testifies to that same divine discernment.

What is truth? Whose truth really is *the truth*? How do you know? Does truth change over time? These are age-old questions. Scripture states that God's power, majesty, justice, love, and holiness are the same today, yesterday, and tomorrow. If that is true, then as Christians and scripture confirm, all corresponding truth relating to each is the same today, yesterday, and tomorrow. Since all truth is derived from God's present authority (and his authority is always present), we can confidently say that truth does not change. It is definable because he proclaimed and defined it through scripture. It is defensible because his Son gave witness and explanation for it, and it is dependable because it exists independently, outside the reach of human attempts or ability to coerce or subvert it.

The matter of whose truth is a moot point if you accept there is no separate objective truth that exists outside or inside God's authority. There are certainly different understandings or interpretations, but there can only be one highest objective truth.

Certain politically correct authorities want you to believe that relativism, pragmatism, and subjective reasoning are the best determinants of what is right for you and our culture. By using a social consensus or political majority as the statistical moral norm, the politically correct want us to believe that their one-sided subjective data or logic that leads to false correlations prove that the new normal morality is now the new correct or normal ethical standard. If you accept any false correlation between morality and ethics, based on subjectivism, you are relying on "cooked" truth and have become seduced into accepting what is scripturally invalid as the new norm. *Radical corruption* would better describe what relativism, pragmatism, and situational ethics have in common. Without fixed, unchangeable core values, everything is subject to violation.

One widely respected theologian, R. C. Sproul, the former president of Ligonier Ministries and a prolific writer and author of numerous books on Reformed Christianity, helps to clarify the above in his book *How Should I Live in This World?*

> Ethics is a normative science, searching for the principal
> foundations that prescribe obligations or "oughtness."

Morality is a descriptive science, concerned with "isness" and the indicative. Ethics defines what people ought to do, morals describe what people actually do. When morality is identified with ethics, the descriptive becomes the normative and the imperative is swallowed by the status quo. This creates a kind of "statistical morality." In this schema, the good is determined by the normal and the normal is determined by the statistical average. The "norm" is discovered by an analysis of the normal, or by counting noses. Conformity to that norm then becomes the ethical obligation. It works like this:

Step 1. We compile an analysis of statistical behavior patterns, such as those integral to the groundbreaking Kinsey Reports of the twentieth century. If we discover that most people are participating in premarital sexual intercourse, then we declare such activity "normal."

Step 2. We move quickly from the normal to a description of what is authentically "human." Humanness is defined by what humans do. if the normal human engages in premarital sexual intercourse, we conclude such activity is normal and therefore "good."

Step 3. The third step is to declare patterns that deviate from the normal to be abnormal, inhuman, and inauthentic. In this schema, chastity becomes a form of deviant sexual behavior, and the stigma is placed on the virgin rather than on the non-virgin.

Statistical morality operates according to the following syllogism:

Premise A—the normal is determined by statistics.

Premise B—the normal is human and good.

Premise C—the abnormal is inhuman and bad.[3]

Situational ethics is another infamous ploy that man embraces—the philosophy that right or wrong is fluid, according to circumstances and context. A mindset that insists pragmatic individual judgment should be the determining factor has great appeal to the masses and is given wide latitude in a live-and-let-live society. We are all searching for the truth—not *our* truth, not someone else's truth, and surely not what passes as political truth. No, we want to say, with unshakable confidence and absolute assurance, that what we understand to be the truth, what we discern as the truth, is indeed the *truth*. The intensity of our search, and the perseverance of our efforts and the processes we use to obtain objective facts as supporting evidence will take us a long way. But there is more to truth than facts or gathered evidence. Our ability to sort it out, to differentiate, requires more than institutional, scientific, or legal authoritative truth. It demands that the arrived-at truth is universal, not local, not regional, and not subject to change, time, or political environment. It stands alone on its own merit, its own unassailability, and its own proven historic authenticity. There is only one place to which you can look and find ultimate truth—and that is God.

This increased identity-group demand for some sort of political action now begs the question: why wasn't the pent-up anger and angst addressed before it became a nationally divisive moral issue?

If something was stewing or percolating over time, what was the catalyst that drew enough attention to it to address it, one way or the other? Where, in any moral or social issue, is the tipping point that forces either positive or negative political intervention? What determines which direction the moral wind blows? Should the identity group's passion, the majority view, the legal scrutiny, the leaning of the ruling political party, or scriptural obedience take precedence?

The scriptural problem with the "correct" position is that God's sovereignty is *absolute,* and his adjudication of legal and moral standards are not subject to human wisdom or reasoning. No one and nothing can overcome, change, or defeat his laws or authority. Yet the politically correct seem to think their free will—their autonomy—is outside God's authority and is not limited by it or even subject to it. They have convinced themselves and others that human institutions and governments are superior to any scriptural influence and that God has no special rights or authority to override theirs.

Christianity's heart and soul are God's truth and grace and our gratitude that he has set us free. Our attitude of gratitude reveals itself by confessing our sins and by our humble submission, fervent prayers, and actions that will bring honor and glory to Christ for his ultimate sacrifice in granting us eternal life. Scripture alone, in and of itself, through the revelation of the Holy Spirit, contains God's Word of life, allowing us to defeat death. Our religions, spirituality, human-rights exhortations, even our goodness or correct thinking cannot save us or give us abundant life.

Whether or not you are a Christian, knowing the truth and all that it requires is not enough. In James 2:19, we read, "Even the demons believe— and shudder." The key for God and you is this: do you embrace it and love it? Does your faith lead you to proclaim it and witness to it? The awful truth for those who cannot or will not be read in 2 Thessalonians 2:9–12:

> The coming of the lawless one is by the activity of Satan with all power and false signs and wonders, and with all wicked deception for those who are perishing, because *they refused to love the truth and so be saved. Therefore, God sends them a strong delusion so that they may believe what is false*, in order that all may be condemned who did not believe the truth but has pleasure in unrighteousness. (Italics added)

John Newton's "Amazing Grace" exemplifies why Christians do not cower or bow down to correct thinking that is so overwhelmingly prevalent in this world. Meditate on these powerful but comforting words that resonate in every true believer's heart and soul: "Twas grace that taught my heart to fear and grace my fears relieved."

The reference or source of authority from here on will be the necessity, sufficiency, and authority of scripture, as revealed by the Holy Spirit that addresses our needs and hopes in the here and now and in eternity. The Westminster Confession of Faith 1.10 and 1.4 will help guide us in our searching and understanding as it declares and clarifies the following:

> The supreme judge by which all controversies of religion are to be determined and all decrees of councils, opinions of ancient writers, doctrines of men and private spirits are to be examined. and in whose sentence, we are to rest; can be no other but the Holy Spirit speaking in Scripture

> The authority of Holy Scripture, for which it ought to be believed and obeyed, dependent not upon the testimony of any man or church, but wholly upon God (who is truth itself), the Author and therefore, it is to be received, because it is the Word of God.[4]

Christianity is not so much about religious positions, human rights, goodness, or correct thinking; it is about God's core truth and grace, passed down for two thousand years through Jesus, the apostles, and the discipleship of the believers. It is a Spirit-inspired truth-and-grace revelation, confirmed in divine writing—scripture! It is a truth that requires public demonstration via words and actions that lift Christ as the Son of God; a faith that calls us to witness to Christ's words and actions in every situation where it is contested and distorted. It is acknowledging God's grace that we do not deserve and expressing our eternal gratitude in the way that we live to honor him.

Scripture states that we were created by God to exult in glorifying him above everything else, as all other glory and praise is fleeting and ultimately does not satisfy the human quest for meaning and purpose. As individuals and as a nation, we are all guilty of seeking glory in ourselves, someone, or something, due to our false worship of human philosophies and standards. We have created and worshiped other images, gods, and authorities, thus breaking several of the Ten Commandments. God's instructions are clear and his warnings stern:

> You shall have no other gods (idols, authorities) before me, you shall not make for yourself a carved image or any likeness of anything that is in heaven above or that is in the earth beneath or that is in the water under the earth. You shall not bow down to them or *serve them*, for I am a jealous God, visiting the iniquity of the fathers on the children to the third and fourth generation of those who hate me," but showing steadfast love to thousands of those who love me and *keep my commandments*. Exodus 20:3–6, (italics added)

Some believe there is no moral or natural law, but if there is, they are not bound by it. Others might say no one can prove there is or is not a God; therefore, no one authority has all the answers or ability to save or condemn anyone. Because we want to believe we are in control of our destiny and that the various beliefs and religious persuasions are similar in nature and are equal in the eyes of the law, we each have the option to pick one or more authorities to guide us in our moral and spiritual journeys. The belief is that, in the end, if we try hard to do the right thing and live a good life, we will be rewarded with eternal life in some form.

What do most of us do? We see what various religious, political, or moral authorities offer on what to believe and practice. We take from various sources what we consider to be the correct moral standards and lifestyles that appeal to our personalities or mindsets. We then use specific authorities that we trust or respect, which are on what we consider as the right track. They become our defense reference to justify what we say and do. Since many opposing opinions and beliefs are accepted as part of the human experience, we all cannot be right or ethically correct. How can so many variations of truth and so many sources of authority that differ on social morality be considered valid by one group and invalid by another? Is there an ultimate source that is universally in control and has all the answers to our problems? Have you found it?

If so, what or who is it? If not, it does not matter what you or anyone thinks or believes is true or right because one view is as good as another if there is no rhyme or reason to human existence. From my perspective, each of us is responsible for developing an ethically coherent defense of our sources of authority, their foundational precepts and values that justify a particular view or action, and a logical system of checks and balances that ensures, as much as possible, that everyone receives just reward for their honor, integrity, or merit or receives discipline and punishment for their sloth, lust, or indifference to everything or everyone that is motivated to live a life of purity, honesty, and obedience, as required by a just universal presence.

The problem we cannot seem to resolve is the *who* or *what* decides or defines universally correct values and actions that apply equally to all people, regardless of whether they accept them or believe them. In other words, we all must live with the premise that humans will never come to an agreement or accept a one-size-fits-all truth imposed by any human authority. Since that has been proven over thousands of years of human history and experience, either there is no hope for universal peace or justice, or we will have to look outside human ability to reason or use logic, which so far, has failed miserably.

The widespread and widely held belief that men and women are basically good at heart and will normally do the right thing is the foundation for promoting moral autonomy. The politically correct give their faithful followers the benefit of the doubt as to their goodness, intentions, and integrity. In their minds, there is no one right way to do things, but if you do them the "correct" way, they assure you that they have your back, and you are free to go your own way, regardless of any negative consequences that might be associated with the belief or act. If you subscribe to their system, you will worship or revere what is human, you will sanctify the system that supports your godlike ability to decide right and wrong, and you will proactively reject all other ethical systems that reject your arrogance.

Is social justice the same as moral justice? What happens when differing political viewpoints determine it is not? If social justice or moral justice do not match up with scriptural justice, how do you determine which is correct and which should be applied? All human-oriented justice, legal or moral, is subject to personal or political bias, framed by civil, criminal, or constitutional law. Each component evolves over time, subject to the quality of the moral character of those who advocate change. Can a subjectively grounded ideology stand scriptural scrutiny and change its spots to become objective, equitable justice, as defined and demanded by God?

In our day, social justice is equated with moral justice because it is frequently oriented around social equality, as defined by the politically correct. In other words, what is seen as correct is determined by what is equally fair and equally right in the eyes of the morally correct ideology, not scriptural justice. When social justice or equality is assigned to scriptural violations, Christians have the dilemma of siding with legal justification or scriptural faithfulness. Are you guiding and directing others to sanctify and obey God's laws first or human laws?

The church is tasked with speaking God's truth to the lost and unfaithful Christians. All sins have negative consequences but what needs to be emphasized is that there are no sins that can prevent you from gaining heaven. John Piper, a prominent Reformed theologian, puts it this way, "No sin must keep a person out of heaven. What keeps a person out of heaven is the unrepentant pursuit of sin, and the rejection of God's provision for its forgiveness in Jesus's death and resurrection."[5] Sins can be forgiven, the rejection of Christ cannot.

Humans have determined, falsely, that human autonomy affords us greater authority over deciding what we believe is true and what is right, rather than what God requires. Every sin is worthy of punishment. It is here where God's patient grace allows us to repent. In our depravity, we determine there is no need to change our attitude or lifestyle. In our earthly existence and dying destination, we receive God's justice for that depravity, for what amounts to cosmic treason. Justice for some; grace to others. The difference is the indwelling of the Holy Spirit, given to those who receive his grace. Grace alone, predestined by God, is the ultimate factor. We do not deserve it, but—thanks be to God—we can eternally worship his glory and holiness! How or why God chooses some over others is not explicitly described in scripture, but we do know it is his right and good pleasure, as the Creator of all things human, to allow or ordain whatever happens, according to his will and purpose.

Idolatry is a word we often associate with primitive cultures. If you are Christian, you know that the Old Testament has many situations and environments where idolatry was the foundation of the people's beliefs. The Ten Commandments speaks to that when it says, "You shall have no other gods, before me." What is forgotten in our day is that a political ideology, moral fixation, or social movement all can be idolatrous. Anything we put before or above God or that we prioritize ahead of our commitment to Christian theology and practice, in God's view, is an idol.

Jesus himself made the point that having the Spirit inside you was better than his being beside you:

> Nevertheless I tell you the truth. It is to your advantage that I go away; for if I do not go away, the Helper will not come to you; but if I go, I will send Him to you. (John 16:7)

That is both a startling premise and promise. We need to rethink our understanding of the importance Jesus placed on having the Spirit within us to have a right relationship with God and all our other relationships. It is the Spirit within us that correctly and faithfully interprets and applies the warnings and promises of scripture so that our responses to social and political issues are more his and less ours.

What has transpired in our day is the newly allowed freedoms and entitlements have unleashed the unrestrained identity groups to indulge their baser natures under the guidance and approval of the politically correct party. In many instances, abortion, homosexuality, and mass entitlements have become a forum for moral transitions, moving from the divine to the perverse. Moral accountability is no longer in fashion for millions. By degrees, "correct" morality has become pragmatic, pluralistic, and ideological equal; worship who or what you want and live accordingly. Many are indulging in moral depravity and sanctifying those who practice it. Today, rights and freedoms granted by the state that fall outside scriptural requirements—promoted as equally acceptable—should be called out as idolatry!

Finally, human rights and human correctness must always be subordinate to Christian standards of obedience. There are no unresolvable social issues that cannot be resolved with obedience. Abortion, homosexuality, transgender issues, addiction problems, violence, entitlements, etc., reflect that individuals and society prefer their truth, their perspectives, to God's. The good news, though, for Christians is that God's truth will march to his drumbeat, regardless of whether the band members march in step. If you are marching to your own beat, you might want to consider that the band leader created all the instruments, knows the parade route, and expects every member to play in the key to obedience.

The idea that any state, whatever its political makeup or will, can solve social or ethical issues by legislation, economic programs, redistribution of wealth, or special entitlements is pure dreaming. Civilization has been around for seven or eight thousand years, and not one nation on earth has ever been able to permanently overcome its internal or external shortcomings by money, military power, political skills, scientific prowess, or judicial renderings. All attempts, even with the best intentions, are only cosmetic when underlying, required, godly core values are short-circuited by applying human wisdom, motivation, and resources for curing or overcoming individual or nationalist sins.

There are no human cures using human ways and means alone. There is no hope that human nature can rise above itself and become more godlike of its own volition. The best of governments, the best of motivations, are doomed to varying degrees of failure right from the start when God is not part of the process. The only viable way to become more godlike is to live more Christlike.

Without the Spirit's prompting and empowerment, everything originating from humans is subject to God's built-in ethical buffers or checks and balances, which reduce any good intended from human originators because of its sinful association. To God, liberal and conservative ideologies are proof positive that humans, left to their own devices, will seek to separate themselves, by decree or degree, from God's core truths. God's ordained greatest good and supreme values require submission and humility. Humans, by their inherent moral disposition, will forever seek to find the ways and means to get around God's values. They will attempt to justify it by declaring their own separate version of what is true as equally valid.

The fact that God loves you does not mean you are saved or safe. You may be a good person and a compassionate being. You might be obeying all the laws of man, an upstanding citizen serving others, yet that is not enough. You may be sincere in what you believe is morally right but that does not put you in God's good grace. All of the above are not enough. You can't earn it, you can't achieve it on your own. Scripture is clear that Jesus alone is your only hope for your salvation. In John 14:1,6,11, Jesus, speaking to his disciples, emphasizes "Let not your heart be troubled. Believe in God, believe also in me. I am the way, the truth and the life. No one comes to the Father, except through me. Believe me that I am in the Father and the Father is in me." The Spirit alone draws you to Jesus. It is God who sends the Spirit. Ask, better yet, pray He will open your heart to see, hear and embrace His truth.

Just as scripture declares there is only one way to enter heaven and achieve salvation (despite what you hear from liberal theologians and moral autonomists), there is only one scripturally valid way to seek, find, and practice the core truth of any matter—and that is through the revelation and power of the Holy Spirit. There are no human laws or culturally accepted morals that have the power, wisdom, or eternal staying power of the Spirit. Either you do it the right way (through the Spirit), or you do it the wrong way (through your own devices). One way or the other, you will discover that when God is not the genesis or driving force of any doctrine or pursuit, Murphy's Law will follow!

I pray that the Spirit empowers you to triumph over a worldly spirit in all. Know the truth; it defines and refines what is right in the sight of the Lord. Ask the Spirit to empower you and guide you as you put the truth into play. Think of God as a loving Father, as a holy God. No matter where you are in your faith journey, scripture tells us to trust and obey the letter and spirit of the wisdom revealed in it and in the process of that discernment, you will find the peace that passes all understanding! Amen.

God wants to bless you. But, His blessing comes with a cost. He will bless those who bless Him and his son, Jesus. God's covenant with Israel reached its fulfillment with the coming of Christ. Our salvation today depends on our fulfilling Christ's requirement that we believe, trust and obey. There is no other way. For those who trust and obey the new covenant with Christ and all that entails, the following words of blessing and comfort given to Israel by Moses through the Spirit of God in Numbers 6: 24-26 hold promise for us today. These words of comfort and blessing given to the people of Israel are used by Christians today as a benediction; depicting a gracious God who blesses faithful Christians with "the peace that passes all understanding."

The Lord bless you and keep you;

The Lord make his face to shine upon you and be gracious to you;

The Lord lift up his countenance upon you and give you peace.

NOTES

Chapter 1

1   Westminster Confession of Faith, *The Reformation Study Bible*, Reformation Trust Publishing, Sanford, Fl, (2015). 2436.

2   Ibid.,2436

3   Ibid.,2436-2437

4   Daniel Webster. (n.d.). AZQuotes.com Retrieved April 01, 2022, from AZQoutes.com Web site: https.//www.azquotes.com/quote/1310763

5   Adolf Hitler. (n.d.). AZ Quotes.com. Retrieved April 1, 2022, from AZQotes.com Web site: https://www.azquotes.com/quote/566434

6   Vladimir Lenin Quote. (n.d.). BrainyQuote.com. Retrieved April 1, 2022, from BrainyQuote.com Web site: https://www.brainyquote.com/quotes/vladimir_lenin-153238

7   Rev. Burk Parsons, "The Religion of Secularism," *Tabletalk*, Ligonier Ministries, Sanford, FL (March 2017).

8   William Voegeli, "The Case Against Liberal Compassion"-*Imprimis*, Hillsdale, MI, (October 2014)

9   Bruce Bawer, "The Victims Revolution: The Rise of Identity Politics and the Closing of the Liberal Mind," The *New York Times*, (12/23/2015).

10 Mark Lilla, "The Problem of Identity Politics and its Solution," Imprimis, Hillsdale, MI (November 2017).

Chapter 2

1   Attributed to Elihu Root, secretary of state for President Roosevelt; secretary of war for President McKinley; 1912 Nobel Peace Prize.

2   J. Gresham Machen, *Christianity and Liberalism,* Macmillan, New York, NY, (1923).

3 Attributed to Benito Mussolini, "Mussolini on the Corporate State–Political Research," 1932, https://www.politicalresearch.org/2005/01/12/mussolini-corporate-state.

4 Edmond Phelps, *Mass Flourishing: How Grassroots Innovation Created Jobs, Challenges and Change,* Princeton Univ. Press, (2013).

5 Charles Spurgeon, *Spurgeon on the Holy Spirit,* Whitaker House, New Kensington, PA. (2000).128

6 William Barclay, *The Daily Study Bible Series* Westminster Press, Philadelphia, PA (1975), 386.

7 Rev. Jason Stellman, *Tabletalk,* Ligonier Ministries, Sanford, FL (February 2011).21

8 John Calvin, "John Calvin Quotes about Soul," A-Z Quotes, https://www.azquotes.com/author/2355-John-Calvin/tag/soul.

9 James Allen, *As a Man Thinketh,* Hallmark Cards, Inc. Kansas City, MO (1968).

Chapter 3

1 Albert Einstein Quotes, (n.d.). BrainyQuote.com. Retrieved April 1, 2022, fromBrainyQuote.com Web site: https.//brainyquote.com/quotes/albert-einstein-130982

2 William Barclay, *The Daily Bible Study Series*: Westminster Press. Philadelphia, PA 1975, 176.

3 Ibid., 202.

4 Charles Stanley Quotes. (n.d.). BrainyQuote.com. Retrieved April 2, 2022, from BrainyQuote.com Web site: https://www.brainyquote.com/quotes/charles-stanley-181227

5 A. J Tozer, *The Pursuit of God: The Human Thirst for the Divine,* Christian Publications, December 1982

6 C. S. Lewis, *God in the Dock,* William B. Erdman Publishing Co., Grand Rapids, MI (1983). 109.

7 C. S. Lewis, *Mere Christianity,* Barnes and Noble, New York, NY, (1952). 51

8 Corrie Ten Boom, "The Safest Place to Be is in the Center of God's Will," Corrie ten Boom Quotes. https:"quotefancy.com/quotes/789863

9 Martin Niemoller: "First They Came for the Socialists," Holocaust Encyclopedia. United States Holocaust Memorial Museum. Retrieved July 25, 2018

10 "John Calvin: Commentary on Habakkuk, Zephaniah, Haggai," Calvin's Commentaries, Book 29, Christian Classics Ethereal Library, June 2009

Chapter 4

1   Dr. Justin Holcomb, "Ethics of Personhood," Tabletalk, Ligonier Ministries, Sanford, FL (March 2013).

2   Charles Spurgeon, *Spurgeon on the Holy Spirit,* Whitaker House, New Kensington, PA (2000). 55,56

3   Attributed to St. Augustine, Microsoft Bing, https://loveand knowledgeblog. wordpress.com/2015/11/19.

4   G. K. Chesterton, *Orthodoxy,* Waking Lion Press, (July 2008)

5   G. K. Chesterton, *The Trees of Pride,* Barnes and Noble, (2014).

6   G. K. Chesterton, G.K. Chesterton Quotes, Good Reads. https.www.goodreads. com/author/quotes/7014283

7   Martin Luther, Lib Quotes, libquotes.com/martin-luther/quote/lbc4q6v.

8   Martin Luther, "There He Stood: Luther at Worms," *Tabletalk,* Ligonier Ministries, Sanford, FL (April 2021).17

9   Zim Flores, "Don't Gut the Fish." *Good News,* The Woodlands, TX (March 18, 2021).

Chapter 5

1   Mike Lowry, "Back to our Future," *Good News,* The Woodlands, TX (September 2021). 10

2   Jonathan Edwards, "Reflections of Jonathan Edwards View of Free Will," https://thirdmill.org/files/english/html/th/TH.h.

3   William Barclay, *The Daily Bible Study Series,* Westminster Press, Philadelphia, PA (1975). 290

Chapter 6

1   Wikipedia contributors. (2022, January 22). William J.H. Boetcker. In *Wikipedia, The Free Encyclopedia.* Retrieved April 6, 2022, from https://en. Wikipedia.org/w/index.php?title=William-J.-H.-Boetckeroldid=1067218010

2   Matthew Henry, www.biblegateway.com/resources/matthew-henry/Prov. 3:7-Prov. 3:12.

3   Michael Youssef, *Hope for the Present Crisis,* Frontline Publishing, Windsor Mill, MD (March 2021).

4   St. Augustine, Augustine Hippo Quotes and Sayings, Top 100 Augustine Hippo Quotes, https://quotesayings.net/topics/augustinehippo/

5   J. I. Packer, Christian Quotes, 41 J.I. Packer Quotes. https://christianquotes.info/quotes-by-author-j-i-packer-quotes/

6   Alexander Carson, "A quote by Alexander Carson" (n.d.). theysaidso.com. Retrieved Mar. 4,2021. https://theysaidso.com/quote/alexander-carson-as-god-can-protect-his-people-under-the-greatest-despotism

7   John Quincy Adams Quotes. (n.d.). BrainyQuote.com. Retrieved April 6,2022, from BrainyQuote.com Web site https://www.brainyquote.com/quotes/john_quincy_adams_401812.

8   Dr. Carl Trueman, BukRate. Com. Carl Trueman Quotes, https://bukrate.com/author/Carl-a-trueman-quoteshttps/h

9   John Calvin, "Approving Evil." Ligonier Bible Study, (April 16, 2021). https://servants of grace.org/approving-evil

10   E. J. Dionne, "The Case Against Liberal Compassion," Imprimis. Hillsdale, MI (February 26,2017).

11   Robin DiAngelo Quotes. (n.d.). BrainyQuote.com Retrieved April 6, 2022, from BrainyQuote.com Web site: https://www.brainyquote.co/quotes/robin_diangelo_931786.

Chapter 7

1   Sean Trende, *The Problem of Identity Politics and Its Solution*, Matthew Continetti, Imprimis, Hillsdale, MI (Nov. 2017). 6

2   Westminster Confession of Faith, The Reformation Study Bible, Reformation Trust Publishing, Sanford, FL (2015), 2435.

3   Charles Spurgeon, *Spurgeon on the Holy Spirit*, Whitaker House, New Kensington, PA (2000). 54

4   Reinhold Niebuhr, *The Kingdom of God in America*, Willett, Clark, and Company, (1937).

5   Dr. John MacArthur, *Final Word—Why We Need the Bible*, Reformation Trust Publishing, Sanford, FL (2019). 59

6   John Wycliffe, "The Aquila Report," Forerunner of the Reformation, Burk Parsons. www.theaquilareport.com/forerunner-of-the-reformation. (July 8, 2014).

7   C. S. Lewis, *God in the Dock, First and Second Things*, William B. Erdman Publishing Company, Grand Rapids, MI (1970). 270

8   Alan Redpath, "No Victory without Vigilance," Greg Laurie Daily Devotion, https://www.crosswalk.com/devotionals/harvest daily, (April 27, 2019).

Chapter 8

1   Chicago Statement on Biblical Inerrancy, The International Council on Biblical Inerrancy, Chicago, 1978, https://www.moodybible.org/beliefs/the-chicago-statement-on-biblical- inerrancy.

2   C. S. Lewis, *Mere Christianity*, Macmillan Publishing, UK, (1952).

3   Rick Warren, *The Purpose Driven Life; What on Earth am I Here for?* Zondervan, Grand Rapids, MI 2002

4   The Westminster Confession of Faith, *The Reformation Study Bible,* Reformation Trust Publishing, Sanford, FL (2015). Chapters 1,2,3,11,16,23.

5   Ligonier Ministries, "Statement of Faith—What are your doctrinal standards?" https://connectfaqs.ligonier.org/en/articles.

6   Ibid.

7   William Barclay, *The Daily Study Bible Series,* Westminster Press, Philadelphia, PA. (1957). 215

8   Ibid., 190.

9   John Bunyan, The Pilgrim's Progress. (2021, October 23). In *Wikisource*. Retrieved April 8, 2022, from https://en.wikisource.org/w/index.php? Title-The-Pilgrim%27s-Progress&oldid=11806164

Chapter 9

1   William Law Quotes. (n.d.). BrainyQuote.com. Retrieved April 7,2022, from BrainyQuote.com Web site: https://www.brainyquote.com/quotes/william-law-158259

2   C. S. Lewis, "A Slip of the Tongue" https: cs80.wordpress.com/about/cs-lewis-the-weight-of-glory/cs-lewis-a-slip-of-the-tongue

3   John Dos Passos, "The Ground We Stand On: The History of a Political Creed," Harcourt Brace, San Diego, CA (January 1941).

4   Charles Spurgeon, *Spurgeon on the Holy Spirit,* Whitaker House Publishing, New Kensington, PA (2000). 102

Chapter 10

1   H. Richard Niebuhr, "The Kingdom of God in America" Wesleyan University Press, Middletown, Ct (October 1, 1988).

2   Malcolm Muggeridge. (n.d.). AZQuotes.com. Retrieved April 05, 2022, from AZQuotes.com Web site: https://www.azquotes.com/quote504848

3   Reinhold Niebuhr, "A quote by Reinhold Niebuhr" (n.d.). theysaidso.co. Retrieved Feb. 26, 2021, from theysaidso.com/web site: https://theysaidso.com/quote/reinhold-neibuhr-ultimately-evil-is-done-not-so-much-by-evil-people-but-by-good

4   C. S. Lewis, (n.d.). AZQuotes.com. Retrieved April 4, 2022, from AZQuotes.com Web site: https.//www.azquotes.com/quote/402360

Chapter 11

1   Dr. Robert Godfrey, *Tabletalk,* Ligonier Ministries, Sanford, FL (January 2019).9-10

2   Charles Peguy, "Notre Patrie," *The New Criterion* (1905). https://newcriterion.com/issues/2001/11/charles-peguy.

3   R. C. Sproul, "How Should I Live in This World?" Ligonier Ministries, Sanford, FL, (2019).

4   The Westminster Confession of Faith, *The Reformation Study Bible, Reformation Trust Publishing, Sanford, FL* (2015), 2434–35.

5   John Piper, Juicy Ecumenism – The Institute on Religion and Democracy's Blog. *'God is Queer,' Duke Divinity Students Proclaim*, https://juicyecumenism.com/2022/04/05/queer-god-duke-divinity/

Printed in the United States
by Baker & Taylor Publisher Services